Bradley's Metaphysics and the Self

Bradley's Metaphysics and the Self

by

Garrett L. Vander Veer

New Haven and London, Yale University Press, 1970

*This Book is Dedicated in Gratitude
and Friendship to*

Brand Blanshard

Contents

Preface

This book represents an attempt to clarify and defend some of the theses central to Bradley's metaphysics. Part I is concerned mainly with the theory of relations and Bradley's notions of appearance and reality; Part II considers the major philosophical theories of the self in order to defend Bradley's theory of the self within his metaphysical scheme. By bringing Bradley's metaphysics into contact with contemporary discussion whenever possible, I hope to demonstrate my conviction that there is philosophical life in what most philosophers consider moribund issues.

My debts are many, but I can mention only some of the more prominent ones. During 1966–67 a leave of absence from Vassar College and a travel grant from the American Philosophical Society enabled me to complete the bulk of this book while in England.

I have benefited both from the encouragement and the criticisms of my colleagues at Vassar and am particularly grateful to Professor Steven Cahn for reading the manuscript and for making important suggestions about it.

Because of the excellent editorial work of Mrs. Jane Isay, philosophy editor, Yale University Press, the book is far more coherent and concise than it otherwise would have been, and I have benefited at every stage from the common-sense suggestions and editorial advice of my wife, Delma. The several revisions of the manuscript went more smoothly than expected because of my typist, Mrs. Lester Tubby.

I have expressed my indebtedness to Professor Blanshard in the dedication. I only wish to add here that my interest in Bradley and whatever of value there is in this book stems from the model

of clarity and philosophical commitment which he has established
both in his writings and in his teaching.

GARRETT L. VANDER VEER

Vassar College
August 1969

Introduction

This is a book about a metaphysician, about metaphysics, and, most importantly, it attempts to develop elements of a metaphysical position along the lines of what is called Absolute Idealism. I make no apologies for doing philosophy in a way that will seem to many to be quaintly, even absurdly, old-fashioned, for it is my opinion that philosophy's future rests with genuinely speculative ventures. And I think that we may well be witnessing the re-entry of metaphysics into the mainstream of philosophy. If I judge correctly, there is an increasing restiveness among many philosophers with the restrictions imposed on the methods and aims of philosophy by the orthodoxies of the last forty years. Thus, the time is ripe for a new surge of metaphysical interest out of which should emerge, chastened by the austerities of recent years, a new and more vital metaphysical spirit. Already, there have been significant efforts at doing what is called "descriptive" metaphysics by philosophers themselves heavily influenced by the antimetaphysical utterances of Kant and Wittgenstein; it is the major claim of this book that a case for a broader metaphysical effort, these criticisms notwithstanding, can be made through an examination of the fundamental elements of Bradley's philosophy.

In order to accomplish this goal, however, two preliminary obstacles must be overcome: the general apathy felt by most contemporary philosophers concerning the issues that seemed of central interest to Bradley and the belief of many that the theory of meaning promoted by logical positivism has shown conclusively that all metaphysical assertions are meaningless.

It is understandable that, if philosophy is to remain vital, it must have its new causes and relegate its old slogans and battle cries to the past. But it is clear that this attitude is both mistaken and unfortunate as regards Bradley, mistaken because the arguments brought to bear on Bradley's important theses generally have treated them in a grotesquely distorted form. At the same time, it is often assumed that these criticisms have shown definitively that Bradley's philosophy rests on rather elementary confusions. One of my tasks in what follows is to unearth the real meaning of some hotly contested and now ignored doctrines, so that one can see how weak and misguided most criticisms of these views are.

The neglect of Bradley is unfortunate because the problems with which he was concerned are issues that philosophy can ill afford to ignore. Most philosophical issues are interwoven, and as long as one's less explicitly held views remain unexamined, the related theories that reflect them cannot be much more than uncertain conjectures. It is clear, for example, that critics of Bradley's theory of internal relations have their own epistemological and metaphysical presuppositions; there is no satisfactory way of evaluating these criticisms until one has some notion of the validity of the underlying views from which they derive. At the very least, one must credit Bradley with trying to take a critical look at such first principles; more strongly, the arguments Bradley presents to support his claims have not been shown defective by even the most acute criticism. The strength of Bradley's positive claims is not realized by most contemporary philosophers.

The second obstacle to a proper appreciation of Bradley's metaphysics can be traced to the influence of the verifiability theory of meaning. It is not fashionable these days to discuss the problems surrounding this theory, but it would be wrong to conclude that the point of view expressed therein is no longer a force in philosophical thinking. On the contrary, it seems clear that many contemporary theses (the private language thesis, or the close association of meaning and use) and methods of argument (proving that a claim is meaningless by showing that it does not allow its key terms to have meaningful contrasts or to be open to possible counterinstances) rest more or less heavily on some form of this principle. Because of the influence of Wittgenstein, most philosophers are no longer concerned to find a single, acceptable defini-

tion for 'verifiability', because that search smacks of the same metaphysical urge that he wanted to treat and dissipate. Nevertheless, there is sympathy both with the aim of verifiability—the
rejection of metaphysics—and with its connection of meaningful
discourse and empirical exemplification. The result is that it is
tacitly assumed that metaphysics by its nature is a fruitless under-
taking, even though one may have doubts about the theory that is
supposed to show this.

For this reason, it is necessary to recall some serious problems
facing the verifiability theory. These can be placed into two
rough classes: those arising from the application of the theory to
itself and those arising from the application of the theory to other
assertions.

When the theory is stated, one can immediately ask whether
the theory can be judged meaningful by its own criterion. This
seems a fair request, for the theory has made a claim about all assertions and is itself an assertion. Many theories will not do precisely because they cannot be accounted for within the limits of
their own claims. For example, how is Hume's *Treatise* to be
saved from the flames if all our ideas can be traced back to impressions and if only assertions about matters of fact are to be
saved from destruction?

There seem to be only two main ways to avoid evaluating the
verifiability theory by applying it to itself. One might claim that
the theory represents merely a stipulation as to how one is going
to use 'meaningful' and, because stipulations are not true or false,
the theory cannot be criticized for failing to meet the standards
that normal assertions must meet. Or, one might argue that any
such criticism of the verifiability theory necessarily occurs at a
higher "level" than does its application to other assertions and,
therefore, cannot call into question that application. If the verifiability theory is a mere stipulation, then indeed it cannot be true
or false. But then it has no force over those who wish to construe
'meaningful' differently. The theory is of interest only if it truly
gives us the criterion of "meaning" in the ordinary sense. The second avenue of escape is equally hopeless. The application of the
theory to itself is a "higher" operation than its application to
other claims, but I do not see how this could save the theory from

such self-criticism. After all, one can ask for the criterion of 'meaningfulness' on this higher level, and presumably it must be 'verifiability'. If this is denied, it is incumbent on the verification-ist to say in what way our criterion on the "higher" level is differ-ent from the one he is advocating.

Isn't it clear, then, that the statement of the theory must be considered meaningless? There are no observations that, in fact, seem to establish the claim that only verifiable assertions are meaningful, even when 'establish' is taken in its weakest sense. And a little reflection shows that there could not be any such ob-servations. No empirical evidence could possibly weigh either way on the question of whether an assertion must be verifiable to be meaningful. My sense experience cannot tell me that there is (or that there is not) more to the meaningful than the verifiable. And in fact, once one abandons the simple identification of meaning and verification, which the verifiability theory itself does, then one wonders what conclusive arguments can be pro-duced to show that the meaningful must be limited to the verifia-ble.

This criticism illustrates that the verifiability theory is as meta-physical as the theories it attacks. By eliminating certain meta-physical alternatives, whether by showing that the cases are weak or by showing that they are meaningless, one is indirectly advocat-ing a metaphysical view of one's own. This is why the theory can-not meet its own standards.

A. J. Ayer tries to meet this point. He claims that he avoids the charge by making the verifiability theory a "rule which deter-mines the literal significance of language" and not a "psychologi-cal hypothesis" in the manner of Kant:

> Our charge against the metaphysician is not that he attempts to employ the understanding in a field where it cannot profitably venture, but that he produces sentences which fail to conform to the conditions under which alone a sentence can be literally significant.[1]

But there is no purely linguistic criterion by which metaphysi-cal sentences could be condemned as insignificant. One could know

1. A. J. Ayer, *Language, Truth and Logic* (New York, Dover, 1946), p. 35.

that they lacked significance only if he presupposed both a belief that meaningful utterances must refer to some object and a belief that there are no metaphysical objects. If so, the theory has a metaphysical base though denying that such knowledge is possible.

It seems clear that Ayer's attack on metaphysics is merely a stronger version of Kant's criticism, for Ayer's claim is that it is logically, not merely factually, impossible to have metaphysical knowledge. But then we are committed to the view that all there could possibly be is what we refer to in our verifiable assertions. Ayer's linguistic antimetaphysics turns out to be a proof for an empiricist metaphysics, for his limitation of 'significance' makes sense only as emerging from an unstated positive view about what there is. Ayer's metaphysics is not so overt as Kant's, but it is an integral part of his argument. He is denying that metaphysical knowledge is possible, and, as Bradley knew, that makes him "a brother metaphysician with a rival theory of first principles." [2]

When we turn to an evaluation of the verifiability theory's success in dealing with metaphysical assertions, we find that the theory is torn in two different directions and cannot make these two tendencies consistent with each other. On the one hand, there is the (negative) desire to show that metaphysical assertions are meaningless because unverifiable; on the other hand, there is the complementary desire to show that law-like scientific claims fall within the sphere of the meaningful. The former purpose indicates that a strict sense of 'verifiable' is what is called for, whereas the latter purpose seems to demand a broad, generous sense of that word.

The framers of verifiability apparently did not find any intrinsic difficulty in compromising between the impulse to be restrictive and the impulse to be generous. Thus, if an objection is raised to a specific formulation of the theory, the verificationist tries to deal with this objection by adjusting his statement of the theory to meet the objection. A good example of this process is to be found in Ayer's reformulation of so-called "weak" verifiability.

My concern, however, is not to point out new ways of avoiding the intent of Ayer's latest statement of the verification thesis, for I

2. F. H. Bradley, *Appearance and Reality* (Oxford, The Clarendon Press, 1955), p. 1.

think that such a move tends to obscure the fundamental reason why the new formulation fails. Rather, my concern is to isolate the basic reason why all the forms of verifiability have exceptions and why, therefore, none can possibly succeed in restricting metaphysical claims, and only metaphysical claims, to the rubbish heap of meaninglessness.

This reason is to be found in the assumption of verification theorists that no experience is relevant to the truth of metaphysical claims. Yet, the assumption is clearly wrong: metaphysical theories are not made without regard to experience. Rather, they are suggested by experience; they emerge as solutions to problems that reflection finds inherent in experience, and they give expression to what the metaphysician believes to be characteristics of experience. For example, the belief in an ego is the result of trying to explain the facts of memory, activity, and self-identity, and the doctrine of internal relations is an extension of the dependence that some related things seem to have on one another. Both monism and pluralism make features of experience seem plausible, and each theory finds the facts on which his opponent relies troublesome and in need of explanation.

But if experience suggests metaphysical theses, then when this evidence is taken in conjunction with the metaphysical claim, certain other experiences should provide additional evidence for the theses. And this is what happens. If the ego theory is an attempt to account for self-identity, then the fact that in memory I remember that *I* felt so-and-so is more evidence for the theory. And if our attempts to explain events reveal that there are always hidden connections between seemingly discrete events, the internal relations theorist can feel that experience is on his side. Thus, though scientific theories and metaphysical theories are related to experience in different ways, the difference is between what is more closely bound and what more loosely bound to experience. Metaphysical assertions are thought to be unverifiable because whatever facts one metaphysician claims favor his theory can always be explained away from the point of view of a rival theory; metaphysical arguments cannot be resolved by the appeal to experience.

Nevertheless, it cannot be doubted that experience is relevant to metaphysical assertions; the looser relation to experience does not in itself make metaphysical utterances meaningless. Why should the relative independence of metaphysics from experience, as compared with scientific claims, condemn the former? After all, scientific claims are themselves "further" from experience than observation statements; yet, we do not want to say that they are meaningless. The sharp division between science and metaphysics, envisioned in the verifiability theory, is based on a misunderstanding of the origin of metaphysical speculation.

More generally, one wants to ask whether there is any way of determining, in general, that certain propositions are meaningless. Indeed, is there any reason to think that the question "Are metaphysical assertions meaningful" has a single, clear meaning? The assumption behind the question seems to be that metaphysics is one kind of thing, which is to be condemned or sanctioned as a whole. This belief plays an important role in discussions of the possibility of metaphysical knowledge, and I show later on that it is as mistaken as is the belief that metaphysics has nothing to do with experience.

The basic problem with verifiability is the criterion of meaningfulness. We will accept any general criterion only insofar as it accords with our general sense of whether we know what we mean when we make a given assertion, and verifiability fails this test in two ways. When we try out a metaphysical claim, such as that there is life after death, we are more certain that we know generally what we mean than we are of any theory that tells us that we mean nothing when we use such words. We can know what we mean by a claim when we have no idea of any possible way of determining whether what we have claimed is true or false. And the assertion that a proposition is meaningful only if it is verifiable seems to our pre-analytic sense of what is meaningful to be exactly backwards. Surely, we believe, a proposition can be verifiable only if it is first meaningful. Verifiability rests on the determination of meaningfulness and not the other way around.

I wish now to consider two alternative accounts of metaphysics, both of which attempt to justify metaphysics against the claim that it is nonsense while accepting the positivist's belief that all knowledge is derived from sense experience. The first view, advo-

cated by W. H. Walsh, sees metaphysics as the promotion of interesting new perspectives, thereby removing it altogether from considerations of truth and falsity. The second account, advocated by
R. G. Collingwood, sees metaphysics as an empirical study and,
thus, as not subject to the criticisms of positivism. These views
merit consideration, because if either is correct, the conception of
metaphysics that pervades this book is fundamentally mistaken.

According to Walsh, the job of the philosopher is just to make
sense of the world he experiences by assessing the "relative appropriateness of rival conceptual schemes" for understanding the
world around him. Thus, he formulates a system of "categorical
principles" that can be used to interpret experience and that embody his own "imaginative picture" of the world. In so doing, he
is practicing what Walsh calls "immanent" metaphysics and is
avoiding the danger of lapsing into the nonsense that results from
the attempt to practice "transcendent" metaphysics, which Walsh
calls the attempt to get "news from nowhere."

For example, materialism may have been thought of as a doctrine that tells one the "true" facts about the world and that denies much that we ordinarily believe. However, it need not be
taken as a transcendent doctrine. Can we not see it as the claim
that "it is out of the question that there should be anything that
cannot be satisfactorily explained in scientific terms?" [3] If so, materialism makes perfectly good sense, and we will have found a compromise between a flat denial that metaphysical utterances are
meaningful and an endorsement of the extravagant claims that
philosophers have made about transcendent worlds.

Several important conclusions follow from this view of what
metaphysics is or ought to be.

1. The basic principles that characterize any particular metaphysic are not the kinds of things that, strictly speaking, can be
true or false. This is because they are "prescriptions" that may be
"advocated," and they are to be distinguished from empirical
propositions, which are "read out" of, and verified by, experience.
As Walsh says of categorical principles, "it is our refusal to give
them up in the face of unfavourable evidence which differentiates

3. W. H. Walsh, *Metaphysics* (London, Hutchinson University Library, 1963), p.
67.

them from highly general empirical laws" (*Met.*, 169). Thus, metaphysical principles are not propositions at all, but instead are bits of advice to take things in a certain way. They do not assert anything about the world at all.

2. Because metaphysical principles are not true or false, it is not surprising that they cannot be proved true. They cannot be established by an appeal to the facts, partly because there is no agreement on what the facts are and, more basically, because such principles supply the framework within which questions can be answered by an appeal to the facts. Neither, however, can basic principles be proved by some logical method. There is no absurdity in the opposite of any metaphysical position; therefore, no such position can be "logically compulsive."

3. It might seem that the conclusion to draw at this point is that metaphysics is nonsense. Walsh, however, sees a way that it can be rehabilitated. Thus, he rejects the nonsense claim for two reasons, one negative and the other positive. First, the person denying an accepted assumption, such as "every event has a cause," cannot be shown either to have asserted a logical contradiction or to have denied a matter of fact. But then, *pace* logical positivism, such a denial must be some third kind of creature (as is the assertion that every event has a cause) and cannot be dismissed as nonsense.

Second, a model may be provided in terms of which we can understand the nature of metaphysical statements and their relation to matters of fact. In the past, the problem with metaphysics was that metaphysicians took as their model mathematics and science, and this led them to think that they discover necessary truths about the world. In fact, Walsh argues, the model for metaphysics ought to be poetry and literary criticism, for metaphysicians would then see the futility of their claim to tell us of a transcendent world. Of course, there are important differences between poetry or literary criticism and metaphysics; the metaphysician is interested in producing a set of basic concepts, and poets are not. But the crucial similarity between poetry and metaphysics is that they both rest ultimately on a "central vision," and neither metaphysicians nor literary critics rely on "knockdown" proofs to establish their claims.

That is not to say that facts play *no* role in the acceptance or rejection of philosophical, historical, or literary hypotheses. Philosophical theories are said to be "suggested" by experience and should be rejected if they do not seem able to account for the facts. And if philosophical arguments are not "knockdown," at least they can be said to "incline" one toward a certain conclusion. The difference between philosophical theories and scientific hypotheses, then, is one of degree and not of kind; metaphysics is "further" from experience than is science, but it is not altogether out of touch with facts. Thus, although metaphysics is not a "superscience," and although its claims are not true or false, Walsh insists that it has some significance after all. He suggests that we might speak of metaphysical systems, as we tend to speak of literary theories, as "illuminating" or "authentic," thus stressing the personal element, the central insight, characteristic of both fields.

4. It follows that metaphysics is not a source of information about the world. As Walsh says,

> There is no such thing as a special stock of knowledge accessible only to metaphysicians, nor is it the case that some metaphysicians have a grasp of fundamental truths of fact which are unaccountably lost sight of by others. We all confront the same world, but we differ in our ways of taking it (*Met.,* 169).

What can be said about Walsh's attempt to reformulate metaphysics along immanent lines? If I stop and ask myself what I am doing when I claim that reality is rational, I find that I am not merely advocating a point of view; I am making a claim about the way things are. When I speak of reality, I know that I am not using a "theoretical construct" that I find useful; I am simply asserting something about the world as it is. Thus, the comparison Walsh draws between the concept of God and that of an electron as a theoretical construct is misleading.

It follows that metaphysical statements are not "prescriptions" or "exhortations," because they are true or false. How do I know that metaphysical statements are true or false? In the only way that I can decide such things. I notice that in uttering them I mean to say something about the world and not to say what attitude one ought to take toward that world. And if it be said that a metaphysical statement can be translated into the advice "adopt such-and-such an attitude if you want to make sense of things," I know that this will not do; for I know that my metaphysical assertion is primarily about the world and only by implication about what I ought to do, whereas the reverse is true about the translation. Therefore, the translation cannot capture the sense of my assertion.

Walsh holds, regarding metaphysics, that "There is no such thing as a scientifically authenticated interpretation to which we are all required to subscribe whether we see anything in it or not" (*Met.*, 180).[4] Philosophy cannot be a science because it ultimately rests on the personal vision of the metaphysician, a vision that colors the facts and makes objective, decisive proof impossible. But, surely, these statements by Professor Walsh constitute his philosophy, namely, the philosophy that philosophy is persuasive in the manner of the arts, rather than objective in the manner of the sciences. And he seems to regard his position as a "scientifically authenticated" interpretation of philosophy and its method, for he cites evidence from philosophical arguments and conducts arguments himself to convince the reader that his interpretation of philosophy is correct, in opposition to the claims of transcendent metaphysicians.

Why, then, is not the same thing possible for the philosopher who believes in the possibility of "decisive tests"? Or, why is the metaphysician alone caught in the net of his subjective vision? Does not Professor Walsh have such a vision, albeit a vision about philosophy and not about the world? It seems to me, in short, that either Walsh is involved in an outright contradiction, in denying that philosophy is decisive while assuming that his philosophy is decisive, or he is saying that philosophy has a necessary, subjective element while his metaphilosophy does not. But why is the latter so different from the former? Walsh produces no reasons to explain this difference, and I see nothing to indicate that Walsh's philosophy is not as much the result of his own basic attitudes

4. This assertion is made about the arts and criticism, but it is clear that Professor Walsh means it to apply equally to metaphysics.

as is any metaphysical scheme. If one cannot be scientific because of the intrusion of "personal testimony," then neither can the other.

Now, what reasons are there for thinking that metaphysics "cannot be a science at all?" Walsh seems to rest his case on two main reasons: the element of vision and the diversity of opinion on metaphysical matters. As to the first point, we may well agree that every metaphysician, indeed, every theorist, has an insight of what the world is like and that a failure to understand his point of view will often make criticisms of the theory irrelevant. But by itself, this does not show that metaphysics is subjective. Even Walsh admits that a "vision" may be tested by its ability to cover the facts adequately. As he says, eventually the "pressure of facts" forces an "honest" metaphysician to abandon his vision if it does not do the job of explanation.

What Walsh means, I think, is that philosophy can do no more than this, whereas science and mathematics can offer "knock-down" proofs for their claims. But this claim against philosophy can be proved only by examining the claims of philosophers, and the weight of Walsh's assertion falls on his analysis of attempts to establish metaphysical claims with logical certainty.

Walsh suggests that such attempts have failed for three reasons. The first is that the logically compulsive is never about fact. But this very statement about some kinds of facts (statements) seems to Walsh to be necessary; if not necessary, then it is possible that logically necessary assertions can be about fact, and it would remain to be seen whether a particular claim was about fact or not.

Second, Walsh holds that "there is no possibility of showing that those who advocate alternative sets of first principles are involved in self-contradiction." (*Met.*, 166). This is an important claim and one I consider at some length in chapter 9. Let me say here only that the claim for the logical coherence of reality seems the best candidate for an exception to Walsh's assertion.

Third, Walsh appeals to the "babble of discordant voices" as evidence that metaphysics involves no certainties. When Bradley claims that positions other than his are self-contradictory, he does not mean that this must be obvious, nor does he claim that the noncontradictory character of terms and relations is obvious. In addition, philosophers have differed greatly in the degree to which they have felt the demands of theoretical completeness and consistency. And, strangely, metaphysics seems for many to have emotional significance. Given these factors, it is not surprising that there should be wide disagreement in philosophy or that similar positions should recur again and again. Nor must one forget the rather amazing agreement of many philosophers, centuries apart, concerning many fundamental matters.

In short, I see no reason to assume that the diversity among philosophers proves the unscientific character of metaphysics. That claim would have to be argued on other grounds, by showing that no metaphysician could prove his assertions, and I do not think that Walsh, or anyone else, for that matter, has done this.

Walsh says both that philosophers encourage us to look at things in a new way so that we can "make sense of them," that such points of view can be "revelatory" when they enable us to see the facts with a new "significance," and that metaphysical propositions are not true or false. But how does metaphysics "make sense" of the facts unless it is by telling us the truth about them? What does metaphysics "reveal" if it is not reality? How can a philosopher be "illuminating" other than by showing us the truth in a new point of view? It is hard to see what these words can mean in this context if we are to dismiss the ontological claims of metaphysics. The programmatic utterances of philosophers tell us that they seek the truth about things, and necessary truth at that. If, in fact, they cannot have been doing this, what they have been doing is foolish and "reveals," if anything, only their lack of understanding of their own craft.

Professor Walsh fails to find a middle ground between assertions that all metaphysics is nonsense and the claims of metaphysicians to have a special knowledge about things. It fails because there is no justification of metaphysics that falls short of the knowledge claims that metaphysicians have made. Thus, Professor Walsh "justifies" metaphysics by making it into a kind of mythology in which some schemes please us more than others. But this is to discredit the seriousness of metaphysics. On the matter of greatest philosophical importance, namely, "Can metaphysical propositions be true?" Professor Walsh sides with the positivists;

but he stops short of saying that such propositions are nonsense. I
have argued that he has not proved that some metaphysical assertions are not true and that his distinction between immanent and
transcendent metaphysics does nothing to show that such assertions
could not be true.

There is another way to justify metaphysics within the general
strictures of logical positivism: by saying that metaphysics is a
purely empirical study, thus avoiding the difficulties of defending
its "loose" ties to experience. This view of metaphysics—Collingwood's—would dissolve the transcendent character that has both-
ered both its defenders and critics, while legitimizing the possibility of metaphysical knowledge. The advantages of such a position
are both obvious and important.

According to Collingwood, metaphysics is the historical study of
the "absolute presuppositions" that have formed the background
of various types of thinking. Thus, it deals with assumptions that
are never answers to questions posed by the thinker in question,
for absolute presuppositions are merely presupposed by all the
questions a given thinker asks. Such presuppositions, Collingwood
asserts, cannot be considered propositions and, therefore, are not
capable of truth or falsity.[5] "Pseudometaphysics" is the attempt
to determine the truth or falsity of absolute presuppositions, and
the result is nonsense, "the kind of nonsense which comes of
thinking that supposing is one of the attitudes we can take up toward a proposition" (*EM*, 48).

If we accept his claims, metaphysics will retain an important
place in human speculation by becoming a completely empirical
study. One could, however, begin voicing reservations by wondering how Collingwood might justify his sharp distinction between
'propounding' and 'merely supposing'. Surely, to suppose anything is to suppose that it is *true,* and suppositions are unques-
tioned when their truth is thought to be beyond question. Of
course, we may not "propound" certain assumptions we make, for
propounding involves overt assertion; but we may still hold them
to be true. The notion of "merely supposing" seems clearly self-
contradictory. And Collingwood's likely reply—that because abso-

5. R. G. Collingwood, *An Essay on Metaphysics* (Oxford, The Clarendon Press,
1940), pp. 31–32.

lute presuppositions "work" in our thinking with "the light of consciousness never falling on them" (*EM,* 43), they are not held to be true—seems equally dubious. Assumptions do not affect me mechanically and from the "outside" as Collingwood suggests.

This leads to my second criticism of Collingwood. How might one show that such apparent assertions as "God exists," "Every event has a cause," or "Reality is rational" are presuppositions and not propositions? Surely if one assumes X he assumes that X is true, and the mere fact that there are some assumptions that one never questions is not a good reason for saying that they cannot be true or false. For example, Bradley argues that we assume, and cannot but assume, that reality is rational. This "postulate," he believes, cannot be questioned without assuming that it is valid. But, if so, what reason is there for saying that this assumption is not even the kind of thing that can be true or false? Bradley has much the better of it when he argues that because we must make this assumption, therefore we must accept its truth.

If one could make an assumption without believing it to be true, then perhaps there could be such things as Collingwood's absolute presuppositions, and one might try to give a dispositional analysis of 'assume' in order to make his theory plausible. Collingwood might be right if "A assumes *x*" could be interpreted to mean "A is willing either to assert *x* at a later time or at least will assert propositions that logically depend on *x*." However, it is hard to see how such an analysis could give one the meaning of 'assume' in the active sense that Collingwood needs to make his theory significant. For then to say that I agree to *x* at a later time is not what I would mean by presupposing *x* at an earlier time. In general, there seems to be nothing that I could do or say at a later time that would be the earlier presupposing. Perhaps, if I do presuppose *x,* I might be inclined to do or say certain things, but then the presupposing is different from the later doing or saying.

Of course, in anything I say I am committed logically to an indefinite number of propositions that were not at all "in my mind" when I made my assertion, but can it be said that I have "presupposed" them? They form the logical background of my claim, but they are not part of what I would, even on reflection, grant that I was presupposing when I made my claim. If one denies this, then there seems to be no difference between what an assertion logically entails and what a given person assumes when he says something. But, if so, what job is there left for 'presuppose' to do?

Collingwood's thesis thus fails in one of two ways. Either his absolute presuppositions are not presupposed at all, and that is the reason they cannot be true or false—rather than their "absoluteness"; or, granting that they are "assumed," there is no reason for believing that one cannot question the truth or falsity of any set of absolute presuppositions. (Here, 'cannot' is used in a logical sense.) If Collingwood replies that this makes them relative and not absolute, then one need only point to his own examples of absolute presuppositions, for example, "Every event has a cause," and "God exists," and ask why they cannot be evaluated. One suspects that the only kind of answer Collingwood could give would rely on the verifiability criterion and would, therefore, contain the same problems that plague it.

There is one final criticism Collingwood's theory must face: What status should be accorded to the claim that metaphysics is the study of absolute presuppositions? Is it, for example, an absolute presupposition for Collingwood? If so, it cannot be a true assertion about metaphysics, for it is not an assertion at all. But if the statement is taken as true, then is it not reasonable to take it as a metaphysical claim? It is neither empirical nor analytic, and as a general characterization of metaphysics must it not at the very least be considered metaphysical? Yet, in Collingwood's view, metaphysics is the empirical, historical study of absolute presuppositions. What place is there for his own theory in such a scheme?

The upshot of these remarks is that none of the three theories shows that substantive metaphysics is impossible. But what kind of metaphysics is possible? The purpose of this book is to show that Bradley's approach to metaphysics both establishes the proper character of metaphysical inquiry and leads to certain important and defensible metaphysical assertions. It is because of these contributions that Bradley's philosophy should be considered a source of living philosophical issues and not a musty, antiquated relic.

Part I

Bradley's Metaphysics

I

The Theory of Judgment

Bradley's theory of judgment can be seen as an attempt to mediate two extreme views: empiricism and the theory of propositions, the former being the view that concerns Bradley and with which he contrasts his own theory. According to many empiricists, ideas are nothing but images, slightly dim copies of sense impressions: To think of anything is to have an image of it. It follows that, when I am thinking of a group rather than an individual, this cannot be explained by saying that I have a group-like image. For as Berkeley saw, the close tie between images and sense makes the notion of an abstract image an absurdity. Images are concrete existences; how, therefore, can they contain within themselves the conflicting properties that a general concept must in some sense have? Yet, one wants to ask, how can the idea be the image if the image can refer to something more than it represents? Has not the idea become the way in which we use the image? [1]

The empiricist account of inference and reasoning is simply the view of thinking applied sequentially. Thus, to reason is first to have the image that is the thought of the first "element" and then to have the image that is the thought of the second element, and so forth. The so-called laws of reasoning will be the laws describing the succession of images. Logic and epistemology become psychology, the empirical study of the association of ideas. [2] The problems in this area are thus empirical and are best handled by the scientist; so philosophers have shown themselves to be trespassers or amateurs in a field once thought to be their own.

1. See Brand Blanshard, *The Nature of Thought* (2 vols. London, Allen & Unwin, 1939), *1*, 578.

2. See Richard Wollheim, *F. H. Bradley* (London, Penguin Books, 1959), Ch. 1, for an excellent statement of the empiricist account of knowledge.

A second view of thought, developed in opposition to the empiricist theory in an attempt to save knowledge from the psychologist, is the theory that in thinking I assert propositions, and propositions are timeless entities, independent of my awareness of them and intersubjective. They are not physical or mental, are different from my thinking, facts thought about, and the sentences in which I express my thoughts. They occupy a "third realm," forming inexhaustible combinations of whatever can be thought. Propositions are said to be true or false in the most fundamental sense: true if there are facts that exhibit the same structure and content as a given proposition and false if the facts do not "correspond" to the proposition.[3]

On the proposition view, to think of something is to apprehend or assert a proposition; and to reason is to apprehend the relations of implication and exclusion that hold timelessly between propositions. In this way, logic and mathematics are emancipated from psychology, for in them we study genuinely objective entities whose characteristics are independent of the way events occur "in my head." In addition, the timeless character of propositions seems to account for the timeless character of logical and mathematical truth. Without propositions, it is believed impossible to explain what I am thinking of—the content of my thought—when I think falsely. False assertions are perfectly meaningful, and what they are about—for this is the condition of their meaningfulness—are propositions that have no factual counterpart.

Bradley is not concerned explicitly with the theory of propositions, as he is with the empiricist account of thinking, but I think his view can be best understood as an attempt to take the best from both theories without allowing himself to be caught in the more extreme consequences of either. He devoted a substantial part of *The Principles of Logic* to exposing the errors of the empirical theory: Because empiricists tend to limit themselves to a consideration of one kind of symbol only—images—they misunder-

3. This is not always the case. For example, G. E. Moore declared that the world was formed of concepts or propositions and that the latter were the only objects of knowledge. Thus, he was forced to define truth as a certain "specific manner," immediately apprehended and indefinable, in which the concepts of a proposition are combined with the concept of existence. Existence is to be defined in terms of

stand the nature of symbols generally. If one notices that words, flowers, and the like have meanings only because we have given them those meanings, it becomes clear that there need be no "natural" connection between a symbol and the thing symbolized. "A sign is any fact that has a meaning, and meaning consists of a part of the content (original or acquired), cut off, fixed by the mind, and considered apart from the existence of the sign." [4] If a rose can mean love, then why cannot an idea symbolize its object without having to be a copy of that object?

In fact, Bradley continues, even when thinking involves images, the content of the image is never the idea, for then it could only be an idea of its original. Rather, the idea is whatever part of the image content we take to symbolize its object. In addition, something can be a symbol only if it is of a certain kind. It is not the particular sound I utter or the particular marks I write that are symbols; the *word* that is expressed in these ways has the meaning. Yet, an image is a "hard particular," a particular fact among other facts. As such, it cannot be a symbol.

Bradley's criticism of images-as-thoughts is summed up by saying that such a view ignores the fact of meaning. Everything that exists has two aspects—existence and content. Things exist with a certain character, and this is as true of images as of anything else. But an idea must "mean" something other than itself, and it is hard to see how it can do this while remaining an individual thing. Only universals can mean; only that taken apart from its existence can stand for something other than itself.

As empiricism has misunderstood what an idea is, so it has misrepresented what thinking is: Empiricist accounts of thinking ignore the aspect of judgment. The "having" of an image must mean that an image occurs or happens in me, but to think or judge is to do more than to have something happen in my mind. To judge is to refer an idea to the world, and, without this reference, there is no judgment. Bradley's early view was that one

---

truth and not vice versa. For Moore, truth is nothing at all other than concepts and their relations. G. E. Moore, "The Nature of Judgment," *Mind*, n.s., *8* (1899), esp. 176–83.

4. F. H. Bradley, *The Principles of Logic* (2 vols. Oxford, Oxford University Press, 1950), *I*, 4.

could have ideas without referring them to an object, but this later view was that there are not two things, 'having' ideas and 'referring' them; ideas are judgments on the later view.

Empiricist accounts make nonsense of reasoning and inferring. If all reasoning is mere association, then we never think as we do because the "logic" of our subject seems to demand it. Rather, our past associations always cause us to have one thought after another. The chance experiences that we have had of things, rather than the logical demands of things, govern our reasoning. One thought is the mere result of another; there are no conclusions in any significant sense.

This view would mean the end of our belief that thinking at its best is rational and that some thinking is more rational than other thinking. 'Rational' would lose its distinctive, logical sense when applied to thinking, and it is hard to see how we could consider reasoning to be a process in which we seek out the truth. A hypothesis of such vast consequences should not be adopted lightly. And our experience of thinking is that of a purposeful activity in which conclusions are reached because they are logically demanded by what has come before. If so, we cannot accept an account of thinking that treats it as just another causal sequence.

Because Bradley develops his own view in opposition to empiricism, he does not stress his ties to it. Nevertheless, one can find two general areas of agreement. First, he agrees that ideas must have an aspect of existence. At first, this seemed to mean for him that all thinking involves images, that an idea is part of the content of an image. But in a later edition of the *Logic,* he rejects this position, and he was wise to do so. For thinking seems quite possible without images, and, as Blanshard has pointed out, it is hard to see how it could be true both that an image is a "hard particular" and that an idea is a "part" of that image. This is especially hard to understand when Bradley says that ideas do not exist either "inside" or "outside" one's head and are not phenomena.

In addition, this early tendency of Bradley's seems to conflict with his emphasis on the arbitrary character of symbols in relation to what is symbolized. Thus, we do not always characterize an object with a part of the content of a sign. As Stout said,

"When a forget-me-not is regarded by me as a sign of faithfulness in love, I do not mentally qualify faithfulness in love as being blue, or having stamens and a corolla." [5] Nevertheless, Bradley continued to insist that ideas were never completely without an aspect of existence.[6]

Second, Bradley is in sympathy with the empiricists' belief in the concreteness of what exists. For this reason, he says, "The belief in universal ideas does not involve the conviction that abstractions exist, even as facts in my head" (PL, 1, 6). To begin with, there certainly are no abstract substantives, such as the Platonic Forms, in Bradley's view. Abstractions are ideas and in judgments are referred to what is concretely real. Bradley's way of stating this fact is to say that ideas imply the separation of content from existence. But where this division occurs, we have appearance and not reality for the very reason that abstractions seem secondary to Bradley. Ideas or concepts are only "of" reality; they never can comprise it.

Bradley's reaction to the empiricist account of thought makes it easy to anticipate his reaction to the theory of propositions. He supports its attempt to distinguish psychology and logic, to justify the objectivity and eternality of truth; no philosopher has stressed more than Bradley the extent to which thinking at its best is under the guidance of the nature and structure of the real world. On the other hand, he objects to several tendencies in the proposition theory. He rejects both the notion that real things are composed of propositions or concepts and the notion that truth can be defined without a reference beyond concepts.

5. G. F. Stout, *Studies in Philosophy and Psychology* (London, Macmillan, 1930), p. 197.

6. "There is, generally, no truth without an aspect of existence, however much for our purpose [in logic] that aspect may be ignored" (PL, 2, 550, n. 18). See also *The Principles of Logic*, 1, 38, n. 8. Blanshard argues that Bradley's mature view is that ideas can be regarded from two points of view, each of which by itself is more or less abstract. One can consider ideas as events or as essences, as one does in psychology and logic respectively. When I think, objective essences or concepts appear in my mind as the content of mental events. Such events-with-content are ideas. Thus, an idea is both temporal and nontemporal, rather than partly one and partly the other. Bradley admits (PL, 2, 550) that we cannot understand how this is possible, but unless it is so we shall fail to do justice to either psychology or to logic and truth. See Blanshard, *The Nature of Thought*, 1, Ch. 13.

He rejects the tendency of this theory to conceive of thinking as primarily the apprehending of propositions, rather than as the apprehending of facts. For Bradley, thinking is always "of" the world, not "of" concepts; concepts are means, not ends. Instead of saying that when one judges falsely one is correctly apprehending a false proposition, why not say that one is merely failing to apprehend the true character of things? There is a content, other than the real, that one asserts of the real and that is excluded by it. But it is misleading to speak as if there were knowledge of the content (proposition); there is no knowledge at all.

To the extent that propositions are distinct from facts and "correspond" with facts, and to the extent that our primary apprehension is of propositions, we seem to be back in the dilemma of a Lockean representative theory. Either we know the facts directly, in which case propositions are superfluous, or we seem unable to break outside our 'iron curtain' of propositions.[7] In Bradley's view, there must be some identity between idea-as-content and the reality "meant," if knowledge is to be possible. A third realm, of whatever nature, makes knowledge inexplicable.

Finally, the sense in the proposition theory that the same proposition can be believed, doubted, and so forth, that the same proposition is asserted by two persons using the same sentence, and that a given proposition is either true or false seems far too clear-cut and rigid to Bradley. His concept of degrees of truth—to be discussed in chapter 7—implies that our ideas are closer to or further from reality, but that they are not perfectly adequate or totally inadequate to the real. The proposition theory merely reflects in this case our normal attitude toward truth and falsity, to which Bradley's criticism also applies.

So far, we mainly have been concerned with what Bradley's theory is not. Let us now explain what it is. I shall select four claims for emphasis. (1) All judgment involves ideas. (2) All judgment involves an act of referring. (3) There is always a reality "beyond" the act and about which we judge, that is, to which we refer our idea. (4) All judgments are hypothetical.

1. The claim that without ideas there is no judgment might be

7. See Gilbert Ryle, "Are There Propositions?" *Aristotelian Society Proceedings,* n.s., *30* (1930), 106–08.

objected to because of the particular interpretation that Bradley gives to 'idea'. More radically, it might be objected to as being wrong in principle. Bradley's notion of an idea can be understood best if we consider some alternatives to it. Is an idea an image? But persons can think without images, and what is asserted in my ideas often bears little resemblance to my images. Are ideas mental acts? But then the object of an act, no matter how fanciful, must have some place in the world at large, and, in any case, the sharp distinction of act from content is suspect. If ideas are different from their objects, we seem caught in the difficulties of representative theories; but if they are not different, then we seem to believe that the thing thought about is literally the content of my thought. This seems absurd, and it makes a mystery of error.

Bradley's solution to this problem, only stated in his later work, is to hold that an idea is a 'universal content', which exists only insofar as it is used and which is identical in content with the character of things thought about (PL, 1, 38, n. 7). But Bradley's additional claim is that, despite this identity of content, our ideas never capture the "form" of what is the case; in thinking, we must deal in abstractions, and abstractions mutilate the connectedness and concreteness of things. Thus, ideas both are the same as things and are different from things, and if this be branded as a paradox, the answer is that the sense in which identity and difference are asserted reveals the claim to be necessary if we are to explain knowledge.

Cook Wilson has raised the more serious objection: If by 'idea' we mean something that mediates our apprehension of objects— that "stands between" objects and ourselves and is our means of knowing obejcts—then either there are no such things as ideas, or if there are, they are not used in knowing. Cook Wilson's position is that

> Even if there exists in my mind an 'idea' of the reality A, whatever such an idea may be, at any rate my apprehension of A is my apprehension of A and not my apprehension of my idea of A: if I know A at all, then what I know is just A itself, and not some idea of A which I have in my head.[8]

8. Richard Robinson, "Cook Wilson's View of Judgment," Mind, n.s., 37 (1928), 307–08. See Ryle, "Are There Propositions?" pp. 110–11, for a similar criticism.

Bradley's answer runs as follows. Of course knowledge is "of" reality and not "of" my ideas. But this does not mean that knowing can dispense with ideas, for in erroneous thinking there obviously is something asserted, and this "something" cannot be identical with any fact. If so, are we to assume some radical difference between true and false thinking? How can ideas be used in the one case but not in the other? Even when I know something, it is always possible that I may be in error. Are not ideas needed to account for this possibility? And, Bradley thinks, no thought of mine can ever be simply identical with the real, for immediate experience testifies to the concrete character of reality, beside which ideas appear as lifeless abstractions.

One may insist on the realistic attitude in thinking, but what one intends or means cannot bridge the gap between ideas and things. The belief that there is a state of mind called "knowing" in which there is a "direct confrontation" between a mind and an object seems a myth made possible by our failure to notice the distance between what I intend in judging and what I accomplish thereby.

2. About the act of judging, two points need to be made. Judging or inferring is not to be thought of as something that *I* do *to* a content "before my mind" when I am 'free' from the constraint of that content. If mental acts are activities that *I* initiate from the "outside" onto some content, then judging and inferring are not mental acts for Bradley.[9] Rather, in rational judgment or in inference objects "develop in my mind," or move to the center of my consciousness. Thus, Bradley defines inference as the "ideal self-development of an object" (*PL*, 2, 597). If thinking is not under the constraint of its object, then how will we ever know that that which we must think is also true? I think it is reasonably clear that whatever the difficulties in Bradley's "objective" view of mental activity, the alternative yields nothing but a self-refuting skepticism.

It has been said that the reference in judgment to a "distant" reality results in a paradox. According to Loewenberg, in judging we refer to an object by describing it. But then we are faced with the following dilemma. Either the object we refer to is the one we

9. Blanshard (*NT*, *1*, 409) gives a vivid description of the relation between act and content for Bradley.

describe, in which case there is "no object outside the one immanent in judgment meant or intended"; or the object referred to is not the one we describe, in which case it must either be a nondescript object of which nothing could be known; or it is the one described in a previous judgment, and we are faced with the first step in a vicious infinite regress.[10]

The first point raised by Loewenberg is not troublesome, because truth need not be based on some simple, certain, nonjudgmental apprehension, which forms the basis of knowledge. For, as Bradley says, "My experience is solid, not insofar as it is a superstructure but so far as in short it is a system." [11] The second point is harmless because the thing to which I refer is no Lockean substratum. If it is 'beyond' judgment, in that no set of judgments is adequate to it, it is equally 'in' my judgments, which express its character with greater and greater accuracy. It is something whose content I only partially and confusedly experience in judgment.

The object is both within judgment and beyond it. Any specific judgment can refer to its object because that object has been previously articulated; all judgments refer to an object that they are 'of' and that is, therefore, 'beyond' them. But if the 'beyond' be not less than what I know in any judgment but, rather, that that previous judgments have already characterized, the thing referred to need not be a blank, characterless 'it.' In Campbell's words,

> The "immediate subject" . . . is for the idealist analysis, in an important sense, *both* "ideal" *and* "real." It is "ideal" in the sense that it is always part of the ideal content affirmed of Reality as subject. It is "real" in the sense that it is always *that* part of the ideal content which, on the basis of past cognitive experience, the judging mind *already accepts as correctly characterizing Reality*.[12]

It is true that, for Bradley, when I say, "This cube of sugar is white," I am further qualifying the real cube of sugar. In that

10. Jacob Loewenberg, "An Alleged Escape from the Paradox of Judgment," *The Journal of Philosophy* (September 25, 1930), p. 545.

11. F. H. Bradley, *Essays on Truth and Reality* (Oxford, The Clarendon Press, 1950), p. 210.

12. C. A. Campbell, "The Mind's Involvement in 'Objects': An Essay in Idealist Epistemology," in *Theories of the Mind*, ed. J. M. Scher (New York, The Free Press, 1962), p. 394.

sense, my judgment rests on and assumes the truth of other judgments I have made—that this is an object, a white object, a piece
of sugar, and so forth. And it is also true for him that the real object is "beyond" any judgment or possible set of judgments. It is
that which they are "of." Yet, neither assertion yields Loewenberg's paradox.

3. There are four points to be made concerning Bradley's claim
that in judgment we always refer to a reality existing "beyond" our
idea. First, it implies that in judgment there is a single idea. The
theory that judging is a synthesis of ideas is wrong because it
omits the reference to reality that is implicit in all judgment.
This is not to say that our idea must be absolutely simple; it is
only to say that judgment is the predication of *an* ideal content to
something else. Second, the subject of our judgment need not be
the same as the subject of the sentence in which we express the
judgment. To know what we are talking about we may have to
change the sentence we have used quite radically, for the actual
subject of the judgment may not even appear in the sentence in
question. This is a lesson that some philosophers would have done
well to learn.

Third, the doctrine implies that all judgments are of the subject-predicate form. Of course, this does not mean that Bradley
was unaware of the existence of relational judgments, or even
that he thought that a relational judgment could be reformulated
into a subject-predicate judgment. For example, he says that, in
the case of the judgment "A and B are equal," "It is unnatural to
take A or B as the subject and the residue as predicate" (*PL*, 1,
13). Bradley is only claiming that in every judgment some idea is
being asserted of something that is not an idea but a real thing.
As we shall see, there is a sense in which my "real" subject does not
appear in either relational or subject-predicate judgments.[13]

Finally, what can we say of the subject of judgment? We must,
Bradley insists, distinguish between the immediate and the ultimate, or metaphysical, subject. My judgment is always of a "se-
lected reality." It is always *this* object or *this* group that I am thinking about. And I assume that this subject is something real, that

13. See the discussion of this matter in C. A. Campbell, *On Selfhood and God-
hood* (London, Allen & Unwin, 1957), pp. 209–13.

is, at the very least, that it exists with a certain character independently of my thinking about it.

But, Bradley contends, this does not end the matter. He insists that the ultimate subject of judgment is always reality, so that the proper formula for judging is "Reality is such that S is P," rather than "S is P." Now, part of the meaning of this new formulation is merely a restatement of the fact that I assume my limited subject to be real. I judge about a real thing, an element or part of reality. But this means that I am thinking about reality when I think of this real thing, although, to be sure, I am thinking of only a limited part of reality.

However, in addition to this, there is implied in Bradley's formula his particular theory that reality is a continuous whole, a theory discussed in detail later. This metaphysical theory leads him to believe that in thinking we are never theoretically content to characterize one aspect of the real. Rather, our limited judgment is to be seen as the start of a series of judgments in which we try to characterize reality ever more widely, all the time trying to fit our judgments into one coherent system.

Our ultimate aim as thinkers, then, is to see our single assertion as a necessary component of the whole reality, as following from the nature of that reality. It is for this reason that Bradley says, "The judgment affirms reality, and on my view to affirm reality is to predicate of the one Real" (ETR, 254). Bradley is not saying that the one reality is explicitly the subject about which we judge. He is claiming that this reality is implicitly present in all thinking, presenting us with an ideal of knowledge and urging us on to its completion. Practically, we are satisfied with less than all-inclusive knowledge, but as thinkers we know that with less we have stopped short of our goal. It is obvious, I think, that the full justification of these claims must await the defense of Bradley's metaphysics.

4. The above makes clear, in one sense, why Bradley holds that all judgments are hypothetical or conditional. If the one reality is our ultimate subject in judging, then our limited judgments must be understood in the light of this larger context of which they are a part. We assume that the reality outside our judgment is so-and-so, for we must take something as "solid" on which we can base

our judgment. In short, judgments rest on factual evidence, which is merely another way of saying that all judgment involves inference.

But this background is suspect, for it rests on its own background, and we have no way of making this explicit in judgment. Thus, the most we can say in judging is "If so-and-so is the case (and that is doubtful because my judgment that it is so rests on unknown conditions), then S is P." Only if pluralism were an adequate metaphysics (which, we shall see, it is not), could there be simple judgments that were categorically true because they did nothing more than report a given fact. As it is, all judgments rest on grounds more or less unknown and subject to change.

In Chapter 2 of *The Principles of Logic,* Bradley tries to show that all judgments are hypothetical in a sense slightly different from, but closely related to, the above. The argument is difficult to follow, partly because Bradley develops his own view dialectically against that of Herbart, without often distinguishing the two clearly enough and without saying precisely what he accepts or rejects from Herbart's doctrine. I shall try to reconstruct the argument briefly.

According to Herbart, a judgment is the synthesis of ideas. Thus, in every judgment, all I can assert is that if S, then P. No judgment categorically asserts something to be the case of some particular thing. Rather, all judgments are restricted to asserting that if one supposes a certain property or universal, then another property or universal follows. But the judgment says nothing about any actual, existing matter of fact. The conclusion is that in no judgment is any fact stated directly or simply.

As Bradley elaborates Herbart's doctrine, the same conclusion might be reached in a slightly different manner. One has only to notice the vast difference between ideas and concrete, individual things. The former are abstract universals and are adjectival; the latter are concrete existences and (apparently) are substantives. Assume now that judgment is merely a synthesis of ideas. It follows that no judgment can express a given fact, and, if not, no judgment can be categorically true (*PL*, 1, 46). Our judgments, or at least our true ones, will imply a real fact that they are about, and we will mean to refer to that fact in our judgment. But all we will succeed in expressing is a connection of universals. The reference to a particular fact is never a "part" of the judgment. Judgments are hypothetical because by their nature they cannot "state fact."

Bradley, then, rejects the premise of the argument that judgments are syntheses of ideas, but he insists that universal judgments are in fact hypothetical because they do refer to facts only indirectly. And though he seems at first to argue that singular judgments are genuinely existential and categorical, he finally argues that they, too, are hypothetical and only indirectly existential.

Universal judgments are to be understood as merely asserting "If S, then P." No existing fact is asserted by them. Yet, they do affirm something of the real, for they are judgments. "What is affirmed is the mere ground of the connection; not the actual existing behaviour of the real, but a latent quality of its disposition" (*PL*, 1, 87). We assert of the real whatever makes our connection of elements true. But, of course, this something is more or less unknown to us, and we certainly *say* nothing about it in our judgment. And, Bradley adds, though we can make the grounds of our assertion relatively explicit, "There is in every case a certain amount of unknown condition (*x*)" (*PL*, 1, 112, n. 45). Our actual universal judgments are never directly true of the real.

Singular judgments certainly seem to be different. And Bradley shows at some length that in singular judgments the subject is always something real. In the judgment "This bird is yellow," "It is the fact distinguished and qualified by 'this bird' to which the adjective 'yellow' is really attributed" (*PL*, 1, 58). In addition, Bradley argues that though no idea or set of ideas can express the absolute uniqueness that any real subject has, the fact that an object is given makes it unique.[14]

Thus, because Bradley insists that even such words as "this" and "now" represent ideas, and very abstract ideas at that, he sees a way out of our imprisonment in abstractions. As long as one treats judging as if it were the linking of ideas, no judgment can refer to a specific fact. But if one realizes that in saying "this" we

14. "It is unique, not because it has a certain character, but because it *is given*" (*PL, 1,* 64).

are using an idea to refer to an object that is unique because it is given, then the reference to a specific fact seems to fall within the judgment, and direct, categorical judgments seem to be saved.[15] As Bradley says, "We escape from ideas, and from mere universals, by a reference to the real which appears in perception. It is thus our assertion attains the uniqueness without which it would not correspond to the fact" (*PL*, 1, 69–70).

Having said this, however, Bradley argues against both the categorical and the existential claims of singular judgments. He raises several objections to the categorical claim.

What we assert about the given fact is necessarily only a fragment of that fact, and the fact itself is only a fragment of a larger context. Our judgment fails to be categorical in two ways: We cannot assume that what we assert—a mere "arbitrary selection"— is true as such, when it does not come to us by itself and when, positively, it exhibits its relativity to the whole; because our fact is conditioned by its context, and because that context is omitted from our judgment, we must be asserting that S is P on the assumption that the context does not contradict our assertion. But, if so, our assertion is hypothetical.

When we use 'this', we mean but fail to express "our reference to the object which is given as unique" (*PL*, 1, 66). Thus, Bradley writes, "That which I designate, is not and cannot be carried over into my judgment. The judgment may in a sense answer to that which I feel, but none the less it fails to contain and to convey my feeling" (*ETR*, 207). Bradley's mature view is that in thinking one approaches the world only through ideas, and, thus, only in terms of abstractions whose claim to truth is never without qualification.

In Terminal Essay Number 4 of *The Principles of Logic*, Bradley turns his back on perceptual uniqueness. There he says that uniqueness in its fullest sense is the same notion as 'individuality', and individuality in turn involves "self-containedness" and "the positive inseparable oneness of 'what' and 'that'" (*PL*, 2, 647). Only reality can be unique in this full sense, for any "thing" shows its dependence on its context and is, therefore, "ideal" to

---

15. This impression is heightened when one also states that "The idea of 'this,' unlike most ideas, can not be used as a symbol in judgment" (*PL*, *1*, 67).

some extent. The "this" has one aspect of uniqueness, that of being immediately given, but it cannot make good its claim to full uniqueness. Thus, we are correct in thinking that knowledge requires us to break out of our "iron ring" of ideas and confront our unique, real object; we are wrong in supposing that we actually do this in preception and that we could have no knowledge unless we do confront the real in perception and can report our awareness in categorically true judgments. We need sensible awareness to give us our contact with the real, but we do not need it as a source of certain truths. And it cannot provide us with any.

This last point explains Bradley's claim that singular judgments also lack existential reference (*PL*, 1, 103–07). Once we see that knowledge seeks a grasp of the whole, seeks to place a particular judgment in the context of reality (reality is such that S is P), we will see that singular judgments are, in fact, first attempts to find a connection of content that will hold good within the real. Thus, "This rose is red" means "If something is a rose, that is, if there are certain characteristics existing together, then they entail red." Of course, this statement is false, and so we must find the conditions under which it is true and bring them into our assertion. Precisely what connection of content we are trying to assert, and under what conditions it holds, will become clear only as we proceed to discover what connection logically follows from the way things are. In short, the singular judgment is a low form of scientific law (*PL*, 1, 104).

Let me try to summarize Bradley's view. When he says that singular statements are hypothetical, he seems to mean two things. First, no judgment can adequately express or refer to the particular fact it seems to be about. Because of the generality of all thoughts, there is a necessary gap between the real and our ideas of the real.

Second, this does not imply that knowledge is lost because it cannot be tied down categorically to particular facts. An analysis of judgment and its ideal reveals that we never really mean to speak of that individual fact. We think we do, and we try to indicate the individual fact by the use of 'this'. But we think this only because we have misunderstood what we are doing as thinkers, a mistake engendered by focusing our attention on a certain kind of judgment. In fact, our fundamental aim as thinkers is to show that what we assert follows from the fact that reality is the way it is. But this means that our ultimate aim is to characterize the whole as a necessary whole. Our singular judgments are first and halting approximations to this ideal.

The evidence for this view is that, as thinkers, we find singular judgments intellectually unsatisfactory unless we can say why they are true; but the spelling out of this "why" involves the transformation of our factual judgment into a necessary truth. As Bradley says, all judgments are both categorical and hypothetical: categorical in that they assert something of the real; hypothetical in that they do not ascribe their elements as such to the real (*PL*, 1, 106). Thus, it seems unimportant whether he holds that judgments are hypothetical because every judgment depends on the truth of other judgments or because what one asserts is abstract and cannot, as such, be true. In either case, the task of judgment is to bring within the judgment the conditions that do away with the distance between the asserted content and the real asserted-of; and, in neither case, can we do this in a way and to the extent that we desire.

Is Bradley's definition of judgment circular? Cook Wilson claims that the idea-theory presupposes, and does not explain, knowing. When we try to explicate the reference of the ideal content, we must reintroduce the judging we are claiming to define.[16] But this seems to be merely a point about the nature of judgment. 'Judgment' can mean either what is judged or the activity of judging; thus, in asking about either the ideal content or the reference in Bradley's definition, we find we must fall back on some form of 'judgment'. But there is no circularity here, because neither the act by itself nor the content by itself is the whole judgment that we are defining. They are aspects of judgment—yet, aspects we can refer to only by using the same word as we use for the whole. Bradley's point is merely that neither acts nor propositions by themselves are all there is to judgment in the fullest sense, and, in making this point, he merely wants to indicate the elements that comprise judgment.

16. Richard Robinson, "Cook Wilson's View of Judgment," p. 308.

Cook Wilson also attacks Bradley's view that in some sense judgment involves "making." He claims that it is a fundamental mistake to conceive of knowing at all on the analogy of practical activity, for knowing is incompatible "with any such *action* upon or *suffering* in, the object known." [17] It is simply a contradiction to think of truth as being "produced."

This criticism rests on a misunderstanding of Bradley's theory of judgment. Bradley's view is that whereas the world as I take it to be is a construction that I have "made" and that is more or less true (*ETR*, 46), the reality that is the subject of my judgment is not made by me. Thus, Bradley says, in as "realistic" a way as Cook Wilson could wish, "If my idea is to work it must correspond to a determinate being which it cannot be said to make" (*ETR*, 76). What I can be said to "construct" is the way the world seems to me, and this is not and cannot be the ultimate subject of my judgment.

Yet, Bradley insists, though this is a necessary assumption for the possibility of truth, it is in itself a one-sided truth. For it is also true that "Apart from its aspect of truth the reality would not be the reality" (*ETR*, 117). Knowledge must make some change in reality when it "happens"; if not, then to what does it make a difference? And because reality is the ultimate subject of judging, there must be a sense in which knowing does alter its object, even if this is not the sense Cook Wilson had in mind. We are faced, Bradley continues, with two "truths," neither of which can be abandoned, but which cannot be made consistent. Reality must be present both in knowledge and beyond it, but we are unable to say how both assertions can be true in any way that is ultimately satisfying.

17. Ibid., p. 206.

2

An Introduction to
the Theory of Relations

Bradley first develops his theory of relations in *The Principles of Logic,* where he asserts that understanding our given experience consists of analyzing a given whole into a series of discrete parts. In so doing, we destroy the unity of the given, for the given is not a collection of "parts." In the second stage of understanding, we take our "parts" and "relate" them, thereby attempting to make good the whole we have destroyed. We "recognize" additional "parts" in our original whole and assign them the task of bringing order to those "parts" that we now call "terms." This is what Bradley means when he says that all thinking involves both synthesis and analysis.

But we are now faced with the following difficulty:

> If the units have to exist together, they must stand in relation to one another; and, if these relations are also units, it would seem that the second class must also stand in relation to the first . . . If relations are facts that exist between facts, then what comes *between* the relations and the other facts? The real truth is that the units on one side, and on the other side the relations existing between them, are nothing actual (*PL,* 1, 96).

And why are they "nothing actual"? Because the given whole from which relations "emerge" cannot be resolved without remainder into terms and relations. Over and above the terms and relations, which do not convey adequately the sense of diversity-within-unity given us in immediate awareness, there is always a "felt background."

Bradley's puzzles over relations are not peculiar to him. In fact, classical, substance-oriented philosophers were extremely perplexed about relations. For example, in the *Phaedo,* Plato tries to assimilate relations to the model that he has already given for qualities, whereas Leibniz' metaphysics reflects his attempt to reduce relations to qualities. Neither attempt was noticeably successful.

Bradley agrees with the tradition that relations are not totally unlike qualities, for they do "qualify" the terms they join. But he denies that relations can be reduced to terms or qualities, for a relation is "external" as well as "internal"—it "stands between" the related terms. As such, it does not "make a difference" to its terms and is more like a "third thing" than anything else. Thus, for Bradley, though there is no relation that fails completely to make a difference to its terms, it is equally true that there is no relation that accounts completely for the character of the terms in question.

Thus, a term must be something in addition to the relations in which it stands. The relations must be "external" to it. Yet, because relations express the unity found in our immediate experience, it must be true that terms are "made" what they are by their relations. Every relation is "internal." But can something with such a two-faced character provide us with an intellectually satisfactory account of reality? When Bradley says that relations are self-contradictory, he means that they fail to provide such an account.

The classic statement of Bradley's theory of relations is found in the third chapter of *Appearance and Reality.* He claims there that our use of terms and relations to explain any state of affairs is no justification for our belief that our theories capture the real nature of things. Instead, we must try to see whether this use meets our standards of intelligibility. The terms and relations complex would be "intelligible" if relations join terms in a way that does not violate the law of contradiction. (And that involves whether or not relations provide a sufficient ground for seeing "how" qualities are joined. We shall explore this point shortly.) If we find ourselves lost in insoluble puzzles or contradictions when we try to understand the union of terms and relations, then we can be certain that terms and relations do not adequately reflect the nature of things.

Bradley begins by arguing that neither qualities nor relations can be understood apart from each other. Qualities cannot be conceived apart from relations for two reasons. First, in our consciousness, awareness of qualities arises from a process of comparison and differentiation, and these are nothing but ways of relating. Therefore, we never, in fact, find qualities apart from relations, and there seems no possibility that there might be such independent qualities. The fact that we can consider a quality apart from its relations proves nothing, for it shows only that we can abstract a term from the conditions in which it is found. It is even more obvious that relations are impossible apart from terms.

We must consider, then, both relations and qualities to see if we can make sense of their union. Unfortunately, we cannot. Because relations and terms are mutually interdependent, neither can be reduced to the other. Terms are entities that "stand in" relations; thus, they cannot be "made" by relations nor "precipitated" by them. It is true that "For thought what is not relative is nothing," but it is also true that "Nothings cannot be related, and that to turn qualities in relation into mere relations is impossible" (*AR*, 25). And because terms are "beyond" relations, we must make do with both in our account of the world.

This is precisely where the trouble lies, for terms and relations are both distinct from each other and mutually interdependent. Thus, every quality has two aspects: it "must be and must *also* be related" (*AR*, 26). And these aspects cannot be joined harmoniously. As Bradley says, "A is both made, and is not made, what it is by the relation; and these different aspects are not each the other, nor again is either A" (*AR*, 26). But this variety within A presupposes a relation within A, in order to connect its two aspects. Each aspect has become "against our wills" a new quality standing in a relation to its partner. And these new terms "fall hopelessly asunder." Our new subterm, call it A_1, cannot be completely either independent of, or dependent on, the relations in which it stands. It is divided within itself, thus leading to an "endless fission" of new terms and relations—and Bradley's infinite regress.

Unless one of these two claims about terms and relations can be shown to be mistaken, we are faced with Bradley's infinite regress.

Let us assume that there is a difference between terms and relations. It might still be claimed that they are not interdependent in the way Bradley thinks they are. But surely they are interdependent in the sense that neither could be unless the other also was, and this seems to mean that neither could be as it is unless the other was also as it is. The character of the one is "made" by its connection with the other. This does seem to lead to a genuine puzzle and one that the usual objections to Bradley's theory hardly touch on at all.

In addition, relations themselves are troublesome. Bradley insists that they "make a difference" to their terms. But how is this possible? A relation does not make a difference to its terms by being an adjective of one or of both the terms. It is not a property of each term, for then it could not relate the terms; neither is it a common property, for then it would obliterate the very distinctness of the terms that is essential to their being related. A relation seems to be "something itself," a thing or entity quite different from the terms, but a thing nevertheless. And we need a new relation to express the duality within the relation of making a difference to the terms and being something independent of, and distinct from, the terms. That is, we need a new relation to link the relation-as-independent-entity and the terms in need of relating. As Bradley asks, "Being something itself, if it does not itself bear a relation to the terms, in what intelligible way will it succeed in being anything to them?" (*AR*, 27–28).

We might try to conceive of relations as not quite different from terms and, yet, as something almost different from them. But this seems to be a meaningless compromise. We must, Bradley insists, conceive of relations as "solid" things, for they are as much a part of our experience as are terms. But, if so, we are faced with explaining how they can also link terms to one another, and we seem to have no other method at our command than the invention of new relations, which then are in need of new links, and so on.[1]

Bradley claims that the infinite regress of terms and relations means that relational complexes are "inherently self-contradic-

1. See F. H. Bradley, *Principles of Logic*, 2, 98, for a good statement of this process.

tory" and are, therefore, incapable of giving us things as they are. But how is Bradley using 'self-contradictory' when he applies this concept to relations?

The law of contradiction is usually taken to mean that contradictory propositions cannot both be true (epistemological sense) or that a thing cannot have two opposing properties at the same time and in the same way (ontological sense). We must be clear about what 'contradictory', or 'opposing', means if we are to know what the law forbids. On one extreme view, it forbids thinking or asserting that a thing is anything but itself. As long as we produce tautologies, our assertions will not be "self-contradictory," but as soon as we make synthetic statements, we contradict ourselves. For A is not B; it is simply A. Thus, to say that A is B is to say that it is what it is not, and this is to contradict oneself.[2]

Bradley does not accept this interpretation of the law of contradiction. He states the law as follows:

> A thing cannot without an internal distinction be (or do) two different things, and differences cannot belong to the same thing in the same point unless in that point there is diversity. The appearance of such a union may be fact, but it is for thought a contradiction (AR, 501).

Thus, it is not the uniting of differences per se that the law of contradiction prohibits, for thinking just is the bringing together of differences into a certain kind of unity, and it is nonsense to believe that the law of contradiction would deny the very possibility of thinking. What the law does forbid is the uniting of these differences in a way that conflicts with thought's ideal.

And what is that ideal? "Thought demands to go *proprio motu,*

2. There is one charge leveled against Bradley again and again that has no foundation whatever. It is often said that Bradley's difficulties with thinking result from a confusion between the 'is' of predication and the 'is' of identity. Bradley thinks that we contradict ourselves when we say that A is B because he interprets the 'is' in the second sense, though it obviously is meant in the first sense. But, as Campbell points out, Bradley's case rests not on this obvious mistake but, rather, on the assumption that all thinking involves the uniting of different elements. And quoting Campbell, "Indeed the bare union of differents turns out, when we reflect upon it, to be *tantamount* to their identification" (SG, 390). The 'is' of predication is as much of a problem for thought as is the 'is' of identity. Bradley calls into question what is held in common between the two kinds of 'is'. Therefore, any criticism based on their distinction can have no force against Bradley.

or, what is the same thing, with a ground and reason" (*AR,* 501). As thinkers, we are unsatisfied until we can see why A is B, as contrasted with knowing merely that A is B. Thought desires insight into necessary connection, and it is presupposed in all thinking that reality will satisfy us on this score. Because we do not have this insight to begin with, we must achieve it, and the way we do this is to find a reason by means of which we can pass intelligibly from A to B. This ground is, in some sense, "beyond" or "behind" the facts as they are given. It is a principle or law.

Here is where our difficulties begin. The ground or reason we use to explain the mere conjunction of two facts (for example, the fact that the sliding metal roof of my car jams on a hot summer's day) itself involves the synthesis or connection of two elements, a connection that is not at all self-evident (for example, the law that metal expands when heated). The result is that

> The intellect is obliged therefore to ask *why,* to look for some ground for this new connection; and obviously it has not secured a satisfactory ground for the *first* connection to be explained if it has not secured a satisfactory ground for this *second* connection, in terms of which it sought to explain the first (*SG,* 394).

Whatever principle we choose will contain a connection of elements as unintelligible as the one with which we began. Thinking must work with elements that are merely "given" to it, for it cannot "make" the elements with which it starts. As thinkers, we must try to account for the divisions and conjunctions that we find in our experience. The distinctions that we find are, unfortunately, unsatisfactory as they stand.

Thought is as impotent to make sense of what it has found as it is to "create" its own "material." Perhaps if "Thought in its own nature possessed a 'together', a 'between', and an 'all at once', then in its own intrinsic passage, or at least somehow in its own way and manner, it could reaffirm the external conjunction" (*AR,* 504). This means that thought does not have the power to reassemble the parts it has extracted from the given into the kind of whole it finds theoretically satisfactory. In attempting to bring the perceptual facts into a logical whole, thought makes its own distinctions. In Bradley's words, it "cuts away a mass of environing

particulars, and offers the residue bare, as something given and to
be accepted free from supporting conditions" (AR, 503). And once
this analytic bit of work is accomplished, thought finds it impossible to do anything but "explain" the mere conjunction of facts
in terms of the mere conjunction of some other, usually wider,
set of facts—the grounds of our first conjunction. In the end, we
affirm a conjunction of different elements, and this is precisely
what it means to contradict oneself.

The paradox of thought can be summarized in three propositions. (1) Thought rejects tautologies as its means of expression.
(2) Judgments are unities of different elements. (3) However, no
uniting of different elements is self-evident. Therefore, none is acceptable as a principle on which we can rest.

As thinkers, we are able to recognize that the self-contradictory
character of our assertions is owing to the way in which we deal
with the world and not to the character of that world. This means
that "No intrinsical opposites exist, but that contraries, in a sense,
are made. Hence in the end nothing is contrary nor is there any
insoluble contradiction" (AR, 505). It is this insight that enables
one to distinguish between appearance and reality.

We are also able to conceive in a general way of what would
satisfy us as knowers. In fact, it is this very vision that makes it
possible for us to recognize that our thoughts give appearance and
not reality. As Bradley states this ideal:

> If the diversities were complementary aspects of a process of con-
> nexion and distinction, the process not being external to the ele-
> ments or again a foreign compulsion of the intellect, but itself the
> intellect's own *proprius motus,* the case would be altered. Each as-
> pect would of itself be a transition to the other aspect, a transi-
> tion intrinsic and natural at once to itself and to the intellect.
> And the Whole would be a self-evident analysis and synthesis of
> the intellect itself by itself (PL, 2, 507).

Such a system would satisfy the law of contradiction because in
it "There is no point which is not itself internally the transition
to its complement, and there is no unity which fails in internal diversity and ground of distinction" (AR, 507). However, Bradley
is quick to point out that he cannot "verify" this ideal in detail.

Our intellect in its actual operations is discursive, meaning that it goes from point to point, lacks a power of intuition, and works within a material that is given and "external" to it. The result is that all thinking is in part "mere" synthesis, the linking of different elements that are external to one another. This lack of an intellectual "together" is expressed in thought's use of terms and relations, for these cannot be united in a way that does away with externality.

When Bradley is developing thought's inability to find adequate grounds, he is simply echoing Hume's theory of intellectual synthesis. Like Hume, he argues that the most the intellect can do is to see things as conjoined; it can never, finally, see the "why" of anything. Yet, he opposes Hume in stressing that thought demands more than mere conjunction. This sense of unrealized purpose in our thinking colors Bradley's doctrine with metaphysical hues only hinted at in the Appendix to Hume's *Treatise on Human Nature*.

Bradley is far from being a simple follower of Hegel, but he does accept the Hegelian notion of an "identity of opposites" as the ideal we try to realize when we think. However, he denies that this ideal can be realized by thought. This implies that thought cannot in some way be identified with the real, an assertion Bradley attributes to Hegel. In Bradley's view, Hume places too much emphasis on the actual results of thinking, thereby misjudging the essential character of both thought and reality. Hegel, on the other hand, places too much emphasis on the ideal of thinking, thereby misjudging what thought can actually accomplish. From one point of view, *Appearance and Reality* is an attempt to mediate these extremes.

When we try to make our experience orderly and rational, we relate terms to one another in order to see why they are arranged as they are. We do this whenever we say that one thing is the cause of another, or distinguish between primary and secondary qualities, or between quality and substance. But this is just to say that relations are grounds. The difficulty with relations and grounds is the same; it is the failure of the intellect to realize the vision of wholeness that alone can completely satisfy the impulse to know.

3

The Realist Criticism of
the Theory of Relations

The most charitable comment that one hears contemporary philosophers make about Bradley's theory of relations is that it represents a last, hopeless attempt to construe the universe in terms of the classical subject-predicate model. Thus, when Bradley proclaims the "unreality" of relations, he succeeds in doing no more than indicating that relations are neither terms nor predicates and that puzzles arise when they are so conceived. In fact, his critics maintain, there are no puzzles about relations, their reality, or the act of relating of the kind Bradley claims to discover; relations do relate, and any theory that insists that they do not should be rejected. The realist reply to Bradley is most forcefully stated in the writings of C. D. Broad and John Cook Wilson. In what follows, I argue that they are not so decisive against Bradley as is generally believed.

Broad vs. Bradley

Broad puts his case as follows:

> Bradley's argument depends on insisting that the relations shall behave as if they were particulars like the terms which they relate. It is plain that Bradley thinks of A and B as being like two objects fastened together with a bit of string. He then remembers that the objects must be glued or sealed to both ends of the bit of string if the latter is to fasten them together. And then, I suppose, another kind of glue is needed to fasten the first drop of glue to the object A on the one side and to the bit of string on the other. . . . Charity bids us avert our eyes from the pitiable spectacle of a

great philosopher using an argument which would disgrace a child or a savage.[1]

Indeed, the argument is pitiful. But Broad's criticism ignores the fact that Bradley employs no such argument to prove the point attributed to him by Broad.

In fact, some further remarks by Broad himself show this. He goes on to cite Bradley's "real" objection to relations—that there are "unities" prior, both logically and psychologically, to terms and relations. This belief leads Bradley to view any set of terms and relations as an abstraction from such a "unity." As Broad says, "Consequently the notion of terms which could exist independently of each other and of the wholes in which they are parts, and which could then, by 'coming into relations,' constitute these wholes, is a complete perversion of the real order" (EMP, 1, 86–87). When Bradley condemns relations as "unreal," he means to point up this disparity betwen the wholes that are given to us in sense and that which we say or think about such wholes and the parts of such wholes.

It is clear that Bradley did object to the adequacy of relational schemes for precisely the reason suggested by Broad (PL, 1, 95). The view that relations and terms are the products of analysis forms the basis for Bradley's criticisms of relations in the first part of Appearance and Reality. But Broad is quite incorrect in claiming that there is no connection between such criticisms (for which he has no sympathy) and the above view of "unities," with which he has at least some sympathy. In fact, this view forms the basis for the criticism of relations.

We have seen that Bradley does claim that terms and relations are mutually interdependent and partially independent. Interdependence is the reflection in our thought of the unity of perceptual experience. Independence is the reflection, present in thought, of the emerging qualitative distinctness of the "aspects" present in immediate experience. And Bradley claims that we cannot understand how relations can combine within themselves

1. C. D. Broad, An Examination of McTaggart's Philosophy (Cambridge, Cambridge University Press, 1933), 1, 85. See A. C. Ewing, Idealism, A Critical Survey (London, Methuen and Co., 1961), pp. 147 and 443, for the assertion and subsequent recantation of this same view.

the qualities of dependence and independence in a way that we find logical. Thus, relations, though "facts" beyond a doubt, are said to be "unreal," to be combinations of different elements without a sufficient reason.

Perhaps a concrete example will help to clarify matters. Consider an individual person, Smith. There is something about Smith that he owes to his relations with others, such as his attitudes toward morality, and politics. Equally, however, there must be something about Smith that he brings to his relationships with others, for he is not simply the product of his environment. After all, it is Smith who is "friend of," "smarter than," and so forth. If not, then there are just relations relating other relations, and that is nonsense.

A person somehow combines diverse elements but still remains one person, and this is not doubted by Bradley. The question he raises is whether we can give an adequate theoretical account of this unity.

Perhaps the qualities that derive from Smith's relations with others are less essential to Smith being the person he is, whereas the characteristics or attitudes that he brings to these relationships are more essential. Thus, we may establish a relation between the two sets of qualities. But have we solved our problem? The less essential qualities are still aspects of Smith, and how they relate to the more essential qualities is not explained satisfactorily by giving one group a "higher" title than another. As Bradley says, "Nothing is actually removed from existence by being labelled 'appearance.' What appears is there, and must be dealt with" (AR, 12).

Furthermore, are the "essential" qualities not affected in any way by the beliefs and attitudes acquired from the relations one has with others? Surely Smith is not divided into two water-tight compartments that have no influence on each other; once such a claim is made, Smith has become two persons rather than one. But if there is some real connection between the two aspects of Smith's character, the distinction of essential and nonessential must be used again to explain the hitherto unnoticed division within the so-called essential qualities. It is this reappearance of our original problem—the explanation of the combination of the different into a single whole—that signifies our failure to understand the "how" of such a combination. And it seems clear that the regress is endless.

The preceding, I believe, is a fair statement of Bradley's case against relations (and terms) being an adequate conceptual means of expressing the nature of reality. Nowhere do I find the kind of simpleminded error that Broad attributes to Bradley, namely, that of assuming that relations are not relations and then of finding to his horror that they do not relate. It is true that Bradley assumes that relations are different from terms; it is also true that he asserts that terms and relations taken together do not form a whole in which the intellect can find ultimate satisfaction. (This is the sense in which relations do not relate.) But neither of these claims is equivalent to a gross begging of the question or to an obvious and prejudiced misconception of the question.

There are two main confusions in Broad's attack on Bradley. First, Broad assumes that for Bradley relations can be thought of as existing completely apart from their terms. This is precisely what Bradley denies when he shows the futility of conceiving of relations as terms and when he denies that the notion of external relations makes any sense at all. Second, Broad believes that Bradley is denying the obvious fact that terms are related to one another. Inasmuch as relations do relate, there must be something seriously wrong with Bradley's argument. But Bradley does not intend to deny any such obvious fact. What he is doing, on the contrary, is showing what happens, both to terms and to relations, when relations do relate.

Bradley is questioning whether terms and relations can give us full intellectual satisfaction. No fact of observation is being denied in this question; the question relates to the rationality of the facts themselves. For these "facts," though creations of the intellect, do not in Bradley's view satisfy the intellect's demand for coherence. The question Bradley is asking cannot contradict common sense, for it is a question that common sense has no need of asking.

Cook Wilson vs. Bradley

Perhaps the most searching criticism of Bradley's position on relations is offered by John Cook Wilson. He argues that the so-called infinite regress generated by terms and relations is, in fact, an illusion. In order for there to be a genuine regress, there must be a new relation generated by the difference between A (term) and R (relation). Call this new relation R_1. Then R_1 must be a new entity so that the statement " 'A stands in relation R_1 to R' should be new and not a part of the original statement which gave R as the relation between A and B." [2] Otherwise, R_1 will turn out to be nothing but a repetition of R, and the regress will be purely formal and harmless. Cook Wilson finds the fallacy in Bradley's position in the assumption "that if two somethings are different from one another they must stand to one another in a relation which is different from either, not identical with nor included in the separate nature of either." In fact, when one asks what the relation is between A and R, one asks a question without any meaning, for "the idea of a relation cannot be applied, as is proposed, to a relation and a term of that relation itself" (*SI*, 2, 692–93). When A equals B, if one asks what the relation of R is to A, one can reply only that A does, in fact, equal B. All that we seem to have said is that the relation of R to A is the relation of A to B. We do not conjure up a new relation, R_1. Rather, we merely restate the fact that R is the relation in which A and B stand, and in so doing we seem to confess that the question, as put to us, cannot be answered. If A causes B, then A is related to causality through the latter being the relation that joins A and B.

Thus, Cook Wilson is making two points against Bradley. (1) To know how A and B are related is to know how R stands to A and B. Because these are the same, one provides the same information as the other, and there is no infinite regress of new relations. (2) It is nonsense to ask for the relation between a relation and a term of that relation. We can ask how the terms are related, but we cannot ask how terms and relations are related, for relations hold between terms and not between terms and relations. These are serious objections to Bradley's view, and there is a good deal of force in both of them.

For Bradley, all explanation starts with the diversity that we find in feeling and perception. This poses a question to our intel-

2. John Cook Wilson, *Statement and Inference*, ed. A. S. L. Farquharson (2 vols. Oxford, The Clarendon Press, 1926), 2, 693.

lect: Why are things diverse in this way rather than in some other way?

Thought tries to clarify the perceptual manifold by distinguishing the things of the perceptual manifold and relating its "things" in a way that it finds satisfactory. But this process faces the following dilemma:

> While the diversities are external to each other and to their union, ultimate satisfaction is impossible. There must, as we have seen, be an identity and in that identity a ground of distinction and connexion. But that ground, if external to the elements into which the conjunction must be analysed, becomes for the intellect a fresh element, and it itself calls for synthesis in a fresh point of unity. But hereon, because in the intellect no intrinsic connexions were found, ensues the infinite process (AR, 507).

Bradley links the "infinite process" to the lack in the intellect of any "intrinsic connections." What does this mean? The intellect tries to provide us with an explicit, rational ground for the facts of experience. But it cannot, for the demands of thought for rational insight are one thing and the power of thought to satisfy such demands is another. Thought can accept synthesis only where there is a reason or ground for synthesis, but thought has no "intrinsic connection" with which to fulfill this demand; it "can of itself supply no internal bond."

In addition, thought demands that its terms be brought into a unified whole, a whole in which the "why" of the connection of things is made explicit; but thought has no power to see things as a whole. Bradley denies that reason has the kind of synoptic power that has been claimed for it by Plato, Spinoza, Hegel, and others. Yet, he insists that such a total view represents the genuine, felt ideal of thinking.

Taken together, these two failures of thinking imply that it is discursive rather than intuitive. Thought cannot hold its elements apart, for they are already together in perception; on the other hand, thought has no "internal bond" by means of which it might unite them rationally or consistently.

Thought would not be dissatisfied with mere conjunction if it had, of its own nature, a " 'together,' a 'between,' and an 'all at once.' " But, Bradley insists, these "sensible bonds of union" do fall outside of the nature of thought as much as do the terms that are to be united. Thus, thinking can find no theoretical satisfaction in such bonds.

As Bradley puts it, thought fails in two ways to explain. First, "The principles taken up are not merely in themselves not rational, but, being limited, they remain external to the facts to be explained" (*AR,* 502). Bradley here takes the view that, when we explain why something happens, we relate the given complex to a general rule or law. But the principle merely states in a general way the fact that the elements mentioned in the principle are conjoined within our experience, and how does our generalization give us insight into why this holds true? Of course, some rationalists have claimed that the basic laws of physics, for example, are simple, necessary truths about nature, but in this regard Bradley cannot be considered as a rationalist of their persuasion. For him, there is no self-evidence in our scientific principles; they do no more than assert that certain conjunctions are ultimate facts about reality. Yet, because they do no more than this, they are not rational and fail to yield ultimate intellectual satisfaction.

Second, Bradley complains that the principle is related externally to the facts that fall under it, which means that the facts must be "brought under" the principle rather than emerging from it. This claim points up the fact that our principles fail to be genuinely comprehensive. There are always facts that, although interpreted in terms of them, seem quite alien to these principles. We force the facts to fit the concepts and laws that have worked elsewhere, and though this may yield success in the form of practical control, does it give us truth? Can we see that the facts demand or entail this manner of considering them, or do *we* impose a scheme on the facts that is foreign to their nature?

Bradley suggests that at some point the latter is always the case; we always see the world from a limited point of view and then try to understand the rest of our experience from that point of view. Such a procedure cannot result in the unity of principle and fact that our intellect demands.

Bradley gives as an instance of this process "the mechanical interpretation of the world." We develop certain principles in physics, and then we try to explain living things and minds in terms of them. But can a mind and its activity be rightly considered within the same framework as the reactions of physical particles? Can there be a "physics" of thinking, or is thinking an end-directed process that eludes the concepts of interaction, association, and so forth? And even within the material world itself, there is not the desired unity between theory and fact. The current emphasis on theories, as means of prediction enabling man to secure control over his environment, Bradley would regard as evidence that our failure to obtain ultimate truth has been recognized and is now being paraded as the only and highest end of thought, rather than its failure. In his view, much of modern philosophy embodies a basic confusion between what thought actually accomplishes (ideas or theories that have "validity," that is, that work practically) and the end thought seeks of its own nature (theoretical satisfaction, logical coherence, truth, the expression of reality in the form of ideas). The confusion is compounded when the former is identified with the latter in the name of common sense, empiricism, science, and, even, in the case of Bergson, mystical intuition.

It seems to me that Bradley's analysis of thinking undercuts the basis of Cook Wilson's criticism. As Cook Wilson states the problem, there does indeed seem to be no really informative answer that one can give to the question of how a relation stands to its terms. But the same matter can be stated otherwise and in a way that does allow of an answer. When we say that friction is the cause of heat, we relate two items of our experience. But we immediately find ourselves asking how friction causes heat.

Two things are said about friction: It is friction, and it is also the cause of heat, and we want to know how these two aspects of friction are related. So we bring in a theoretical account: Friction causes some molecular change, and this causes the sensation of heat. But, of course, the relation of friction to some molecular change is no more self-evident than is its relation to heat; nor is there anything self-evident about the relation of some molecular change to heat.

Thus, we once again attempt to find a reason for the character of our experience. What is the link that will explain the connec-

tion between friction and what it is said to produce? Whatever
form our answer takes, there will be no more self-evidence or necessity in it than there is in the conjunction with which we began.
The regress is indeed infinite, and I see no reason whatever for
denying that the problem is a genuine one or that the answers to it
go beyond the original fact of the conjunction of friction and
heat.

There is a regress because there is a continual search for terms
that entail one another; the regress is real and not merely formal
because we must "discover" new causal relations to explain the
causal relation under consideration, much as we "discovered" the
original causal relation to explain the conjunction of elements
with which we started. Each level brings a new causal relation
and a new content to act as the ground for the content and relation on the previous level; but no level is without need of an explanation for the conjunction of elements on which it is based
and from which we can understand a previously asserted causal
relation.[3]

Finally, is the regress of conjoined elements vicious? Much in the
spirit of Kant, Bradley claims that our intellect seeks the uncondi-
tioned, a comprehensive, detailed grasp of reality as a whole. All
it accomplishes, however, is theories that are limited and inadequate and that demand further conditions to remedy these de-
fects. The regress is vicious because it represents a failure of
thought to reach its own end, that of a comprehensive insight into
the "why" of things.

In general, Bradley's problems with relations arise because of
the inability of terms and relations to express fully the logical, systematic whole that thinking seeks. The connection between the
parts of this whole is more intimate than the concepts 'term' and

3. Schlick makes the same point when he asserts that understanding a causal
relation (as contrasted with merely experiencing a sequence of two events) occurs
when we are able to fill in the gap between cause and effect with "an unbroken
chain of events which are contiguous in space and time." But these events, which
allow us to infer the effect from the cause, are themselves known to follow one
another only because "in the laboratory this has always been the regular course
of things." In the end, we fall back on observed regularity. Moritz Schlick, "Causality in Everyday Life and in Recent Science," *Readings in Philosophical Analysis,*
ed. Herbert Feigl and Wilfrid Sellars (New York, Appleton-Century-Crofts, 1949),
p. 521.

'relation' suggest. The result is an infinite regress resulting either from our attempt to demarcate clearly the terms that are said to "stand in" the relations or from the lack of intrinsic connection between the terms even after they have been related. In short, terms-in-relation do not form the kind of whole that can bring final, theoretical satisfaction; for although every relation does make a difference to its terms, thus suggesting a more intimate kind of unity and bringing about the first kind of regress, no relation gives us an adequate insight into why the terms are conjoined. Thus follows the second kind of regress. The criticisms of both Broad and Cook Wilson, ignoring as they do the philosophic context of Bradley's theory of relations, do nothing to prove that his concept of thinking is mistaken, and it is this failure to consider his theory in its wider setting that explains the ineffectiveness of their criticisms.

4

The Doctrine of
Internal Relations

I

Perhaps a good way of focusing on the doctrine of internal relations is to consider the debate in the pages of *Mind* for 1910–11 between Bradley and Bertrand Russell. Russell there defines the issue as follows:

> The view which I reject holds (if I understand it aright) that the fact that an object x has a certain relation R to an object y implies complexity in x and y, i.e., it implies something in the 'natures' of x and y in virtue of which they are related by the relation R.[1]

Russell's own position is that

> there are such facts as that x has the relation R to y, and that such facts are not in general reducible to, or inferable from, a fact about x only and a fact about y only; they do not imply that x and y have any complexity, or any intrinsic property distinguishing them from a z and a w which do not have the relation R.[2]

The basis of disagreement, as Russell sees it, lies in Bradley's belief that all truths are necessary. This belief, in turn, is the result of Bradley's adherence to the principle of sufficient reason: If there must be a sufficient reason for the truth of every proposition, then no proposition will be "merely true in fact." Russell is quite willing to accept the view that "fundamentally" all truths are "merely true in fact," which is equivalent to denying that a reason must be given, or even can be given, that explains why a

1. Bertrand Russell, "Some Explanations in Reply to Mr. Bradley," *Mind,* n.s., *19* (1910), 373–74.
2. Ibid., p. 374.

given proposition is true. In Bradley's view, if no such explanation is possible, then the truth of the proposition (and the character of the fact contained in the proposition) is fortuitous. He finds this possibility intolerable, and Russell does not.[3]

Bradley's reply to Russell [4] begins by arguing that externality and "mere fact" are things that cannot possibly be observed. What is observed is a whole or manifold that forms the given from which all thinking proceeds, and from this manifold, by a process of distinguishing, qualities and their relations arise. The complete fact is always the terms in relation and the unity or whole from which they emerge. The whole may be ignored and fall into the background of our attention, but it remains the basis or ground for the relating of the terms. The terms seem external to one another only because we mistake the result of our distinguishing for the actual, complete fact. "The supposed fact is really an inference reached by vicious abstraction" (ETR, 290).

Russell's commonsensical argument appeals to what is obviously the case and attempts to express this in theoretical or general terms. As he has no difficulty or ambiguity in deciding what the facts are, and as his theory is a mere transcription into other terms of these accepted facts, there can be nothing questionable about the theory.

Bradley agrees with Russell's implicit assumption that the job of a theoretical statement about relations is to be "like" the facts it depicts. He agrees further that the facts imply a certain theory about relations and that knowing what the facts are is crucial to formulating any such theory. Bradley contends, however, that Russell has confused theory-laden "facts" (that there are "things" that stand in "relations" to other "things") with the real, given facts of perception.

Critical reflection leads to the undermining of a further assumption of Russell's. Russell seems to be sanguine about the possibility of having a theory of relations that will "mirror" relational facts. However, when we reflect on "fact" and "the given,"

3. A more elaborate statement of Russell's position can be found in his *Philosophical Essays* (London, Longmans, Green, 1910), Ch. 6, "The Monistic Theory of Truth."

4. Bradley, "Reply to Mr. Russell's Explanations," *Mind*, n.s., 20 (1911), 74–76.

we may find the world far different from what we at first supposed. And if we include in this critical reflection an analysis of
thinking, and of how thinking stands to relations and to the
given, and an analysis of "reality", and of how both thinking and
the given stand to it, we may well begin to wonder whether any
theory can be considered a mere transcription of the facts.

Bradley admits, further, that Russell's theory correctly embodies a central feature of ordinary belief and perception, namely,
that things remain unchanged in character when their relations
to other things change. But the theory overlooks the possibility
that perception (and the beliefs based on it) involves the "work
of the mind." If this is the case, the facts to which our theory
must conform in order to be true are not as they seem to be in
cases of explicit perception. (In such cases, things seem to be externally related to one another.) For it is just these "facts" that,
in Bradley's view, are the result of our conceptualizing. This is
precisely the point that Bradley made against James' doctrine of
pure experience—that it did not distinguish clearly enough between the really pure and what was, in fact, the initial result of
our conceptualizing the given. Bradley insists on a "tough-
minded" empiricism, a doctrine that is less easy to practice than
either James or Russell imagined.

Of course, Bradley is not saying that it is simply false to believe
that there are things that are the same in different contexts. For
ordinary purposes and for getting on in the world, Russell's
theory does splendidly. Bradley does insist, however, that for philosophical purposes, a far less commonsensical theory is needed because of the failure of common sense to notice the "work of the
mind" in perception. If it could be shown that perception is shot
through with inference, it would tend to undermine the assumption that the facts to be accounted for are "given" in perception. For then, the commonsense world will be seen as a construction based on something more fundamental, and what the
ultimate facts are will have to be reconsidered in the light of this
real given. The distinction between sensing and perceiving is one
way that philosophers have tried to bring out this distinction of
levels.

The second side of the dispute over relations concerns an appeal not to certain perceptual "facts" but, rather, to what *must* be

the case with relations. Bradley analyzes the nature and goal of thinking as that which makes possible the claim that all relations must be internal, even when this does not seem to be the case. Russell has failed to see that the issue might be argued in some other manner than appealing to the given facts found in perception. Bradley avails himself of this second mode of argument, and Russell does not; I shall argue that this difference gives Bradley an important advantage over Russell and over exponents of the external relations theory generally.

This side to the dispute presents a contrast in philosophical methodology. Russell's position seems to rest on the claim that one can notice obvious cases in which terms are not affected by the relations in which they stand, for example, spatial relations. Bradley does not deny that such often seems to be the case. Rather, he tries to show that more basic considerations about the nature of relations and of knowledge lead to the conclusion that all relations must "make a difference," even when we cannot see how.

One might wonder about the status of Bradley's position if no appeal to the facts can either prove it or disprove it. The answer is that, though the apparent facts of perception do not decide the matter conclusively, there are some facts (those concerning the nature of thinking) that at least are relevant. From these facts, one can argue that all relations are internal, for they (the facts) make it possible to grasp the nature of relations in a way that the facts of explicit perception do not. Here we argue from a basis of facts to the conclusion entailed by those facts. What the facts are and whether our conclusion actually is entailed by the facts may be matters of dispute, but one cannot disprove the conclusion that relations are internal to their terms simply by asserting that some relations are external to their terms, for such an assertion may involve an appeal to ignorance.

II

Let us consider some other arguments of Bradley's that attempt to cast doubt on the case for external relations. The question is: What can one say against the possibility that the world is composed of discrete units related by mere conjunction as conceived by Hume? To some degree, this must be how the defender of external relations conceives of things. First, Bradley argues that, even on the level of "thing" and "relation," it is not clear that the "facts" establish Russell's theory. Second, he attempts to show that the notion of an external relation is an absurdity. The former might be called Bradley's empirical argument and the latter his a priori argument.

Bradley points out that it is not enough to show that a certain character remains the same despite the change of a certain relation. At most, such an argument could prove only that this particular relation was external to this particular term; it would not prove that all relations were external. Neither would it prove that this particular term could exist "independent and naked." More importantly, the obvious cases of seemingly external relations (comparison and spatial change) on examination bring the externality of the relation into doubt.

Consider comparison. I compare A and B and find A to be "more beautiful" than B. In so doing, have I not left both A and B as they were before the comparison? The comparison is *my* act and does not affect the terms compared. But, one might ask, why do I make this particular comparison? If there be nothing in the terms that calls for this comparison, that is, if we merely impose the relation on the terms, then how can that relation be true of the terms?

Yet, if the relation is based on a quality found in the terms, then the terms have that relation because of their character, and this character is the reason for the relation. But this is precisely what is meant by saying that a relation is "internal" to its terms; a change in that relation would make a difference to the terms. A might remain A in some sense and not be more beautiful than B, but it would also be a very different A if it no longer stood in that relation to B.

And what of spatial relations, which seem to be a prime case of external relations? A thing can be moved to a new location and still remain the same thing, unchanged in all respects save that of spatial location and the relations and relational properties that went with that location. Bradley wants it clear at the outset that the issue is not whether "for working purposes we treat, and do well to treat, some relations as external merely" (*AR*, 515). Nor does he question the fact that we seem to find complete externality in spatial relations (*AR*, 517).

Nevertheless, Bradley's basic principle that reality is rational makes it impossible for him to accept such externality as ultimate fact. To do so would be to admit that there are some facts for which there is no explanation, and such a state of affairs violates the basic assumption of all thinking. Therefore, when we think that spatial or temporal relations are merely external, we mistake our ignorance for the fact, or an abstraction for the concrete reality.

We do not know how the character of a thing and its spatial existence are so related that they mutually determine each other. This connection is just as unintelligible to us as is the connection between the appearance of qualities and the changes in our brain that are said to "produce" such sensations. But the fact that we cannot see such connections in detail does not prove that they do not exist. That they do exist may be called an article of faith, but it is a rational faith based on an examination of thought and its demands in relation to reality.

Bradley presents his case that spatial change does "make a difference" in a twofold manner. He begins with the nature of space. Space, he insists, is an abstraction from a "more concrete qualitative unity." There is nothing that is merely spatial, for such relations rest throughout on qualitative differences. It seems a short step from this to the claim that spatial relations are mere dim reflections of the more concrete, intimate unity of "differents" that we are aware of in feeling or perception. In this view, no change can be merely spatial, for all change is fundamentally qualitative, and spatial change is an inadequate expression of qualitative change. And it is the metaphysical character of space, that of an "appearance of the more intimate unity suggested in immediate awareness," that guarantees that spatial change does mean a real difference in the terms related. As it stands, the argument is unconvincing, and I shall pass over it without further comment.

Second, Bradley points out that if we begin considering a thing apart from its spatial and temporal context, then of course the "thing" will not be affected by any changes in these relations. We first consider the thing from the point of view of a certain character that it has, find this unaffected by a change of place, and then conclude that spatial relations are external. An example of this occurs in science fiction stories in which people go backward or forward in time. We imagine that we can conceive ourselves living in some remote time, but the "we" is obviously an abstraction from the concrete individual. A concrete thing is determined by its spatial or temporal context to be what it is, and to change these relations would be to change the thing in a significant way.

Of course, this change may be insignificant from a certain point of view, but being, in fact, a change to the thing it is not merely external to that thing. In so saying, Bradley is careful not to reduce the doctrine of internal relations to a doctrine that is trivially true because of the extremely broad manner in which he defines the "nature" of a thing: If any property of a thing is considered part of the "nature" of the thing, then it is analytic to say that all change is a change in the "nature" of the thing. As G. E. Moore pointed out, everything has a property merely as the result of standing in a relation, namely, the property derived from the relation itself. Thus, if Jim stands in the relation "smarter than" to John, Jim has the relational property of being smarter than John. If this property is considered to be part of the "nature" of Jim, then a change in the relation will make a change in his "nature." But this will be true only because you have defined "nature" so as to include all properties.[5]

Although Bradley does not mean that all relational proposi-

---

5. A. J. Ayer seems to take the theory of internal relations in just such a way when he claims "We find that to assert that all relations are internal to their terms is equivalent to asserting, with regard to any relational proposition, that if it is true then it is in fact analytic. And it is not difficult to see that this assertion is false." "Symposium: Internal Relations," *Aristotelian Society Proceedings, 14,* supp. (1936), 175. Russell makes the same claim in *Philosophical Essays,* p. 167. This is most certainly not what Bradley means to say, and Ayer here makes no attempt to prove that it is. In addition, Ayer assumes that it is easy to name some relational propositions that are not necessarily true, just as Russell thought it was easy to cite some cases of things that were related externally. But are not such claims based on assumptions about knowledge, perception, and so forth that cry out for justification, but that, at least in the present context, receive no attention at all from either Russell or Ayer?

tions are analytic when he says that all relations "make a difference," it is easy to see why someone might so interpret him. First, he does not accept the traditional distinction between essential and accidental properties. No property, in his view, is merely accidental, but not because he has defined "nature of X" so as to include all that is true about X. Rather, he claims that a change in X implies a change in the other properties of X, properties that may be more immediately essential to X being what it is. A relation is internal because of what a change in it would mean to its terms generally.

In addition, the doctrine does not imply that all assertions about an individual are analytically true. If Bradley is right, it does follow that all statements about an individual are necessarily true, for if every relation or property does "make a difference" in the above sense, there is no aspect of an individual that does not entail, and is not entailed by, every other aspect. And entailment is a necessary relation. However, unless it can be shown that all entailment is analytic, it does not follow that the doctrine of internal relations would make all assertions trivial.[6] It would follow that no aspect of an individual is without importance to any other aspect and to the whole individual, but this is far from saying that the subject of my assertion "contains" the property asserted of him. Neither is it to say that the "nature" of the subject is simply the sum of all of its properties. Thus, the doctrine of internal relations does not make uninformative our ordinary claims about things.

Returning to our subject, is there any empirical evidence that spatial relations do "make a difference?" If a person moves, does not his new location both reflect and cause differences in him? If so, the new relation must be "internal." And what of the case in which the new spatial relationship creates a "fresh aspect of quality"? If one arrangement of flowers is more beautiful than another, then are not the terms affected by that arrangement? If a musical phrase expresses different moods depending on the order in which its notes are played, does not this temporal order "make a difference" to the phrase and its parts? It may not be obvious

6. For the defense of the view that entailment is a synthetic relation, see Brand Blanshard, *Reason and Analysis* (London, Allen & Unwin, 1962), pp. 283ff.

that absence makes the heart grow fonder, but it does seem clear that absence makes some difference to the parties involved.

Thus, Bradley concludes, a thing's spatial relations are an expression, although inadequate, of the complete relativity of one thing to another. The externality that we seem to find in spatial configuration reveals on closer inspection that such relationships either determine the nature of the terms completely (as in the case of the parts of space itself), partly (as in the above examples), or not at all as far as we can see; but even in the last case we must believe that such determination is present. Bradley summarizes his position with classic brevity when he says,

> But any such irrationality and externality cannot be the last truth about things. Somewhere there must be a reason why this and that appear together. And this reason and reality must reside in the whole from which terms and relations are abstractions, a whole in which their internal connection must lie, and out of which from the background appear those fresh results which never could have come from the premises. The merely external is, in short, our ignorance set up as reality . . . (AR, 517).

Bradley's second series of arguments that purport to show that the very notion of an external relation is an absurdity may be called a priori. Such relations are impossible because they should be thinkable apart from their terms, and they are not. The reason why they should be so thinkable is not stated clearly by Bradley, but I think it is reasonably apparent. If the relation makes no difference to the terms, they must be merely conjoined to it as well as merely conjoined to one another. But this mere conjunction must be mutual; the relation must be as free from involvement with the terms as they are from involvement with it, which makes the relation to be some kind of independent thing. And the notion of relations without terms seems an obvious absurdity.

Of course, we do not ordinarily think that the phrase 'external relation' is meaningless in the obvious way that 'the largest integer' is. However, that is because we are unaware of the full meaning and implications of the theory and the terms in which it is expressed. Bradley exposes the latent difficulties in such phrases as 'having a relation' or 'standing in a relation' and shows how these disclosures make 'external' and 'relation' incompatible notions.

III

What is the philosophic importance of Bradley's doctrine of internal relations? To answer this question, recall that relations are the inadequate expression of a "whole" on which they depend for their existence. The characteristic of a "whole" is that it "qualifies" its parts and is "qualified" by them in turn. Terms are altered by their context, although a quality may remain relatively unchanged through a change of context. And no matter how loose or external a context may seem, the terms are elements in that context and would be different if they were in a different context. Sometimes this is obvious, as when we think of the parts of an organism forming a "whole." Sometimes it is not, as when objects are related temporally and spatially. But all this means is that relations express the wholeness of reality in differing degrees.[7]

The example of comparing is again instructive here. When we compare, Bradley claims, we change that which is compared by abstracting it from the whole in which it comes to us in feeling or perception. In the case of two red-haired men,

> The men are taken first as contained in and as qualifying a perceived whole, and their redness is given in immediate unconditional unity with their other qualities and with the rest of the undivided sensible totality. But, in the second case, this sensible whole has been broken up, and the men themselves have been analysed. They have each been split up into a connexion of redhairedness with other qualities . . . (*AR,* 519).

Both the relations and the qualities are abstractions from the given whole. As such, they reflect the nature of that whole in some degree. At the same time, as abstractions, they cannot do justice to the unity of the whole and may even appear to express no unity at all. But this cannot be the final truth, for there must be a ground or reason in the "background" that explains the particular nature of any relational whole. It is to the explanation of this "must" that we shall have to turn shortly.

In a passage of exceptional brilliance, Bradley describes what

7. Bradley's doctrine of degrees of truth and reality follows directly from this claim.

the doctrine of internal relations implies for the world and for knowledge of that world. He asserts:

> And if you could have a perfect relational knowledge of the world, you could go from the nature of red-hairedness to these other characters which qualify it [for the joining of these characters with red-hairedness cannot be bare change; there must be an involvement of one in the other], and you could from the nature of red-hairedness reconstruct all the red-haired men. In such perfect knowledge you could start internally from any one character in the Universe, and you could from that pass to the rest. [For nothing is as it is for no reason, and a reason means an internal or necessary bond.] You would go in each case more or less directly or indirectly, and with unimportant characters the amount of indirectness would be enormous, but no passage would be external [an external passage would be a passage without a reason and, hence, no passage at all]. (*AR,* 520).

No individual can know himself completely without "passing endlessly beyond himself" in the determination of his relations with others. The "nature" of an individual is to be found in the connections of that individual with his context and, ultimately, with the most inclusive context. A person's certainty that he does not change is often beside the point for Bradley; it is merely the awareness that in some aspect one does not obviously change, and this is compatible with much change in some other regard and with some change in the aspect under scrutiny. We make the confusion between selves as abstracted and incomplete and selves as fully concrete. In this state of mind, we are ignorant of much that we are, and we mistake our ignorance for the supposed externality of the relations that are changed.

IV

We are now in a position to consider Bradley's second argument against external relations, which I called the "higher level" approach to his dispute with Russell. At least, the dispute rests largely on the source of one's ultimate, final "hard" facts, which Russell finds in what is common sense. Obviously, there are some relational situations that have no effect at all on the terms standing in those relations. Indeed, one can show that this is so by any number of easy thought experiments. Move two objects about in space, think of yourself in one social setting and then in another, and so forth. The objects remain the same, and this is conclusive proof of the doctrine of external relations.

This simple, straightforward argument is almost persuasive. It involves an appeal to readily available facts and to a clear distinction within those facts, that between those relations that make a difference and those that do not. Certainly, no one could doubt that the facts seem to be as Russell and common sense say they are. Bradley himself does not claim otherwise.

This appeal to the obvious is a recurring theme in philosophers who defend some version of the external relations theory. Gilbert Ryle argues along these lines: (1) According to the theory of internal relations, a change of relative position should result in a "wholesale" change in the other characteristics of the thing. "But in fact there is no inference from the compass-bearings of objects to their colours, shapes, sizes, etc." (2) It is clear that "From the comparative sizes of two things nothing follows about their comparative temperatures or positions." (3) It is "patent" that no particular matter of fact follows from another matter of fact: "Nature is not just a theorem which happens to be too hard for us to reason out." (4) Finally, asserting that if we knew more, we would (or might) see the internal connection between some relations and terms, although we cannot now see it, is an inadequate reply because we do know *now* that some relations are not essential to some characters in some terms.[8]

Insofar as the first two points are not simple deductions from the third, they seem to be additional appeals to the "obvious." But surely the fact that we cannot now understand the connection between some relations and some qualities does not prove that there is no internal connection there. Apparent externality may, for all we know, merely reflect either a limitation of our understanding of nature or a limitation in the very nature of science itself. As to the first, at one time, people saw no connection between social background and stupidity, but it does not follow that there is no

8. Gilbert Ryle, "Symposium: Internal Relations," *Aristotelian Society Proceedings, 14,* supp. (1936), 158–60, 168.

such connection. Without a theory one misses such connections, and we as yet have no theory that is adequate to the facts that Ryle mentions. As to the second point, even if no theoretical account of the connection of size and color be forthcoming, it does not follow that there is no such connection, for it may be that the interest and/or methods of the scientist preclude the discovery of certain kinds of connections.

Ryle cannot be certain that what seems clear does not seem so only because of the present state of knowledge or because of an approach to nature that may be inadequate as a final account of things. And if there are these possibilities because of reasons derived from reflection on the nature of thinking, reality, the given, and so on, then we may be forced to agree with Bradley that "Somewhere there must be a reason why this and that appear together."

The same line of argument applies to Ryle's third point. It is agreed that there is "apparent externality," but can one be certain that the external is not, in Bradley's words, "our ignorance set up as reality"? Of course, the argument is a long and complex one, but it is not settled by an appeal to the "patent" as long as others find quite the reverse to be equally "patent."

Lastly, Ryle is correct in trying to defend his appeal to the "obvious" by anticipating a criticism that would undercut it. In so doing, he is performing the kind of self-aware philosophical act that we found absent in both Russell and Ayer. Unfortunately, the defense fails, for it is itself simply a repetition of the appeal to the "obvious." Those who question this appeal do so because they question whether we do know that some relations are external; therefore, to repeat explicitly the assumption that we do know this to be so will not help. Only an accounting of knowledge, perception, and the like well help, and Ryle does not defend his view of relations in this manner.

The problem with the appeal to the commonsense facts arises out of its very strength. In its simplicity, it ignores other facts from which doubts can be raised about the ultimacy of the facts that common sense found so convincing. There is, for example, the "fact" of thinking. Bradley's claim is that thought can find no satisfaction in the self-contradictory and refuses, therefore, to accept it as ultimate fact. And it is precisely the external, the mere fact, the mere conjunction, that is for thought the self-contradictory; for thought finds itself paralyzed when it is "confronted by elements that strive to come together without a way of union" (*AR*, 504–05). Thought must always join what is to be explained to other parts of experience with a ground or reason, and the merely external implies precisely the lack of such a reason. When we do not see why things go together as they do, we know that we have failed to understand the way things are.

If one accepts this view of knowing, it becomes very hard to see how it could ever be known that the doctrine of external relations is true. To have knowledge about a state of affairs is to see the connection of this bit of experience with other such bits. To explain is to relate in such a way that we gain insight into the "why" of the unexplained connection. But if external relations are ultimately real, then so is pluralism. And if so, there must be at least some areas in which necessary connection and the insight that it makes possible do not exist. (Presumably, this is what Russell means when he speaks of "mere" truths or "mere" facts.)

But how can we have knowledge that such is the case? The situation imagined is exactly that in which knowledge would be impossible, for there is no necessary connection to be grasped. Conversely, if we do have knowledge in any instance, then the facts must be connected in the way that our intellect demands for its own satisfaction, and that means connected by entailment. How can you know that two facts are related merely externally unless you begin with that assumption? How can you know that it is not your ignorance masquerading as truth, particularly when there are arguments for the internality of relations? One of these is the "apparent fact of feeling with its immediate unity of a non-relational manifold" (*ETR*, 237). If thinking is the attempt to make sense of this manifold, then relations can be true or adequate only to the degree that they represent this kind of intimate unity. Internal relations come closer to this ideal than do external relations.

Thus, if one starts from Bradley's end of the spectrum, the "facts" demand that we view externality as the way that things appear to be when they are not understood fully. Closer inspection will reveal that many apparent cases of externality can be shown to involve internal connections between the terms. Further, it makes sense to infer that this is the case even when we cannot demonstrate an internal connection. The assumption that we have made about reality in the first act of thinking requires this extrapolation beyond our data, for it tells us what must be the case, in spite of what may seem to be the case. Bradley's specific arguments, designed to prove that the external relations advocate has not proved his case, whether by mistaking the nature of the given, by mistaking the abstract for the concrete, or by failing to analyze the notion of relatedness, are all based on his conviction that reality is rational and that "with ignorance and chance the last show of externality has vanished" (*AR,* 520).

In effect, we are asked to choose between accepting a view of the world that seems implausible when we rest on common sense and accepting a view of relations that entails a view of reality incompatible with the demands of thinking.

The theory of external relations asks us to accept "mere" fact as "ultimate" fact. But thought runs into contradiction when it deals with "mere" facts. Thinking is explanation, and all explanation involves synthesis. To explain or understand a fact is to relate it to other facts in such a way that one sees why the first fact is the way it is. Such relating leads to contradiction when the *relata* are "contrary" to one another, and this happens any time we relate two things without a ground or reason. Any B in combination with A can function as a not-A if our passage from one to the other is not internal, is not one of entailment. Because thought rejects tautology and seeks unity-in-diversity instead (which is to say that all meaningful judgment is informative), any judgment is a standing contradiction, or at least a provisional truth, if it omits the ground that makes its synthesis rational.

I think one can go even further in showing the untenability of the doctrine of external relations. As stated above, it leads to a view of the world that the intellect cannot accept, a view that violates the basic assumption of all thinking. It follows that the advocate of external relations is involved in a contradiction in the very statement of his theory. On the one hand, he assumes that if he is correct the advocate of internal relations must be incorrect. That, of course, assumes the validity of the law of contradiction. Yet, the position of external relations describes a world in which thought can find no satisfaction and, in so doing, denies the validity of the law of contradiction. This denial, implicit though it is, means that the position of external relations must imply that the opposite of itself might also be true. But to say this is to say nothing, for meaningful utterances must exclude their opposites from holding true.

In sum, if one accepts the doctrine of external relations, one is involved in denying the very principle that allows for meaningful utterance, the doctrine itself among them. We are then asked to choose between the doctrine and the law, and the choice is already made for us; for every position requires that the law of contradiction hold sway. We must reject the doctrine of external relations on the ground that it is inconsistent with the basis of all discourse.

Bradley's theory, finally, seems to have the advantage of comprehensiveness over Russell's theory, which lends it greater credibility. The theory of internal relations takes into account its opposition and finds a place for it within its own limits: Bradley goes to great lengths to explain why there seem to be "mere" facts and how they relate to the context from which they are abstractions. The claim is that the external relations theorist has misunderstood the weight and direction of his evidence, not that he is without any ground at all to stand on. However, the reverse does not hold. Because the advocate of external relations tends not to discuss his position in a wider metaphysical context, he has no comparable way of showing the "degree" of truth in his opponent's position, with the result that he ignores the real basis of his opponent's argument. The strength of Bradley's position is that in widening the area of discourse he makes the issue one that can be decided, for the strengths and weaknesses of the two theories become apparent only when one considers their metaphysical implications.

V

Three points are worth mentioning in conclusion. First, Bradley is more self-critical than Russell in his approach to the problem of the nature of relations, and this greater awareness gives him a decided edge in his argument with Russell. Second, insofar as Russell's approach to the problem of relations is similar to that of other philosophers who defend the external relations view, Bradley has exposed weaknesses in the doctrine itself, namely its conflict with thought's ideal and the logical confusion of its key concepts. In this case, his argument with Russell has more than merely a historical interest for philosophy.

Third, however, we cannot claim to have demonstrated that the doctrine of internal relations is true for the following reasons. It is obvious that a doctrine is not established by showing that there are weaknesses, even important weaknesses, in the opponent's view; the arguments used by Bradley against the doctrine of external relations depend on his claims about the character of knowledge, the "given," reality, and so on. In this chapter, we have done little more than indicate what these views are, for a defense of them would require a full-scale metaphysical investigation. Yet, without this defense, they stand without justification and, in such condition, cannot serve as adequate grounds for the doctrine of internal relations.

Furthermore, certain problems within the theory of internal relations have not yet been considered. Perhaps the most important is mentioned by Ryle, who indicates that a necessary conclusion of Bradley's theory is that "No universal could have more than one instance." It also follows that "No laws could hold of particulars." [9] There could thus be no identity of a thing or quality in different contexts, and this leads to two fundamental problems: Knowledge is of the universal or kind, and unless there are such identities in nature, it is hard to see how there can be knowl-

9. Ibid., pp. 159–60. It does not seem to follow, however, as Ryle claims, that things could not be similar nor that we could not think that there are true, general propositions—not the former unless it could be shown that similarity must be based on identity, not the latter unless the differences in things caused by their relations must always be visible.

edge. Any view, furthermore, that denies the possibility of knowledge is broken-backed from the start; in denying the independence of things from their contexts, the internal relations view
seems involved in just this absurdity. Second, all reasoning demands that its terms retain their identity in differing contexts.
We can infer that something that has X must have Y only if X
and Y are repeatables whose connection we know from other
cases. If they are only similar to other qualities, then our previous
knowledge or experience will not allow us to conclude that these
qualities must be connected with one another. Yet, the internal
relations view seems to prohibit the existence of such identical
characteristics and, thus, to prohibit reasoning. If so, the view
seems to be self-defeating.

It is my belief that the theory of internal relations can overcome these difficulties with a careful analysis of the kind of identity knowledge and reasoning require and of the sense in which
they require it.[10] In addition, Ryle's criticisms of the internal relations thesis are precisely the results that Bradley claims the metaphysician must accept. Bradley insists that knowledge is inherently defective and that, therefore, his own theory must share in
that defect. In this chapter, I have not shown that a view of such
profound self-skepticism can withstand the test of self-consistency;
but it is clear that Bradley's theory of internal relations cannot be
refuted merely by pointing to certain "absurd" consequences of it,
if it can be shown that these consequences are entailed by the
facts of the matter.

10. In fact, a fruitful effort has been made in this direction. I refer to Brand
Blanshard, *The Nature of Thought, 1,* Chs. 16–17, *2,* Chs. 21–22. Also important is
his *Reason and Analysis,* Ch. 9.

5

The Idealist Criticism of the Theory of Relations

If Bradley's realist critics were dissatisfied with his theory of relations because it was too abstract and intellectual, idealist critics hold that Bradley's theory is not intellectual enough. To the former it seemed perverse to deny the reality and the externality of relations. To the latter, it seemed perverse to deny that our intellect, which works by terms and relations, is able to give us an adequate account of the nature of things. Following Hegel, they were willing to distinguish among "levels" of comprehension and to condemn some levels as inherently defective, but they wanted no part of any wholesale self-skepticism.

To these more orthodox philosophical compatriots, Bradley overstressed the demands of feeling. In fact, much of the time he appeared as if he were a mystic, in contrast to those times when he attacked British Empiricism, defended the coherence theory of truth, and supported the possibility of metaphysics. Surely, it was thought, there is no higher standard than reason from which its result might be criticized. As it was put, "If water burns, whereof shall we drink?"

G. Watts Cunningham

Although an advocate of Bradley's theory of judgment, Cunningham found his claim that reality is suprarelational to be both needless and false. In *The Idealist Argument in Recent British and American Philosophy*,[1] Cunningham offers several important arguments against the claim that reality is not a relational whole.

1. G. W. Cunningham, *The Idealistic Argument in Recent British and American Philosophy* (New York, Appleton-Century, 1933).

If Cunningham is correct, Badley's theory of relations is internally inconsistent, based on false inferences from evidence that is suspect, and leads to unacceptable consequences.

First, he holds that Bradley's argument that immediate experience is a nonrelational manifold is based on a falsely drawn exclusive alternative. Bradley assumes that because experience in feeling is not a "mere congeries of discrete many's," it must be a nonrelational whole. But Cunningham says there is a third alternative:

> Suppose the relational whole be conceived not as a mere congeries, but as a system in which terms and relations are mutually involved, am I then to reject it as self-contradictory merely because I have agreed to reject the congeries as such? (IA, 389).[2]

But it does not follow that either immediate experience or reality must be nonrelational merely because it is shown that it is not a mere collection. Nor does it follow that all relational schemes must be condemned because "mere congeries" are rejected as "inherently contradictory." But this is not Bradley's argument at all. He first shows that relations conceived as external, third things are inadequate. He then proceeds to show that relations taken with their terms are equally plagued with difficulties. This latter point forms the basis for his condemnation of relations in general; the former shows only that one conception of relations is inadequate. Second, Bradley holds that immediate experience is nonrelational, not because of an inference from his argument concerning relations, but because this seems to him to be an adequate description of the given. Mere conjunctions are unintelligible for Bradley, but his argument against relations is not based on this conception of relations as external.

It is Cunningham's view that "there is nothing in the non-relational character of immediate experience which seems to have any implication whatsoever with reference to the structure of relational experience" (IA, 391). But why is this so? If reality comes to us first as a nonrelational whole, if the task of thinking is to

2. By the phrase "mere congeries," Cunningham means either terms with no relations at all or terms merely conjoined to other terms. For him, the two seem to be equal.

understand reality, and if our only basis for knowing what reality is like is to be found in immediate experience, why does it not follow that relational thought will be inadequate to this task? If these assumptions are accepted, we seem forced to conclude that any theory is necessarily deficient, and when Bradley condemns thinking as self-contradictory, he only means to highlight the form that this deficiency takes.

Even if immediate experience is nonrelational, why must we conclude that reality is also nonrelational? The objection here is to the transition from the "non-relational character of the experience to the non-relational character of the "content" of the experience" (IA, 398). Cunningham insists that however nonrelational the former may be, it may still "intend" a content that is "intrinsically relational." Part of the answer may be put off until we discuss Bradley's view of potentiality. For the moment, I think the answer can be given in two parts. In immediate experience, there is not the division between form and content that the objection suggests.³ But this answer by itself is not satisfactory, for Bradley also insists that reality appears only in immediate experience and does not "really" have the character it "appears" to have in that form. Bradley does seem to make the distinction between form and content after all.

Thus we must insist that for Bradley immediate experience is already "ideal," already reveals the working of thought in it and so "intends" the relational. But Bradley's rather complex view does not entail that immediate experience is fully realized at the relational level. To be sure, the relational "is an advance and a necessary step towards that perfection which is above relations, supersedes and still includes them" (AR, 522). But it is an imperfect advance, one that points ahead for its final completion. Therefore, the immediate does point to the relational, but we cannot conclude that reality is intrinsically relational.

Bradley simply will not fit the "either-or" categories of many philosophers. Immediate experience both "intends" the relational and is nonrelational as it stands. Both facts must be considered when we estimate the nature of reality. Cunningham's mistake is in thinking that the former truth somehow cancels out the im-

3. "And what I repudiate is the separation of the feeling from the felt" (AR, 129).

portance of the latter truth. The issue is: Can thinking reproduce adequately the "felt many in one" characteristic of feeling? No one to my knowledge has shown that Bradley's "no" to this question is either muddleheaded or wrong.

For Cunningham, all Bradley's analysis of relational experience proves is that

> any particular type of relational experience is not in itself complete. . . . any type of relational experience is partially abstract and that, when taken as if it were indicative of the absolute, it is mistaken. For it, there is always a 'beyond' or a 'not-yet'; it is never quite all there is (*IA*, 389–90).

Cunningham grants that any relational scheme is incomplete in that it of necessity leaves out of consideration some aspect of experience. But incompleteness is different from inconsistency, and the latter in no way follows from the former. Thus, we might well admit incompleteness without either condemning relations or claiming that reality is suprarelational.

First, Bradley does not deduce the contradictory character of relations from their incompleteness plus the hidden assumption that only if we conceive of relational wholes as "mere congeries" will this incompleteness show itself. In fact, he does not deduce the contradictory character of relations at all. Instead, he goes directly to terms and relations and performs what he calls an "ideal" experiment. He imagines how terms and relations might fit together in a logical way. He finds that none of the alternatives yields such a way, and he concludes that relational wholes are defective for this reason.

Second, there does seem to be one sense of 'incomplete' that does entail 'contradictory', although this sense is not that used by Cunningham. If, as Bradley argues, every relational scheme is incomplete in the sense that it conjoins terms without sufficient reason, then such schemes by their very nature bring a diversity together without explanation. And that is the essence of contradiction. It is not merely that relational wholes fail to include everything, but, rather, that this failure means that what they do include is not conjoined logically. In this sense, incompleteness does lead to inconsistency.

Next, Cunningham argues, if relational experience is self-contradictory and if thought is relational, then we are forced to conclude that the products of intelligence are self-contradictory. But this is impossible. "Can intelligence contradict itself, or can it take for significant that which is contradictory? And what, above all, are we to do with the house which science has built?" (*IA*, 391). These questions are not answered by the doctrine of "degrees." In addition, if the intellect is said to seek a whole above relations, then are we not saying that we can think that that is essentially unthinkable?

There are three questions here. (1) How can thought be a systematic failure, as opposed to being a failure at certain times and with certain problems? (2) Can philosophy condemn science? (3) If reality and thought differ in their nature, must one not admit that reality is unknowable? And is not this result the very opposite of what Bradley desires?

Questions 1 and 3 can be answered in a similar fashion. One must never forget that for Bradley thought has a dual character. On the one hand, "The reality that is presented is taken up by thought in a form not adequate to its nature, and beyond which its nature must appear as an Other" (*AR*, 158). Reality always is "beyond" thought, both in the sense that thought is "of" reality and in the sense that thought does not fully capture the character of reality. On the other hand, reality is the end sought by thinking. It is "the nature which thought wants for itself."

Thus, reality both is and is not foreign to thought. Is it unknowable then? The answer must be both yes and no. It is yes if one means that thought cannot express fully the character of reality. Thinking merely "intends" the real. The answer is no if one means to suggest that all or part of reality cannot appear in conceptual form. As Bradley puts it, "The assertion of a reality falling outside knowledge is quite nonsensical" (*AR*, 114).

Bradley expresses this distinction when he asserts that we know reality in its general character but not in its detail. Thinking proceeds under a limitation, but it does not grope in utter darkness. Thus, it cannot fully realize its own ideal at the same time it is realizing this ideal by degrees as its conceptual schemes become more and more complete. This does not make the real unknowable in any objectionable sense; thought's failure to realize perfect consistency is not a logical embarrassment to Bradley. Thought strives for perfect consistency and realizes it to a degree everywhere. It accepts its products for just so much and must reject them as ultimate truths to the extent that they fall short of this ideal. What is logically unsatisfactory about such a view?

As for Bradley's condemnation of science (point 2 above), he refuses to accept any theory as final truth. But theories can be said to be valid (*AR*, 321, 503). Thus, Bradley does not want to deny either the importance or the truth of science, although this may seem to be the case when he says that its results are self-contradictory. He merely insists that we should not take the theories of science as final, metaphysical truth, for that would be to mistake abstractions for concrete fact. Because the dominant view of science today disclaims any such metaphysical intent for science, it seems that Bradley leaves science where it desires to be left.

Finally, Cunningham argues, what reason is there to believe that immediate experience is nonrelational, when in Bradley's own analysis "the relations which analysis of the immediate experience discloses were already implicitly there in the immediate experience"? (*IA*, 393). How else can immediate experience be said to be the "significant background" for relational experience than by embodying the essential features of that higher, more revealing, experience? Cunningham states the problem in the form of a dilemma.

> Either the nature of the 'that' is progressively disclosed through judgmental predicates and is therefore relational, or the 'qualification' of reality in judgment is a falsification and the predicates merely 'float' (*IA*, 394).

Here, Cunningham raises an important point, one that has significant implications for Bradley's metaphysics. In general, it may be said to reflect the standard idealist objection to this part of Bradley's philosophy: Is it really necessary to hold that reality is suprarelational or that immediate experience is nonrelational? More specifically, Cunningham here questions whether these assumptions are consistent with Bradley's view that the relational is a development from the immediate. Does not this view suggest that the immediate is nonrelational only in that it is not completely relational? Certainly, Cunningham's criticism gains support from the commonsense feeling that our ideas are often true of the world we perceive and the implied assumption that for this to be so the world must be "like" our ideas.

There is no question that Bradley found the above view very tempting indeed, because for him the relational is not "imposed" on either reality or immediate experience as if they were completely foreign to it. But, as we have mentioned, the relational is an "imperfect" development of the "immediate totality." For those who prefer clear-cut answers to reasonable questions, this may seem like an evasion instead of a reply. Can one have it both ways? I do not see why not. There is nothing inconsistent or troublesome in saying that thought does make explicit the nature of immediate experience but not in a way that is completely satisfactory. In our commonsense life, we are accustomed to thinking that truth is an "either-or" matter; an idea is true or it is not. But this attitude is not self-justifying, and I do not find Bradley's correction of common sense to be illogical.[4]

In any case, the relation of immediate experience and thought that we call "potential" does not allow us to conceive of reality as relational. For thought is only a partial realization of immediate experience. Once again, Bradley insists that thought both is and is not the realization of the immediate, thus saving at once the "truth" of thought and the suprarelational character of reality.

Josiah Royce

Royce's criticisms of Bradley's theory of relations are a classic example of traditional idealism. In general, Royce is not concerned to show that anything in particular is wrong with Bradley's analysis of the relational situation, as were Broad and Cook Wilson. Rather, he wants to show that Bradley has misunderstood the import of his own analysis. What Bradley has actually discov-

---

4. Bradley's theory does ask us to make one substantial correction in our ordinary thinking. His notion of 'degrees of truth' calls into question the ultimacy of the law of excluded middle. For him, it is not on a par with the law of contradiction, and this is not a traditional distinction in logic.

ered is the form that successful thinking takes and the form, therefore, that is characteristic of reality. Where Bradley finds weakness and failure, there is in fact success, which Bradley fails to see owing to some pre-existing, arbitrary standard of what a relational whole "ought" to be like. In short, Royce questions not whether there is an infinite regress between terms and relations, but whether this regress is vicious.

Royce's initial concern is with Bradley's wholesale condemnation of thinking. If, in fact, I am able to recognize that the given in perception is such that I can neither make it to suit me nor accept it as it is, then must I not have found, at least in part, a theory in which I can find satisfaction? Is not the judgment that the given is intellectually unacceptable a "contrast" judgment, one that is possible only when I can contrast the given with the theory in terms of which it is seen to be inadequate? As Royce puts it:

> But how is it possible for thought to discover the very fact that it cannot make, and that it declines to receive, certain differences, without itself making, of its own motion, certain other differences, whose internal unity it knows just in so far as it makes them? [5]

There must be a ground for our dissatisfaction with the given, and this ground is to be found in the demands of thought. But how can these grounds provide us with a criterion in terms of which we are able to criticize thought itself?

For Royce, the product of thinking, in response to the problem posed by the given, is in fact the solution to that problem. And if the solution involves a diversity of aspects, then these aspects must be needed to solve the problem. Such aspects are not to be rejected, for they reflect the diversity that thinking needs to fulfill its purpose (*WI*, *1*, 492–93).

Thus, thought sees that the infinite regress between relation and quality is the necessary outcome of its purpose to find a ground for the conjunction of A and B. What reason can thought have for doubting the reality of that in which it finds its purpose realized? There is none.

5. Josiah Royce, *The World and the Individual* (2 vols. New York, Dover, 1959), *1*, 492.

> When thought sees this result of its own efforts, and sees the result
> as necessary, as universal, as the consequence of a relational way
> of thinking, then I persistently ask, Does not thought here at least
> see in one instance, not only that identity and diversity are con-
> joined, but *how* they are this time connected (*WI, 1,* 493–94)

The regress of terms and relations is thought's own creation and,
as such, should provide us with a paradigm case of the kind of intellectual product that thinking desires. The regress does not indicate a failure for thought and so is not vicious.

Royce carries his anaylsis to its logical conclusion. If the infinite regress of terms and relations is not vicious, then it should
give us a clue as to the nature of reality. As such, it provides us
with a reason for accepting Bradley's analysis of relational complexes without accepting his further claims about the suprarelational character of reality. Royce begins by agreeing with Bradley
that reality, whatever else may be true of it, must be an all-inclusive whole whose elements are so combined that the intellect finds
the combination to be logical. An adequate conception of reality
must show how the elements are the expression of a single unity
and how that unity finds expression in just those elements.

But a process in which a single purpose creates an "infinite process" discovered by reflection is just the notion of the diversity-in-
unity that we claim for reality. Royce defines such an operation as
"recurrent" or "iterative," one that "reinstates, in a new instance,
the situation which gave rise to the operation, and to which the
operation was applied" (*WI, 1,* 496). Only the philosophic preju-
dice, arising from a lack of training in modern mathematics,
against the "actual" infinite prevented Bradley from seeing that
the regress of term and relation is a model of an acceptable concept of reality. Reality is both infinite and a whole; it is a "self-rep-
resentative" system, a whole in which a single purpose finds expression in an infinity of other purposes that themselves find expression in other purposes and so on endlessly.

I do not find Royce's case convincing. That the regress between
term and relation means defeat and not victory for the intellect
can be shown, I think, if one considers the reason for the regress.
The reason is not, as Royce suggests, that the regress expresses a
development or a deepening of our understanding. Rather, the
reason is that we find our attempt at a synthesis of the given

yields a mere conjunction of independent elements. Because this is what is meant by contradiction, we must try again to find an acceptable means of synthesis. Because we try to find unity without doing away with the independence of the terms, we can never avoid mere conjunction.

The failure may be, as Royce himself says, universal and even necessary, but why is it less of a failure for all of that? We just do not see how or why things must go together as we find them or put them together. Thought points to but does not reach a synthesis in which the "why" is made fully explicit, and this means that reality is always a step ahead of our concepts.

H. H. Joachim

In the work of Joachim, we find the purest form of the Hegelian objection to Bradley's theory of relations. Criticism of the intellect was not foreign to Hegel and his followers, the distinction of the understanding and the reason being an example. The products of the understanding, including the attitudes of common sense and the theories of science, were said to be incapable of grasping the nature of reality. Reality was said to be "organic," and only thinking that employed categories and methods adequate to organic wholes could grasp the real. One must look to art, religion, and philosophy for a clue to the seemingly paradoxical, but inherently logical, nature of reality.

Here the Hegelians part company with Bradley. The intellect is deficient in its grasp of reality only in part. There is a "level" of thought that is adequate to the notional or dialectical character of the real. They charge Bradley with making the mistake of limiting "thinking" to the level of the understanding and ignoring the higher level of thought that reason represents.

Joachim expresses the dilemma he feels arises from Bradley's failure to recognize this higher level of thought:

> The intellect itself has doubled the parts of criticized and critic. And as critic of itself . . . the intellect is using—and therefore must possess—an ideal by which it criticizes and condemns its own imperfect achievement.[6]

6. H. H. Joachim, *Logical Studies,* ed. Leslie Beck (Oxford, Oxford University Press, 1948), p. 281.

For Bradley, the failure of the intellect lies in the "bare identification of the different," and, when we understand the nature of this failure, we make explicit an ideal that could overcome this failure.

Joachim lists three requirements that the ideal must fulfill. It must proceed by means of a ground or a reason; it must not make its distinctions arbitrarily, but must develop the lines of connection present in fact; the connecting links found in fact must be recognized by the intellect to be a "movement natural and proper to itself." The mere fact that a ground or principle seems forced on us is not by itself enough to warrant taking it as final. Because the intellect possesses this ideal, it knows that relational schemes can never give final truth.

Bradley's attitude toward this ideal is complicated. In one sense, it is a mere ideal, unrealized and unrealizable. The intellect simply does not have the means to see its world in the light of the ideal. The intellect is formal, working up a given by means of terms and relations; it has no power of intellectual intuition. On the other hand, the ideal is a sound one in that it can function as an absolute criterion of truth and reality. Our general knowledge of reality is possible only because of this criterion. The intellect is one aspect, but only one aspect, of reality. Because it is an aspect of the real, it can know that reality; because it is only *an* aspect of the real, it cannot do this without distortion.

Is this two-faced concept of thought and its ideal consistent? Joachim thinks it is not. He argues that Bradley must accept one of two exclusive alternatives. Either he must identify the intellect with the analytic, discursive process that he conceives thinking to be—in which case the intellect would be reduced to the intellect-as-criticized and Bradley's view would be indistinguishable from those of Locke and Hume. Or he must identify the intellect with the intellect-as-critic and then must accept the metaphysical conclusions that follow. But, Joachim adds, the first alternative is not open to Bradley, for such an intellect could not conceive of, let alone identify itself with, an ideal of organic wholeness. Because Bradley claims that this is the ideal of thinking, he must hold that there is a "thinking" that is ours and that is more than a "discursive and relational faculty."

What is the result of identifying the intellect with the intellect-as-critic? Is there any reason Bradley should not have made this identification? Joachim answers the first question by saying that such an intellect "being thus the critic of itself, it includes within its total being . . . *both* the 'mere thinking', which is criticized, *and* the aspect of immediacy, for lack of which that 'mere thinking' is condemned" (*LS,* 288). That is, the intellect-as-critic would have to embody the ideal that is brought to light in our discovery of the inadequacies of relational thinking. There would be no distinction between thought and reality, and the problem caused by Bradley's suprarelational reality would be solved.

Joachim is equally unconvinced by Bradley's claim that thought cannot be identified with its own ideal. He agrees that our intellects cannot see in detail how our intellectual ideal is realized in reality. This ideal is not "visible" to us because we do not know everything. But we do not need to be omniscient to know with certainty that our intellectual ideal is realized. And Bradley himself asserts that we know this. All we need to claim is that the general knowledge we have about reality would remain unchanged from a more adequate viewpoint, and such must be our assumption in even claiming to have this general knowledge.[7]

Our thinking expresses an ideal of which, on reflection, it can become aware. We have the power to condemn certain concepts and theories as inadequate to reality, and we have the power to form a concept of what would satisfy us as thinking beings. In Joachim's view, Bradley's claim that reality cannot have the form that finds expression in all thinking makes nonsense of his claim to know with certainty that reality is "harmonious," "individual," or even that the real meets our intellectual demands "somehow."

Bradley's division between thought and reality introduces a note of skepticism that is more far-reaching than he saw, for it extends past our inability to know in detail what the universe is like

7. Joachim puts the dilemma forcefully when he says, "If thought (knowledge, truth, etc.), in being fulfilled in the Absolute Experience, is transmuted or transformed, it is difficult to see how Bradley can be entitled to fix any limits—or what limits—to the transmutation: difficult, therefore, to see what criterion is still available for him by which he is able to decide what is or is not 'impossible'; what does or does not 'stand out', and conflict with, the individuality of his Absolute Experience" (*LS,* 291).

and corrodes the very foundations Bradley thought metaphysics could establish. And, Joachim insists, there is no good reason to promote a division between thought and reality. Bradley's grounds seem to be that he cannot "verify" in detail the presence of the intellectual ideal in our experience. From this fact, he concludes that the intellect does indeed find satisfaction, but only in an Absolute of which all aspects are transformed from their appearance to finite beings.

But, Joachim argues, the conclusion does not follow from the premises. Our inability to see all of reality as it is in no way implies that our intellectual ideal is inadequate to the character of reality. There are good reasons for the failure to comprehend the ideal in detail, and they (the dependence of reasoning on material furnished by the senses for one) cast no doubt on the actuality of thought's ideal. In addition, there are reasons for the identification of the real and the ideal of thinking (including the radical skepticism that would result from any other assumption), and other reasons against the identification of all thinking with the discursive thinking that both Bradley and Joachim assert is inadequate as a clue to the nature of reality.

These latter reasons center around Joachim's claim that the very ability of the intellect to criticize its metaphysical efforts implies that such thinking is more than merely discursive or relational. In order to look back on its efforts as failures, the intellect must already have reached a higher level from which this insight is possible. Because the division in Bradley's thought between thinking and reality is made more plausible by his concept of thinking as merely discursive, a refutation of this concept makes the identification of the two all the more reasonable.

However, the difference between Joachim and Bradley on this point is not so sharp as it might seem. For example, Joachim holds the orthodox Hegelian view that human thinking reflects the order and structure of the real. Yet, he seems to echo Bradley when he insists that this relation between the infinite whole and the finite part must remain unintelligible to us.

But we are now left with the paradox that reality must be both infinite and finite, eternal and temporal, and the latter term of each pair is necessary in some way for the realization of the former. (What sense does it make to speak of the eternal being "realized?") Joachim concedes that this twofold nature of reality, which he believes is forced on us by the nature of thinking, cannot be explained. There is no theory, the coherence theory included, that can escape this ultimate contradiction within experience.

Put in somewhat different terms, a final view of the nature of things would require that the finite mind fully express the world in which it moves and on which it depends. Yet, this is impossible. As Joachim puts it, "And since all human discursive knowledge remains thought 'about' an Other, any and every theory of the nature of truth must itself be 'about' truth as its other." Such a theory is "at most possessed of a 'truth' which we may believe, but have not proved to be 'symptomatic' of perfect truth." [8]

Joachim seems to imply that, because we never have the "other" totally within our experience, it is difficult to ascertain the degree of correspondence between our thoughts and the world. We can, of course, determine the difference between our theories and the ideal of truth that reason sets before us, but because that ideal is a theory, there must be some difference between it and the world it is "about." And unless we can determine the degree of discrepancy, it is hard to avoid the radical skepticism used as an argument against Bradley by Joachim himself.

I am unable to find a substantial difference between Bradley and Joachim on the contrast between thinking and reality. To be sure, there is a striking difference in emphasis. Bradley at times stresses the distance between our thoughts and the world to which they refer, whereas Joachim is more confident that we know what reality is like. But when Joachim also says that we cannot understand the basic character of reality, the heart of Bradley's position seems to be admitted at the same time.

Pointing out the similarities between Bradley and Joachim tends to reduce the force of the latter's criticisms, but I think one can go even further. First, Joachim does not do Bradley justice when he says that the only reason for holding that thought's ideal is not actual is that we cannot verify this in detail. Bradley does

8. H. H. Joachim, *The Nature of Truth* (Oxford, Oxford University Press, 1906) pp. 174–75.

take this failure as a sign that reality transcends thinking, but
only because we have additional evidence that reality has a
"form" that is not relational. The aspect of integral wholeness,
which is characteristic of immediate experience, provides the basis
for Bradley's rejection of the ideal of thinking as an actual fact.
Mere failure to verify the presence of this ideal in our experience
cannot prove that it does not present us with the bare outline of
reality.

A second point concerns the extent to which there is a division
between thought and reality in Bradley's philosophy. As Joachim
recognizes, there is no simple answer to this problem. Truth *is*
reality in that a full realization of thought would be that reality
that thinking is "of"; but thought is necessarily different from
reality, for it is only "of" reality and is too defective to be identified with the real. Even if we admit that the above limitation is
not a barrier in theory to the perfection of thinking and that we
can conceive of the possibility of an all-embracing, logical system
(as Bradley seems to admit in the Appendix to *Appearance and
Reality*), there is a more fundamental objection to the final realization of thought. All thoughts are "ideal"; thought lives in contrast to fact. Yet, that very distinction prevents thought from
achieving perfect consistency, which it must attain in order to
"contain" reality in a proper form. Thinking has no way of qualifying reality that can produce consistency, though, to repeat, it exists only as such a qualification. Thus, the difference between
thought and fact, which common sense takes for granted as an ultimate fact, is used by Bradley to find a basic self-contradiction
within thought.

This position is obviously complicated, but I do not see that it
is inconsistent. Nor do I see that it puts reality so far "beyond"
thought that, as Joachim charges, one is in danger of making reality unknowable. Both Joachim and Bradley agree that our role as
critics of our own theories is possible only on the assumption that
reality is working in and through our thinking, thus providing
the criterion by which we know that certain kinds of theories are
inadequate to the real.

But this does not imply that we must have a perfectly formed
view of the nature of things, or even the power to form such a

view. All that is required is that we be able to *feel* a discrepancy between any theory and the ideal it only partially embodies and that we be able to say in what general way the former falls short of the latter, for example, lack of harmony.

And Bradley's doctrine of immediate experience makes just this point. Thus, in another context, Socrates can say with honesty in the *Meno* that he does not know what virtue is, at the same time being able to distinguish more and less successful attempts to define what he does not know.

On the other hand, Bradley has not separated thought and reality in such a way that we are committed to intellectual anarchy. Metaphysics is possible precisely because our concepts more or less reflect the presence of reality in our thinking. Of course, reality is harmonious in a sense that transcends our idea of harmony, but that we are closer to the truth in claiming harmony and not chaos for reality is explained by the presence of the felt standard in thinking. We know what disharmony is by an analysis of our experience, and we form, thereby, a negative idea of what perfect harmony would be like. The "given" provides positive data for this idea. Together the data and the idea point the way for our theories, but we are never able to see the end of our quest. We always work in the presence of some light, but we never bathe in the full light imagined by Plato, Spinoza, and Hegel.

Bradley does admit in the Appendix to *Appearance and Reality* that the mind has the power to conceive of an ideal that, if actual, would provide satisfaction in full for the intellect. Joachim asks if this is not the reality we seek in all thinking? Bradley answers that it would be so only if reality were a "ballet of bloodless categories," and the character of immediate experience proves that it is not. This ideal does provide us with our best insight into the nature of reality, but it is not entirely adequate to a reality whose character is different from thought's character.

In conceiving this ideal, we seem to transcend the logical difficulties of relational thought that Bradley urges on the reader in the early parts of *Appearance and Reality*. Left to itself, thought can have no objection to this ideal as our ideal of final truth. But in confrontation with reality, thought finds that its "internal" ideal is still not adequate to the world. We must not conclude from this that reality in some way blocks or frustrates the attempt to explain. Rather, he insists, it realizes concretely the abstract ideal of wholeness.

There is one final problem with Joachim's comments on Bradley: Thought has no mysterious power of intuition, or of transcending the "material" that comes to man through his senses; all thinking can do is relate this material in ways that illumine it. It is Joachim who seems to be claiming that there is more to reasoning than this, and the burden of proof for this "more" falls on his shoulders.

For example, Joachim claims that "being thus the critic of itself, it [the intellect] includes within its total being, as moments subordinated to its concrete unity, *both* the 'mere thinking', which is criticized, *and* the aspect of immediacy, for lack of which that 'mere thinking' is condemned" (*LS*, 288). If the intellect can criticize itself, then it must be the very ideal by which it condemns its products; for a merely relational intellect would not ever form the concept of the dialectical ideal.

But Joachim's assertion need not be true, and it is not, in fact, true. First, in order to be aware of the failure of my theories, I need only glimpse reality in some nontheoretical guise. Bradley provides for this glimpse in his theory of immediate experience. Bradley's view both explains the possibility of truth and limits thinking to its proper sphere. We do not fall into either skepticism or abstract intellectualism. The skeptic denies the connection of thought and reality, but his very utterances betray his denial. The intellectualist claims that this connection amounts to a simple identity and, in denying the difference between thought and reality, reduces the world to a "ballet of bloodless categories."

But the connection we must assume between thought and reality, if we are to avoid skepticism, does not entail that our theories be adequate to the real. It only entails that reality is "in" our thoughts in some form and that it is the background against which we evaluate our theories. In Bradley's view, Joachim has stressed the unity of thought and reality to such an extent that he ignores important differences between the two.

Second, Joachim's concept of thinking is not in fact true. When we think, we do seek relations among things in a world that is given to us and that we do not make. In this process, I can notice nothing that includes "within its total being" the given on which thinking depends. Thinking is discursive, and if, as Joachim admits, this condemns it, then condemned it must be. If one stays within the bounds of what we can verify, then thinking seems to lack the element of immediacy and to move among abstractions or ideas. Reality is more than this, but to insist that the same is true of thought confuses the notions of thought and reality.

Once the gross confusions surrounding Bradley's theory of relations are cleared away, it can be seen to be a conservative idea. Bradley seems to be saying something like the following:

> We never manage to say all that we want to say or that we need to say. That is, the reasons that we give for what we observe are always inadequate. At some point, we must rest on a basis of "mere" fact or on a principle that we accept without a sufficient reason. And though this is a necessary result of the limited character of thinking, it also represents a failure to realize the ultimate aim of thinking, namely, a view that is at once perfectly comprehensive and coherent.

Wherever thought must be content with the given, it finds itself involved in contradiction, for contradiction arises when we bring two "things" together in thought without sufficient insight into why they go together.

Thus, when Bradley says that relations are unreal or that they fail to relate, he is not asserting a paradox. He is only observing that we never succeed in understanding our experience in a way that we find completely intellectually satisfying. All explanations fail because the things to be explained retain some independence from the context that supplies the reason for their relatedness. To some extent, we force our explanations on the facts, and the result is that the facts remain in part beyond our theories. It follows that relations cannot be "real," for they never capture the character of the situation or event as they claim to do. It is the "facts" that are "real," and our ideas do no more than approximate them.

No doubt there is much in this view that contemporary philosophers in particular would find impossible to accept. This includes the ideas that there is no truth short of the whole, that thought cannot accept mere fact, that there is a single ideal that all thinking attempts to realize, and that thought is necessarily inadequate to the facts, whatever they may be. These are doctrines that need defending, and Bradley tried to expand on them in his *Essays on Truth and Reality*. But they are not absurd ideas, and their function is to provide a foundation for the theory of relations.

The failure of many critics to notice or stress this connection has led them to believe that the theory of relations is without rhyme or reason, and thus they fail to touch the heart of the matter. It is my view that, with the major exception of Joachim, even those sympathetic to Bradley's general philosophical posture fail to do justice to the subtlety or to the balanced nature of his view.

Certainly, a view is not proved true by the failure of its critics to detect important weaknesses, but a view that can withstand the attacks of astute philosophers of differing persuasions has much to be said in its favor. Final evaluation of the view must await the analysis of Bradley's metaphysics that follows.

Appendix   The Nature of Immediate Experience

Given the importance of immediate experience both in Bradley's condemnation of relations and in his positive metaphysical claims, let us ask whether it is true that in immediate experience we are aware of a nonrelational whole and whether such experience furnishes us with a clue to the nature of reality.

C. A. Campbell questions these claims by arguing that we do not "start from (or, indeed, can even at any time possess) a 'felt unity,' a 'many felt in one.' " He agrees with Bradley that experience is not merely identical with "consciousness" and that thought presupposes, rather than establishes, the "unity of our experienced world." But he insists that this unity is not given in feeling, for

> Feeling may be *in* itself a unity, no doubt. But that is not to be a feeling *of* unity. . . . The appreciation or recognition of unity, in short, implies the activity of the mediating or 'relational' consciousness. There is no unity 'given' in feeling.[9]

9. C. A. Campbell, *Scepticism and Construction* (London, Allen & Unwin, 1931), p. 52.

And, he asks, "How can feeling, as such, make us aware 'of' any-thing?" Campbell concludes that reality "comes to us in 'ideally interpreted feeling' " and that this fact does away with the claim that we have a direct, even if unsatisfactory, experience of reality in immediate experience.

Campbell's criticisms fail to touch Bradley because they attrib-ute to him a view he did not hold. In fact, I find it hard to distin-guish Campbell's account of immediate experience from Brad-ley's. Bradley does not assert that there is any immediate experi-ence totally apart from conceptual experience; he does not claim that without ideas feeling could be "of" anything at all. On the first point, he insists that "facts which are not ideal, and which show no looseness of content from existence, seem hardly actual" (*AR*, 146). And on the second point, he explicitly states that to speak of the feeling "of" anything, when by 'feeling of' we mean the 'simply felt', is illegitimate, for in such a case the "of" "does not belong to the feeling. It belongs solely to an outsider who adds ideas true or false." [10] All Bradley claims, and all he needs to claim, is that we can have a sense of things-being-together that is unlike the way they are "together" when we theorize about them, that in this state there is no explicit distinction be-tween subject and object (or of anything from anything else), and that this sense provides a background against which we can see the failure of our theories to give us the unity we have expe-rienced.[11]

Why are we to conclude that such experience does not tell us something about the real because it is not "pure" and involves ideas in some implicit way? As far as I can see, all Bradley is say-ing is that to "feel" is one thing and to know about a feeling is another, and I can think of no good reason for doubting this.

10. F. H. Bradley, *Collected Essays,* ed. H. H. Joachim (2 vols. Oxford, Oxford University Press, 1935), *1,* 197.

11. Ward claims that in immediate experience "cognition and feeling ought not to be called 'implicit' because the knowledge of them may be so." James Ward, "Bradley's Doctrine of Experience," *Mind,* n.s. *34* (1925), 16. But how, in immediate experience, can one distinguish between our knowledge of cognition and cognition itself, for how can we distinguish 'seeming to be' from 'is'? In feeling, Bradley insists, "This whole is 'known' and is experienced, though as a whole it is not an object" (*CE, 2,* 399).

One might add some general comments in defense of the notion of immediate experience as conceived by Bradley. Must there not be something, some 'content," that is given? How could we have any ideas or make any judgments if there were not some source of information and basis of our judgments? If there be a given, never experienced as such but approached in nonreflective moments, we must wonder about its character. Because concepts bring certain elements in our experience to our attention and, in so doing, isolate these elements from the rest of our experience, it seems reasonable to think that immediate experience is continuous and a "whole," rather than discrete as Hume believed.

There are certain logical arguments, to be examined later, that indicate that the world cannot be as common sense thinks it is, that is, as many-but-related things. But if reality cannot be discrete in this way, then what reason is there for thinking that our immediate experience is discrete? Finally, the experience of the unity and continuity of things, reported by poets and mystics, is characteristic of those moments in which we merely "take things in," rather than consciously reflect about them. It seems to me correct to say that the world comes to me as a "whole" when I "feel" it instead of know it. If Bradley's view of immediate experience is accepted, of course, it follows that the radical pluralism of many empiricists can never get off the ground, for such theories will mistake an abstraction for the testimony of experience.

6

Bradley's Philosophic Method
and Common Sense

Implicit in our entire discussion to this point has been Bradley's famous distinction between appearance and reality. There is both confusion as to the precise meaning Bradley attaches to these concepts and considerable criticism of the distinction as he draws it. In the remainder of Part I, I shall explain Bradley's use of these terms and consider critical and competing accounts of what 'real' means. This chapter begins this evaluation by connecting his conception of reality with the philosophic method that supports it.

At the start, it is important to notice the similarities and differences between the ordinary notions of 'appear' and 'real' and the ideas Bradley intends to convey by these same words. For example, as we ordinarily think and speak, it makes sense to say that one thing or quality or event *seems* to be so-and-so, when it really is not, *only* when this distinction might be verified. One thing seems to be another when it shares some qualities of the latter but lacks some as well, so that on closer inspection we see that the thing is other than it at first seemed. And the same thing could be said with little modification of qualities and events.

A plastic object may seem to be a gun because it has the same shape as a gun, or a group of boys may seem to be fighting because they are hitting one another, or a person may seem to be happy because he is smiling. But we can determine by observation that these things are not as they seem. We grab the plastic object and try to shoot it; we hear the boys laughing as they roll on the ground; the person's gestures or the tone of his voice disproves our original hypothesis. What an object "really" is is no more of a mystery than what it "appears" to be, for both are determined by the same kind of evidence.

It is precisely this possibility of confirmation or disproof by empirical means that is missing in Bradley's contrast of appearance and reality. For when he says that space and time are unreal, he cannot mean that these are characteristics that closer investigation will reveal the world does not "really" have at all. He cannot mean that there is some empirical test by which we might determine that objects have some qualities that spatial things have but that they also have other characteristics that convince us that our objects are not spatial at all. Nor can he mean similar things about change and the rest, because there is no conceivable empirical test by which one might determine that things only "seem" to grow older, change, and so forth. It is precisely this fact that makes Bradley's claim that space, change, and the like are unreal seem so strange. What could be "real" if space and time are not? If someone asserts that such things are only appearances, either he is using 'appearance' in a strange manner (and, hence, is not saying what he seems to be saying), or he is saying something clearly false.

Although there is this striking difference between the ordinary use of 'real' and 'appear' and that of Bradley, it would be wrong to assume that there is no community between what common sense and Bradley mean by 'real'. As A. E. Taylor pointed out,[1] we introduce the distinction between what appears to be the case and what is really the case because without it our world would present us with intellectual chaos. In so doing, we insist that what is intellectually unacceptable must be considered less fundamental, less "real" if you like, than what seems to be logically coherent. We just will not consider an inconsistent state of affairs as an ultimate fact. Bradley accepts this meaning of 'real' and 'appear', but he applies the standard of coherence much more stringently than we ordinarily do, partly because of the interpretation he gives to 'contradictory' and partly because of his analysis of relations and terms. The result is that he employs 'unreal' in a far-reaching way not anticipated by common sense. Nevertheless, because common sense and Bradley share a mutual interest in obtaining a coherent view of things, Bradley is well within his rights in believing that he is merely working out the view of the world

1. A. E. Taylor, *Elements of Metaphysics* (London, Methuen, 1961), Ch. 1.

implicit in the broken and fragmentary thoughts of the common man. If the common man does not recognize the results as what follows from his initial distinction of appearance and reality, then the reason is to be found in his inability to see what is implied in the distinctions he unthinkingly employs and not in an imposition on the common sense of a scheme foreign to it.

In fact, Bradley is doing here what philosophers have always done when they have tried to define justice, truth, substance, self, and the like. When he offers a definition of 'real', he intends neither to present the ordinary use of that word, for that use may be unduly limited and only faintly express the philosophical meaning, nor to impose some foreign, "true meaning" on the ordinary man, for that would be to invent an arbitrary definition, of interest only to its inventor, that one tries to pass off as the ordinary meaning.

Bradley is attempting a synthesis of these extremes. What he gives us as the meaning of 'real' is drawn from ordinary usage, but it is not necessarily identical with it; yet, it may emerge from that familiar usage. The job of the metaphysician is to provide us with "true" definitions and theories. He does this by the method found in the Platonic dialogues: Bradley's "ideal experiments."

One begins by asking himself what it means for an act to be just, a thing to be real, and so on, beginning with the ordinary concept of such matters, for what we believe immediately and instinctively is likely to approximate the ordinary linguistic usage. One tests this hypothesis by thinking of concrete instances that are said to be just acts, real things, and so forth. One may find that one's definition or theory needs revision on the grounds that it fails to do justice to the "facts" presented in the examples. One's definition may require one to assert that acts said to be unjust are just, or it may fail to include acts said to be just within its scope, and we may regard either such excess for deficiency as an inadequacy in our initial definition.

However, precisely the reverse may occur. When confronted with our concept or definition, the "facts" themselves may seem to be in need of rethinking; for it may become clear that our examples are derived from another "theory" we hold unconsciously. Thus, we may elect to hold on to our definition, for the time being, as it seems to be more adequate and solid than the "facts" with which it is contrasted, although at this initial stage our allegiance is likely to be with the facts and not with the theory.

The relation between theory and fact is complex, but perhaps a few words about it are in order at this point. The examples we use to confront our theories embody certain pre-analytic convictions that any theory must satisfy or be disproved. Among these convictions, I would list the feeling that a causal relation is more than constant conjunction, that there is some difference between a mental event and a bodily action, that men are responsible for their actions, that judgments about value are true or false, that the truth of an idea is independent of one's wishes or its practical effects, and that there is a common world we confront in theory and practice, a world of physical objects that are colored, shaped, and so forth. There are many others. Although I have no explicit criterion in terms of which I could explain why certain convictions appear on the above list and others do not, it seems certain that we do in fact have such basic convictions and that they form an unshakeable background to our theories. Thus, though there are theories of great contemporary importance that advocate the opposite of the above convictions, it seems to me that such theories are, strictly speaking, unbelievable. We feel that somehow an argument of this kind must be wrong, even though we cannot at the moment locate its error.

These basic convictions often come to the surface only because a theory has been tried and found wanting. On reflection, we may discover that the proposed theory violates a conviction we unknowingly held before. Conversely, a theory that is intellectually satisfying may be found on reflection to be so because it harmonizes with our deepest convictions. We seem to have no power to discern, in a Cartesian manner, the basic beliefs that any theory must account for. We may be passionately convinced that a certain act is just, or that a certain theory of causation is true, but, with reflection and patience, we may find our conviction melting away. Perhaps, in some larger perspective, even our basic "postulates" might need to be modified, but they certainly play an important role in any theory that can win our final assent. When Bradley defined metaphysics as "the finding of bad reasons for what we believe on instinct," he was expressing the view that acceptable theories must express our common convictions. Many seemingly knockdown counterexamples turn out, on reflection, to be unconvincing, for the theory that opposes them may carry more weight than does the example. And even when there seem to be facts that are "hard" beyond question, it remains to be seen what form an explanation of these facts will take. For example, there is some distinction between mind and body, but it remains a question exactly what this distinction is and how it is to be understood.

Our most basic convictions set very general guidelines for our theories, and they appear as facts that can refute any theory opposed to them. But no specific fact is rendered thereby impervious to criticism and modification, and no theory follows automatically and without argument from these convictions. The final stage of philosophic investigation involves an interplay between fact and theory in which each factor is reshaped in order to conform to the other. A mutual criticism and reinforcement takes place between instance and theory; both take part in a process of development, our view of one having a direct bearing on our view of the other.

Our goal is a sort of parity between the two, in which the theory would cover the examples that are the test of its adequacy and the examples are seen to be genuine examples as they are illuminated by our theory. Here the quest for a "true" definition may cease, for fact and theory are in harmony. However, individual notions change as they come to bear on more facts, and no single notion can reach a final equilibrium with the facts until it is seen as part of a total world view.

Thus, one must hold a notion tentatively until it can be seen in relation to other notions. This relating may reveal unexpected harmonies or conflicts. If the former, then our notion is good for so much. If the latter, then we must proceed on this higher level much as we did on the first level. No notion can have an absolute purchase over another, and our reconsideration will move toward the greatest possibilities for harmony. Certainty lies only with the whole fabric of concepts that emerges slowly from their critical interplay. It is ironic that Bradley and Bosanquet, among others, should have the reputation of followers of the high a priori road, when the fluidity of all concepts plays such an important part in their thinking. For both men, the difficulty of philosophy lies in the necessity of seeing one's concept in its larger context and refusing to commit oneself until it is seen to fit in this context.[2]

An example of this process on a large scale can be found in the connection between ethics and metaphysics. Some philosophers are convinced that a contracausal notion of freedom is necessary to account for our belief that man is responsible for his actions. Such a philosopher might also hold the metaphysical view that reality is a coherent whole, but when he compares the two views he finds them incompatible. If some events occur without any reason, then the ideal of reality as a whole in which every aspect is entailed by every other aspect must be false.

Here we have a case of two theories that, within their own spheres, seem to have given adequate expression to our instinctive commitments to freedom and rationality. Yet, their opposition suggests that one or both theories is inadequate when viewed in this larger context. Some reconciliation is necessary, but, at the same time, justice must be done to both commitments our theories reflect. In general, until we have a perfectly comprehensive and coherent view, no philosophical definition or theory can be more certain than its limited success warrants. Thus, Bradley is on sound ground when he rejects the Cartesian ideal of basing philosophical speculation on a set of intuitively known certainties.

This method can be criticized as circular—viciously circular because it denies a firm and independent set of facts by which we can test our theories. We cannot establish our theory until it accounts for all the facts, but we cannot identify our facts without first presupposing a theory. How, then, can we know either what justice is or what acts are just, for does not knowing one presup-

2. In Bradley's words, "Of the attitudes possible in experience I will try to show that none has supremacy. There is not one mode to which the others belong as its adjectives, or into which they can be resolved" (*AR*, 405). Those philosophers who think that Bradley is an extreme rationalist must not have read such passages. In fact, Bradley's philosophy might be characterized as an attempt to avoid the dangers of overintellectualization, while still doing justice to the role the intellect does play in life and in philosophy. See also Bernard Bosanquet, *The Principle of Individuality and Value* (London, Macmillan, 1912), pp. 122–23.

pose that we already know the other? And this circularity seems to protect the theory from criticism, for if we cannot get the facts apart from the theory, it seems that the facts must establish the theory that they already express.

The strength of this criticism lies in the realization of the theory-laden character of the "facts" that we select as evidence. The classic picture of theories standing before the bar of naked facts has no application here, although one doubts if it has application anywhere.

The situation might be seen as the confrontation of two competing theories, one explicitly formed, the other implicitly held and present in the examples we bring forth. As rational beings, we sense in a fumbling manner the theory that we seek, and we feel it as part of that larger theory that would give us perfect intellectual satisfaction. When considering a single notion, such as justice, this feeling of the all-comprehensive system gives direction to our search for an adequate concept of justice and allows us to eliminate or correct alternative suggestions.

The theory we state expresses our vague feeling that we know from the start the answer we seek. The examples we offer contain the same instinctual feeling, and we tend to rest on them as if they were beyond question. Nevertheless, our data involve a primitive attempt to make our felt conviction explicit and, as such, are open to correction.

At times, our theory may be only a fragmentary statement of our conviction, and the need to change it will be highlighted by the conflict between it and the examples that come to mind. At other times, our theory will highlight a feature of our conviction that has been ignored by the specific illustrative instances. The interplay is between the implicit and explicit versions of our theory, and the goal is an explicitly stated theory that will embody without distortion our feelings about the subject. Such a theory will be in harmony with the instances we mention, for our selection of facts will have been changed by our increasing awareness of what we want to say about the theory. Short of that goal, we have nothing that could be considered absolutely true.

If what I have said is correct, Bradley's aim is to reveal what we believe on instinct. When he defines truth or reality he is trying to capture what we would all believe, if only we could reason out our beliefs. Thus, the picture of Bradley as a man who consciously turned his back on common sense is simply not true.

In *Ethical Studies,* Bradley condemns both indeterminism and determinism for failing to provide the conditions under which the common man will admit responsibility for his actions.[3] Indeterminism errs in making a free act not "my" act at all; it claims that a free act arises not from my character but from a "mere characterless abstraction," which is free because indifferent. Determinism errs in accounting for the self by antecedent causes, and thereby destroying it. By ignoring the center of one's "moral being," the theory also makes action, and with it responsibility, impossible.

As Bradley puts it, this separation between our commonsense beliefs and our philosophical theories may lead to one of two results. From the commonsense point of view,

> seeing all we have of philosophy looks away (to a higher sphere doubtless) from the facts of our unenlightened beliefs and our vulgar moralities, and since these moralities are what we most care about, that therefore we also should leave these philosophers to themselves, nor concern ourselves at all with their lofty proceedings.

From the philosophical point of view,

> seeing that the vulgar are after all the vulgar, we should not be at pains to agree with their superstitions, but, since philosophy is the opposite of no philosophy, we rather should esteem ourselves, according as our creed is different from, and hence is higher than theirs.

We cannot "rest with the vulgar," and we cannot "shout in the battle of our two great schools"; but we can join the "battle of philosophy itself against two undying and opposite one-sidednesses; a philosophy which *thinks* what the vulgar *believe*" (*ES,* 40–41).

The task of the philosopher is very clearly set here as that of making explicit our commonsense commitments, but this does not mean that philosophy consists of transcribing or codifying our or-

3. F. H. Bradley, *Ethical Studies* (Oxford, The Clarendon Press, 1927).

dinary beliefs. For one thing, there are some issues on which common sense is silent, such as the degree of intelligence that is necessary before one becomes morally accountable. But the difference between philosophy and common sense is not simply that the latter is incomplete, for one must distinguish what the vulgar "really" believe and what they think they believe, given the practical, realistic character of much of common sense.

No doubt philosophy does involve the transcendence of our commonly held beliefs, if "transcendence" implies extending our general convictions with needed details. It may even involve transcendence if that word connotes a modification of the specific form a common conviction may take. Thus, common sense holds that value judgments are objective. Yet, we may find it necessary as philosophers to reconceive the way in which value judgments are objective, while still preserving the underlying claim that they are true or false. Consider Bertrand Russell's advocacy of the emotive theory in conjunction with his denunciations of war. Surely, Russell does not think that in his role as pacifist he is merely giving vent to a feeling he has about the war. His actions and pronouncements reveal his fundamental belief that he is saying something true when he condemns war, regardless of what theory has won his intellectual assent.

Of course, the most famous and candid admission of the gap that may hold between one's philosophical beliefs and his commonsense beliefs is to be found in Hume's *Treatise of Human Nature*, but Hume there interprets this phenomenon far differently than we have done. He asserts that "the understanding, when it acts alone, . . . entirely subverts itself and leaves not the lowest degree of evidence in any proposition, either in philosophy or common life." [4] Hume interprets these antiphilosophical tendencies as "sentiments of my spleen and indolence," and he describes how, after being away from philosophy for a while, he is able again to try to "establish a system or set of opinions, which if not true (for that, perhaps, is too much to be hop'd for) might at least be satisfactory to the human mind" (*THN*, 272).

It seems to me, however, that what is at work here is not merely

4. David Hume, *A Treatise of Human Nature*, ed. L. A. Selby-Bigge (Oxford, The Clarendon Press, 1955), pp. 267–68.

our animal tendency to avoid the difficulties of philosophy and to accept uninformed opinions instead. Rather, Hume is describing unknowingly the conflict within himself between his philosophical conclusions and his fundamental commonsense beliefs. The philosophy is at fault here and not our feeling that a thoroughgoing skepticism cannot be the final truth about things. As in the case of Russell, the depth of real conviction is measured more accurately by those beliefs on which we can act than by those engendered by our philosophy. Hume's philosophy "transcends" our fundamental convictions in a way and to a degree that robs it of any lasting plausibility.

Bradley, then, is willing to admit that there may be some difference between philosophy and common sense, but it is the kind of difference that matters. The task of the philosopher is to give form and expression to the substance of common belief and to avoid the temptation to turn one's back on common sense in favor of some "higher" realm. The appeal throughout his work is to our "felt commitments," and, in this sense, Bradley should be considered a defender of the plain man.

This is made especially clear when Bradley puts his philosophy in perspective. Though not the result of "mere compromise," his philosophy "makes a claim to reconcile extremes." On the one hand, "That metaphysics should approve itself to common sense is indeed out of the question. For neither in its processes nor in its results can it expect, or even hope, to be generally intelligible" (*AR*, 485). On the other hand, "It is no light thing, except for the thoughtless, to advocate metaphysical results which, if they *were* understood by common sense, would at once be rejected." The results to which he refers, he adds, are not the specific "subordinate" points of a theory, for there is no general, commonsense agreement on these points. Rather, common sense makes its claim on us in a different way. As Bradley says, "I mean that to arrange the elements of our nature in such a way that the system made, when understood, strikes the mind as one-sided, is enough of itself to inspire hesitation and doubt." (*AR*, 485).

7

Contradiction, Degrees of Truth, and Metaphysical Incorrigibility

Before beginning our analysis of Bradley on appearance and reality, it is important to recall what he means by 'self-contradictory'. In his view, all judgment involves synthesis. Certain very general ways of performing this synthesis seem to be (1) forced on us by experience (time and space), (2) natural, instinctive ways of relating elements (substantive-adjective), or (3) given emphasis by developments in science (primary-secondary). The world contains both change and plurality, along with permanence and unity, and our theories must do justice to both pairs of characteristics.

There is no difference in kind between these three modes of synthesis. All three are in need of justification, although the third is most obviously a "way of taking things." The distinction between substantive and adjective has a long history, but it is a "way of taking things" and stands in need of justification. And though it is harder to see how space and time can be considered as "ways of taking things," we must remember that, for Bradley, the distinction between fact and theory is not the final, absolute distinction that we normally believe it to be.

Bradley concedes that there is some sense in which these forms of synthesis succeed, but he questions whether they succeed in a way that metaphysics can find satisfactory. And satisfaction in metaphysics comes from the logical coherence of our explanations, not from their practical value or possible contribution to natural science. "Time" involves the combining of "before" and "after," but does it allow of a satisfactory ground for this union? Does the notion of predicating a "quality" of a "thing" do more than pose the problem of how this unity is possible? If on examination these modes of synthesis fail to provide an adequate reason for the union of elements they assert, Bradley says that they are contradictory.

His concept of contradiction, then, is far wider than that in ordinary use. When we say that someone is contradicting himself, we mean that he is saying that something both is and is not the case, and we reject the contradictory as necessarily false. Bradley's concern is to highlight the essential ingredients that make a judgment contradictory.

To reach this end, he employs the doctrine of negation he had worked out in *The Principles of Logic*. To say that something is not-A, Bradley argues, must be an indirect way of saying that it is something else. Negative judgments, in common with all judgments, must rest on some positive base. Therefore, to know what something is not requires one to know something positively about it. Nothing could be mere not-A, and to think of it as such would be to think nothing of it at all. We use the negative judgment when we know that something is not in one state but not enough to know what state it is in. "There is a reason, a positive character, on account of which 'this' excludes 'that,' and 'that' again on its side is opposite to 'this' " (*PL*, 2, 664).

The doctrine of negation is applied to the notion of contradiction through the meaning given to the term 'opposite'. The opposite of A cannot be the bare denial of A, for there is no such thing. It must then be whatever quality would conflict with A, but this means that A has an indefinite number of "opposites." Once contradiction has been defined in terms of positive conflict, it makes sense to speak of qualities contradicting one another, and not merely propositions, for qualities can be exclusive, although they cannot be contradictory in the narrower sense of that term. And when do qualities conflict? There is the obvious sense in which a given color excludes another color from the same space at a given time. However, Bradley insists that our notion of conflict must be widened along with our notion of contradiction. For him, any two properties may conflict with each other (that is, may be "opposites") if they are united without a sufficient reason. The point follows equally from his belief that, without a sufficient reason, our intellect is dissatisfied and intellectual dissatisfaction is contradiction and that different qualities are made to be contradictory by the manner in which we associate them.

When Bradley says that time is self-contradictory, he does not mean, for example, that when I use temporal expressions I also, of necessity, say the opposite of what I say at first. He does not mean that time expressions are obviously nonsensical. Nor does he assume that time cannot exist because it is a contradiction. He only means that time proves on analysis to be intellectually unsatisfactory. Time is believed to be an ultimate fact in which we must acquiesce. Yet, the intellect cannot accept this unity of elements "from the outside and ready-made." It must digest the "facts" thrust on it by finding the "why" that explains their unity. Bradley claims that the ordinary way in which we speak of things fails to provide us with such theoretical harmony.

No way of looking at things provides us with a final reason either for its distinctions or for the distinctions that characterize other modes of experience. The incompleteness, both "internal" and "external," of all our categories explains their contradictory nature: All theories rest finally on an unexplained conjunction of elements.

In order to understand fully the meaning of this doctrine, we must consider two other theories that qualify and give substance to it. If Bradley is willing to condemn all theories, he does not believe that all theories can be condemned equally, for he is anxious to do justice to our common notion that some theories are better than others. In addition, he does not want to abandon our belief that some claims are absolutely true. The former idea is the doctrine of degrees of truth and the latter is the doctrine of the incorrigibility of metaphysical truth.

The doctrine of degrees of truth fits harmoniously with the claim that all assertions fail to be wholly true, once one is willing to abandon the belief that a proposition must be simply false if it is not simply true. For the doctrine of degrees implies that the law of excluded middle does not apply to truths without qualification. The law does apply in a sense, for though a theory may be both true (to a degree) and false (to a degree), it is so from different points of view. It is true to the extent that the theory has over-

come the difference between thought and reality and false to the
extent that it has not. And the tests of this success are comprehensiveness and coherence.

Nevertheless, the law of excluded middle normally implies that,
if an assertion lacks truth in any way, it lacks it entirely. This
Bradley denies, and the ground of his denial lies in his analysis of
the nature of truth. In ordinary speech, we seem to feel that a certain proposition or theory is either true or false, that it is true if it
"corresponds" to the facts. These attitudes toward truth are incompatible, however, and the incompatibility lies in the vagueness that "corresponds" has for common sense.

In Bradley's view, thinking "corresponds" to reality when it
gives full expression to that reality. But no simple judgment can
be fully adequate to even the simplest fact, for every fact exists in
a context of other facts that condition it. In ignoring this context,
our simple judgment treats the fact as if it were genuinely atomic.
And, because ideas are general and ideas are the means of expressing truth, our fact is represented in our thoughts as if it were
general. Because facts are neither atomic nor general, it follows
that no idea or theory can correspond to the facts.

Here is an example of the philosophic method described above.
Bradley holds that it is a fundamental axiom that "Truth, to be
true, must be true of something, and this something itself is not
truth" (*ETR*, 325). To do justice to this basic claim about truth
requires that one make the other beliefs of common sense consistent with this one. When we make the meaning of 'corresponds'
precise, we find that no judgment can correspond fully with its
object. And, if so, why should truth and falsity be mutually exclusive? To be sure, absolute truth excludes falsity, but then we have
learned that such truth is a mere ideal. Truth and falsity are not
to be identified, but they may express different aspects of the same
judgment at the same time.

Bradley's doctrine of degrees gives formal expression to our
haunting feeling that we never quite say what we mean to say;
there is always more to be said, and the "more" is not external to
what is said, for if it were made explicit, it would change the
meaning of what is already explicit. When theories based on one
set of data are expanded to include more facts, they need to be re-

vised in the light of this new material. Indeed, the meaning of concepts changes as our experience widens, and if the meaning is different, so is the truth. After all, such a change in meaning reflects the adaptability of our ideas to the facts, and truth is nothing but the degree to which our ideas express the character of fact.[1]

In ordinary judgments, however, common sense seems to feel that what is left unsaid affects neither the meaning nor the truth of what is said. Yet, what is the justification for such a sharp distinction? Judgments that we make are based on evidence and extend beyond that evidence. A judgment is a conclusion for which we have a reason. Or judgments are hypotheses awaiting confirmation, and there is no distinction in kind between an hypothesis and a theory. But it is important to realize that what we omit in the case of simple judgments is just as important to their meaning and truth as what we omit in the case of theories.

Bradley's account of degrees of truth has important connections to other, seemingly opposing, philosophical doctrines. He says that theories are true insofar as they "work," which is close both to pragmatism and the modern view of the way "theoretical constructs" function. Both views consider theories as useful or not, rather than as true or false, and we are readier to say that usefulness is a matter of degree than that truth is. Bradley has no quarrel with those who link the concepts 'true' and 'use', but he insists, as the other views do not, that 'use' be defined as the kind of use that is appropriate to theory and not to practice.[2] But with this restriction in mind, Bradley's doctrine of degrees is in harmony with contemporary tendencies to deny the Cartesian doctrine that all knowledge rests on intuitively grasped truths, truths known independently of any context or results to which they might lead.

The doctrine of degrees of reality causes the same kind of perplexity as does the doctrine of degrees of truth, and it can be seen to make sense in the same way. In fact, the concept of degrees of reality provides the rationale for the concept of degrees of truth.

1. For a brilliant elucidation of the doctrine of degrees of truth, see Brand Blanshard, *The Nature of Thought*, 2, Ch. 27 and pp. 309–10, for the point that truth and meaning are organic to each other.

2. See *Appearance and Reality*, p. 135, for Bradley's statement on this matter.

In this case, one asks, "Despite what has been said about truth, is not a thing either real or not real, rather than real to some degree?"

Although a full answer to this question must await our analysis of 'real', we can say that for Bradley the answer is no. He points out that it is difficult to know what one means in saying that something "has" existence or reality, and it is as paradoxical to say that all things equally "have" reality as it is to say that they have it in different degrees. There is less difficulty in saying that a thing may have more influence, more importance, or more "presence" than something else, and it is from this point of view that the doctrine of degrees of reality begins to make sense (*AR*, 318). Reality for Bradley "consists in positive, self-subsisting individuality" (*AR*, 321). And just as judgments are more true the more they exhibit this character in their "internal harmony" and "all-inclusiveness," so different "facts" are more real the more they approximate this standard.

The meaning and significance of something (such as time) becomes clear only when we see it in relation to the rest of our experience. We see how closely its unity approximates the kind of unity found in other areas of experience, and we compare these unified wholes to reality. The task of the metaphysician is "to survey the field of appearances, to measure each by the idea of perfect individuality, and to arrange them in an order and in a system of reality and merit" (*AR*, 433).

The doctrine of degrees explains the notion that all judgments are contradictory, but it is most difficult to see how it squares with the claim that some truths are incorrigible. This assertion means that such truths are certain and, therefore, consistent—precisely what Bradley had previously denied was possible.

The conflict can be solved once one understands the sense in which truths are "incorrigible" for Bradley and the important distinction between finite truth and absolute or incorrigible truth. To be finite, an assertion must have a context that it omits to include within itself, this omission making the assertion contradictory. Such assertions are necessarily true in degree only. This deficiency does not characterize absolute truth, for "With absolute truth there is no intellectual outside. There is no competing predicate which could conceivably qualify its subject, and which could come in to condition and to limit its assertion" (*AR*, 483). The reason for this is that such assertions are all-inclusive. In being absolutely general, they contain implicitly any fact or claim that might be brought before them. Therefore, such facts cannot falsify them as they may finite assertions. To be "set against" absolute truth, an assertion must first be intellectual, and, in that very fact, it has submitted itself to our absolute claim.

As an example of an absolute truth, one might cite the claim that reality is coherent. This claim, if true, gives us a standard by which we can measure all other facts or truths, and, for this reason, it cannot be questioned by facts. One cannot know that there is some element of reality that resists inclusion into the one, coherent reality; for to have such knowledge, one must have an idea of this element, and to have an idea of it is already to have begun the process of joining it to the other elements of reality. Only by an appeal to some "higher" faculty of intuition can one escape this conclusion. And if one does claim such a power, it is fair to ask if he knows that he has it by intuition or by thought. Does one intuit that he has a power of intuition, or does one have an idea that he has this power? Is it a faculty that all men have or only some, and how are we to distinguish its false reports from genuine reports? As I can find no such power in myself, can see no evidence of it in others, and can see no answer to the above questions that gives comfort to the advocates of nonrational intuition, I support Bradley's claim that man has no such power.

One can see the strength of Bradley's position if one recalls Kierkegaard's harsh criticisms of Hegel in the *Concluding Unscientific Postscript*. On what ground does Kierkegaard stand when he insists that, because Christianity is a paradox, belief in it must rest on a "leap of faith" and not on the usual method of evidence and argument or proof? He ridicules Hegel's attempt to formulate a rational, philosophical account of Christianity, and he glorifies the religious for transcending the ordinary limits of the ethical. But if one abandons reason in his beliefs, how is he to know when those beliefs are sensible and justified? If Abraham's readiness to slay his son is said to be justified by a "higher" standard than that that reason can provide, how could Abraham distinguish bad actions from those that only "appear" to be bad from our lower, rational point of view? We all know that from some

limited point of view a belief may appear foolish or an action
wrong that appears quite correct from some more complete point
of view. Bradley's doctrine of degrees insists that this is always a
possibility. But Kierkegaard rejects this kind of transcendence, for
it merely represents the clash of two rational systems. He claims
that there are times when all attempts to account for things must
be put aside in favor of blind action or commitment.

Yet, Kierkegaard is not anxious for us to believe in just any absurdity or to commit just any irrational action. He believes that
Christianity is the true religion, and it is for this reason that certain apparently rash beliefs and acts are to be condoned. But one
wonders how Kierkegaard knows any of these things about Christianity? How does he know that the doctrine of the trinity is true
but nonsensical? How does he know that Abraham's action would
have been justified? How does he even know, and how did Abraham know, that it was God speaking to him at that moment?
How does Kierkegaard know that there is a level "above" reason
that allows us at times to turn our backs on reason?

Surely, it is not reason that makes any of these pronouncements. Is it then a power of intuition that Kierkegaard has but
that others do not? Against this claim, one might place Kierkegaard's own admission that the leap of faith is built on extreme
doubt, for intuition seems to entail certainty. Only hypotheses are
doubtful. And an appeal to intuition will not help in any case,
for an absurdity is that which has no meaning. Therefore, it cannot be true or false. How can one distinguish the "good" absurdities from the "bad" ones, as one must if he is not advocating the
absence of all standards for thought and action?

In trying to go "beyond" reason in both theory and practice,
Kierkegaard has not revealed a new and higher realm to us; he
has instead taken from us the only means by which we can distinguish the true from the false, or the right from the wrong. And
the truth of this assertion rests finally on the obvious absurdities
involved in the very attempt to state Kierkegaard's doctrine. Either he stands with reason, in which case he must submit to its demands for consistency, or he rejects these grounds, in which case
he has taken from himself the basis on which his very rejection
(as well as his subsequent theory) must rest. As Bradley put the
matter, you may avoid the claims of reason if you decline to

think. But "if you sit down to the game, there is only one way of playing. In order to think at all you must subject yourself to a standard, a standard which implies an absolute knowledge of reality; and while you doubt this, you accept it, and obey while you rebel" (*AR*, 135).

It follows from Bradley's doctrine of the incorrigibility of metaphysical truth that his own theory is certain in a way that other kinds of theories are not. He accepts this conclusion, but his attitude in doing so is not at all that of the believer in Cartesian certainty. Bradley's view is certain because "It is impossible rationally even to entertain the question of another possibility" (*AR*, 459). Any alternative system is merely a fragment of Bradley's outline of reality, whose place in that reality has been misunderstood. Because this competing view is different from Bradley's concept of reality, it is thought to be independent of it. What we fail to perceive is that the competing view is a form of the one reality.

Bradley is not neutralizing the claims of rival philosophers by some kind of sleight of hand. Rather, his view is that he has made no claims about reality except those that all men must make whenever they reason. It follows that any view that seems contrary to Bradley's must deny the very assumptions on which it rests and would, if fully understood, be seen to be an uneasy combination of what it assumes and what it professes. Once this is admitted, the next step is to see that it has a place as a fragment of that philosophy that rests on those assumptions we cannot deny.

As an example of this process, consider the view that reality is many rather than one. As Bradley points out, such a view admits, as a matter of course, that the many real things are related; but an analysis of relations shows that they are a means of unity. Therefore, in assuming the ultimate reality of a plurality of related real things, one asserts that the many real things are related while ignoring the fact that their independence is cancelled by their relatedness. When this is understood, we will see that the belief in plurality must accept its proper place within a more logical framework.

Consider the inner workings of Leibniz's pluralistic metaphysics. First, he attempts to deny all "real" relations between monads so as to ensure their mutual independence. Second, he admits of "ideal" relations between them so as to ensure that they will "reflect" a common world. Third, he needs to explain this "harmony" of monads by postulating a cause that has "preestablished" it. Fourth, he needs to show that the connection between this ultimate ground and the monads is not accidental, and so the talk of "fulgurations." Fifth, he attempts to head off the drift toward monism in the name of freedom by speaking of God's choice of the best of all possible worlds. Last, or so it seems to me, he realizes that such a move, if pressed, would destroy the sense in which God is an ultimate reason and would permit the possibility of choices inconsistent with His nature. But God is the "most real" for Leibniz, and no inconsistency can be allowed into the heart of reality. Leibniz's philosophy is driven to this impasse by the conflict between his explicit philosophy of pluralism and his implicit admission of the coherence of reality.

Bradley's philosophy is an attempt to view reality independently of the demands of any single form of experience to be the "true" form. Therefore, any theory that rests on science, or art, or ethics must be mistaking a part of things for the whole. All such theories repudiate or ignore the claims of the rest of experience, which then remains unexplained by our theory and in conflict with the form of experience on which we rest. The result is that our limited point of view cannot express our intellectual demand for an explanation that is both all-inclusive and coherent.

Bradley holds his view to be certain because it is all-inclusive and asserts only that which we all assume about reality. In order for a view to be in genuine opposition to his theory, it would have to call into question the very standards by which we judge all theories; it would have to stand outside of all that there is.

> We are impotent to divide the universe into the universe and something outside. We are incapable of finding another field in which to place our inability and give play to our modesty . . . We, in other words, protest against the senseless attempt to transcend experience (*AR,* 460).

The certainty in Bradley's theory, then, derives not from a special intuitive insight but from the inability of any thinker to do other than his intellect demands.

There remains the last question of how the doctrine of incorrigibility is consistent with the doctrine of degrees. Although, for Bradley, absolute truth cannot be falsified, it is still "conditional." The distinction is that between an assertion that, because it is limited, can conflict with assertions that are "external" to it, and an assertion that cannot be so opposed but that is still defective in the way that all thought is defective. All thinking is abstract and "cannot give bodily all sides of the whole." In this sense, it is true in degree only. Like the meaning of any concept, the meaning of "contradiction" is enriched through experience; the meaning this concept had for Aristotle is far different from that of those who have lived after Hegel. All truths are subject to this kind of change, but only absolute truths are subject only to this kind of change.

The doctrine of absolute truth is an exception to the doctrine of degrees that claims that all truths may be falsified by further evidence, but it is not an exception to that part of the doctrine that stresses the abstract character of thought. However, this is a necessary exception, without which the doctrine of degrees would be self-defeating. Consider the assertion that all truths may be falsified because they are true in degree only. Does one want the assertion itself to be falsifiable? Obviously not, for then it might be false that all truths are falsifiable. Relativism makes sense only when it is limited, that is, when it follows from a basis of truth that avoids the taint of relativism. Bradley's doctrine of absolute truth forms just such a basis, a context within which all that remains of truth can be seen to be a matter of degree only.

8

Appearance

This chapter and the following deal with Bradley's concepts of appearance and reality. Before beginning, let me make two general remarks about the subject.

First, Bradley must accept some of the blame for misunderstandings about his use of 'appearance' and 'reality'; in particular, the organization of *Appearance and Reality* is likely to mislead the careless or hasty reader. Because Bradley begins his "critical examination of first principles" by denying that such familiar things as space, time, change, and relations are real, one is apt to think that some radical denial of palpable fact is under way. It is well known that philosophers are fond of denying the obvious, and surely many readers have dismissed *Appearance and Reality* well before reading its last chapter with the thought that it represents yet another attempt to appear profound by questioning the unquestionable.

Second, by dividing *Appearance and Reality* into two distinct sections, Bradley gives the impression that appearance and reality are similarly distinct; and because those ordinary aspects of the world that we take for granted are dismissed as "unreal," one wonders what reality can be. It seems to be a mere blank, a mere negation of all that we know about the world. Such a view is obviously paradoxical.

But if Bradley is partly to blame for such impressions, his critics are all the more to blame for ignoring what Bradley actually says about appearance and reality. The view that Bradley is an other-worldly philosopher, who claims to know truths about a transcendent reality by some kind of special intuitive power, reflects no reasonably objective reading of Bradley's works.

In presenting Bradley's doctrine of appearance, there are six fundamental points to make. First, to be an appearance, it is not necessary that something actually appear to someone in perception or that someone judge it to be an appearance. It simply must have such a character that when reflected on it is seen to be not fully real. Therefore, 'appearance' is a dispositional notion.

Second, all appearances are characterized by what Bradley calls "ideality." All things have two aspects, content (or "what") and existence (or "that"); though these are distinguishable in thought, they cannot exist independently or even be thought of in total isolation from each other. When a thing exhibits some kind of "loosening" of content from existence, it is said to be "ideal" and an appearance. Existence and content are not two features of the world that merely happen to coexist; rather, they are only aspects of the things that do exist.

Take, for example, a book. It must have a character: a certain color, size, shape, and so forth. These characters, universals all, must "qualify" something, for by themselves they cannot exist. In order to exist, a thing must exist in a certain way; on the other hand, in order for there to be characters, there must be things that "have" these characters. Once these aspects of real things are separated in our consciousness, there seems to be no way to reunite them harmoniously.

Because neither element can be ignored, there seems to be no easy solution to the problem of their union. There is no "pure" existence we might attend to (which explains the hopelessness of existential metaphysics), but neither can we claim that there is nothing to a concrete entity but the features it is said to "have" (which explains the failure of any phenomenalist account of things). Qualities are qualities of something and cannot, by themselves, comprise a thing. We seem frustrated in our attempt to find anything beyond the qualities of a thing when we analyze it, for what could our experience reveal to us other than a quality? Yet, we resist the suggestion that a thing is nothing but a set of qualities related to one another in some way. No matter how we take the qualities, we fail to achieve the unity we believe a concrete thing to have. Indeed, this unity may well turn out to be the missing "that" that things "have" over and above their qualities.

We realize that for anything to be real it must have both content and existence unified into a single whole. How do we know this? In feeling, we confront the world at a level "below" the distinction between content and existence. This experience puts us in direct, if inarticulate, contact with reality. An analysis of judgment—thought in its developed form—reveals that it involves predicating a content of a subject: it involves the "reunion of two sides, 'what' and 'that,' provisionally estranged" (AR, 145). The goal of thinking is to reunite content and existence, and we believe that any completely true theory would present things as they are and realize this goal. Feeling gives us a clouded glimpse of what this ideal implies, and it offers us a positive contrast to the actual state of affairs in our theories.[1]

The distinctness of qualities and the reference of any quality to something "beyond" it exemplifies the ideality of fact. Qualities are absolutely distinct from one another, hence they are also "loose" from one another. As far as one can see, the union of qualities in a thing has no effect on the qualities concerned. The atomic character of Hume's impressions is true to this aspect of experience, for distinctness and externality seem to be merely two ways of expressing the same feature of experience.

But it follows that no thing can have the kind of unity we demand of anything real. We cannot accept this externality as final truth, for it represents the mere togetherness that our intellect rejects. Further, the things of which we speak are finite. But the character of anything finite is relative to the greater context in which it stands and looks to this context for its explanation. In both these ways, the content of a thing transcends its own existence. It is so "loose" from its existence that it is a universal applicable in a variety of contexts, and it looks beyond its existence for its final accounting. As Bradley says, "Everywhere the finite is self-transcendent, alienated from itself, and passing away from itself towards another existence" (AR, 430).

However, although we recognize that the world as it comes to us does not satisfy our intellectual demands, there is little that we

1. It is important to note that the above theory implies a criticism of our ordinary experience. For, as Bradley himself states, "Facts which are not ideal, and which show no looseness of content from existence, seem hardly actual" (AR, 146).

can do about it. Thought is the development of the division between content and existence that characterizes the finite. It "moves and has life" through ideas, and "an idea is any part of the content of a fact so far as that works out of immediate unity with its existence" (*AR*, 144). Our ideas are abstractions that cannot, as such, exist; in judgment, we affirm their unity with the existent; but the unity asserted there is imperfect, for universals simply cannot exist. In short, thinking works within the distinction of existence and content, even though the very act of judging is an attempt to overcome this distinction. Our theories never give us fact, no matter how extensive and coherent they may be, for there is no division of any kind in the real world.

Because man's only approach to reality is through ideas (once feeling has been transcended), there is no way for him to overcome the difficulties that plague thinking. He must work with appearance and try in his theories to remold it in the image of reality; but appearance and reality never coincide. Bradley has been called a mystic, and it is true that, in speaking of the "suicide" of thought as it approximates reality, he seems to reject thought as our means of knowing the real. Yet, Bradley rejects mysticism in denying that there can ever be a "vision" of the real that transcends the powers of thought.

Third, "Nothing is actually removed from existence by being labelled 'appearance.' What appears is there and must be dealt with" (*AR*, 12). When Bradley states that there is no such thing as *mere* appearance (*ETR*, 272), he means to underline the positive character of appearance and to avoid closing his eyes to obvious facts, something he has been accused of doing. As he says, "Whatever is rejected as appearance is, for that very reason, no mere nonentity. It cannot bodily be shelved and merely got rid of, and, therefore, since it must fall somewhere, it must belong to reality" (*AR*, 119).

Fourth, even more positively, Bradley states, "in a word, *appearances* are the stuff of which the Universe is made" (*AR*, 511). Thus, all appearances must belong to reality in some sense, for they have a "positive character" and have "no place in which to live except reality" (*AR*, 114). Reality is all-inclusive. Yet, it is also true that in calling something an appearance we distinguish it from reality and imply that, as such, it cannot be true of reality.

Once again we need the notion of degree. An appearance belongs to reality in the sense that it expresses the nature of the real to some degree; however, as an appearance, it cannot hold of reality without qualification.

The important point is that the "contradictory" character of appearance does not imply some positive feature in appearance that sharply divides it from the real. What is unacceptable to us in appearances is that the elements they contain are united without a sufficient reason. Thus, these elements are "opposites" for us, and the appearance is a "contradiction." But the lack of a sufficient reason is a reflection of our failure to see things as a whole and not a reflection of the nature of things. We cannot know in detail how things are combined to form a logical whole, but our belief that there is such a whole allows us to hold that everything positive in appearance can be accepted as "real" when seen in the light of its larger context.

On the one hand, for Bradley, appearances are the "stuff" of which real things are made and are not "lost" in reality; on the other hand, they lose their "distinctive" natures in reality, where they are said to be "transmuted" or "overcome." Are these two assertions, representing as they do distinct tendencies of human nature, consistent? If Bradley has not solved this problem, at least his doctrine of appearance goes as far as any doctrine in the direction of a solution.

Fifth, appearance, although distinguished from reality, is not to be identified with illusion. Space and time are not figments of our imagination. Because our ideas never correspond exactly with their objects, finite life involves appearance and error, and, when our view of things is distorted beyond this necessary minimum, we have illusion. Because, we feel, reality does respond to the demands of our intellect, the opposition between appearance and reality does not make the former into mere illusion. And if one objects to the notion that illusions have their own degree of adequacy, let me point out that this notion is simply part of the larger conception of degrees of truth and awaits its justification there.

Finally, philosophy, as the work of the intellect, "is but one appearance among others, and, if it rises higher in one respect, in other ways it certainly stands lower" (*AR*, 402). It is this kind of philosophical modesty that irritated Bradley's idealist critics, such as Edward Caird who claimed that Bradley's philosophy was "all blade and no handle" and led to a "manifest self-contradiction." How can philosophy condemn itself without implying that there is something about reality that it cannot know? But in this very self-condemnation, does it not claim to know that there is something that it cannot know? And is not this a contradiction? Bradley himself uses this argument to show that any doctrine that assumes an unknowable must be self-refuting: "It would be much as if we said, 'Since all my faculties are totally confined to my garden, I cannot tell if the roses next door are in flower.' And this seems inconsistent" (*AR*, 111). Similarly, does not Bradley's criticism of common notions imply an absolute knowledge of reality, as Bradley himself claims? If so, then what is the justification of the constant reservations about the adequacy of thought in general and of philosophy in particular? [2]

Like many philosophical arguments that seem "knockdown," this argument is not so strong as it first seems to be. Caird has raised the issue of whether Bradley's restrictions on thought make sense, and I think that, when one sees the sense in which thought falls short of reality, one will agree that the restrictions are justified. The issue turns out to be not one between two exclusive points of view. Bradley's view turns out to be a middle ground, a blend of elements that would be in conflict without the requisite qualifications.

In Bradley's view, neither of two extreme positions can be defended. The theory that there is an absolute unknowable is self-defeating, for more knowledge is implied in the theory than the

2. Caird suggests that there are in fact two Bradleys, an idealist and a skeptic. It is in his latter guise that he denies the basis that makes sense of the skepticism that abounds in *Appearance and Reality*. Philosophy needs a handle, as well as a blade, if it is to cut. As Caird said of Bradley's skepticism, "The very idea which is set up as the test of truth seems to be finally dissolved in the absolute—which, as with Spinoza, is presented as complete reality and yet as the negative of all the 'reals' we know." Sir Henry Jones and John Henry Muirhead, eds., *The Life and Philosophy of Edward Caird* (Glasgow, Maclehose, Jackson, 1921), p. 206.

explicit statement of the theory will allow. Yet, it is also true that
thought and reality are not one and the same, for thought is always "of" a reality that has an immediacy lacking in all theories.
Thus, it seems that there cannot be an "other" to thought and
that there must be such an other. Can we find a ground that will
allow both these claims to be true in a sense? This is precisely
what Bradley does when he says,

> But the Other which I maintain, is not any such content, nor is it
> another separated 'what', nor in any case do I suggest that it lies
> outside intelligence. Everything, all will and feeling, is an object
> for thought, and must be called intelligible (*AR,* 155).

Thought's other is present to thought; there is no feature of it
that cannot be expressed as an idea. But even so, what one thinks
of remains distinct from the thoughts one has about it.

I do not see that this position is self-contradictory. Indeed, it
seems to me to do full justice to our sense that thoughts and
things are different kinds of entities without separating them in
such a way that one creates needless theoretical puzzles. Nor do I
see that in this distinguishing thought and reality Bradley has ignored his previous claim that all criticism implies a positive basis.
His claim is that he knows the general "form" of reality because
the end of thought is that of an "immediate, self-dependent, all-
inclusive individual." In our thinking, we reflect this ideal in a
fragmented and incomplete way.

Thus, the "distance" between thought and reality does not prevent us from knowing the general form of reality. Of course, as
this ideal is present in our thinking, it, too, must be somewhat distorted and in need of further supplementation; but as there is no
way of questioning this ideal, its general truth must be beyond
disproof. It seems to me that this view gives Bradley enough purchase on reality to justify his positive claims, without misplacing
the role of thinking in the nature of things. Perhaps we cannot
know precisely the degree to which our view of contradiction
must undergo change before it would be adequate to the "harmony" characteristic of the real; but we can be certain that the
change cannot be great enough to falsify our claim that reality
avoids contradiction. Bradley's handle is not so detailed as was

that of Hegel, but it is enough to support the actions of his blade.

Campbell claims that Bradley's distinction between thought and reality conflicts with his doctrine of degrees. This alleged conflict arises out of Bradley's view that "Differences are united in reality in a manner intrinsically different from the mode of union which is characteristic of, and inseparable from, the finite intellect" (SC, 31). Campbell asserts that, because for Bradley reality is "beyond" thought in this way, he must admit both a "noumenal" ideal of self-consistency and a "phenomenal" ideal. And Campbell adds, "The contradiction in Bradley's doctrine of 'Degrees' is that he uses the *second* form to apportion degrees of the first" (SC, 32).

We may agree that to be able to assess the "degree of truth" of a judgment we must have a criterion that reflects the way things are. If our intellect has no purchase on the real, we have no way of knowing whether what satisfies it also is true or real. In light of this point, I wish to make two remarks concerning Campbell's criticism. First, Bradley's doctrine allows for a criterion sufficient to establish degrees of truth. Second, Campbell's own view is inconsistent.

Campbell claims to know that reality, "of whose concrete character we know nothing," must conform to a noumenal ideal of self-consistency. But to know even this much is to know something of reality, and, thus, we must be able to distinguish true assertions about the real from false ones. Yet, how can we do this without applying the "criterion and positive guide in our actual intellectual operations"? If the real were as different from our thinking and its criterion of truth as Campbell makes out, we could never know that it was so. And if we do know it, it cannot be so. Metaphysical solipsism is no more intelligible than is the common variety. As Bradley has said, "The intellect, if you please, is but a miserable fragment of our nature, but in the intellectual world it, none the less, must remain supreme" (AR, 454).

We answer the first point by noting that the difference between thought and reality is only one side of Bradley's theory. He stresses equally their identity, the presence of the real in thinking, and the fact that thought has its own ideal, the actual character of the real. Campbell's criticism of the doctrine of degrees ignores this qualification of the "distance" that exists between thought and the real, and this qualification provides a rationale for that doctrine. Bradley has succeeded, I believe, in providing a theory within which both a judicious skepticism and a self-saving degree of knowledge are possible. Reality is not closed to thought, as Campbell claims Bradley holds, nor is it transparent to thought. If a metaphor is needed, let us say it is translucent to thought.

9

Reality: Coherence and Value

I

A major premise of Bradley's philosophy is: Reality is coherent. The defense of this view, put forth by H. W. B. Joseph and more recently by Brand Blanshard, proceeds in two stages. First is the establishment of the law of contradiction as absolute, and second is the proof that this law covers all things and not thought alone. The latter is necessary, I believe, if the former is to seem to be more than a trick. Yet, it has been criticized for feeding on the "logicocentric predicament" much as Berkeley made use of the "egocentric predicament" to make it seem that he had proved that things cannot exist unperceived.

The first point is simply a reformulation of Bradley's claim that his philosophy is absolutely true, and it contains a weaker and a stronger claim. As a matter of fact, no one ever does doubt the validity of the law of contradiction. When we reason, we always assume that we have failed to get at the bottom of things if the facts seem to be incompatible. Apparent exceptions to this rule must be merely apparent. For example, some philosophers speak of the irrationality of things, but they mean, one gathers, that things lack the kind of purpose that men have believed in for so long. The philosopher who glories in irrationalism wants to stress that a realistic and, one assumes, rational account of things will expose the teleological pretensions of the past. Kierkegaard speaks often of the 'paradox', but even he does not claim that things generally are paradoxical. And when we say that a situation "just does not make sense," we do not mean quite what we say. We mean, as we would admit if pressed, that *we* cannot see any explanation for what has happened. Obviously, this claim is not inconsistent with the belief that there is an explanation.

One might argue that we cannot call the law of contradiction into question even if we wish to. Yet, this is precisely what the defenders of conventionalism in logic intend to do, for if the traditional laws of logic are mere conventions, then it should be possible to deny them and to construct logics based on opposed laws. As Blanshard points out, however, the conventionalist is stopped in his venture before he begins.

> In the very assertion of the thesis, it is assumed that the position is false, for we are supposed to understand that the logic used in establishing the conventionality of logic is itself somehow exempt from the conventional character ascribed to other logics. For example, we are offered as true the statement that all logic is conventional, and expected to accept without question that the contradictory proposition, "some logic is not conventional," is false. But if the law of non-contradiction is really only a convention with alternatives, why should we be expected so firmly to take this contradictory as false? If there really is an alternative to the law, *both* sides of a contradiction may be true, and to insist on either to the exclusion of the other is dogmatism (*RA, 275*).

Assertions, whether positive or negative, must proceed from some ground or evidence. But from what ground could we question the law of contradiction? Without it, we cannot say anything to the exclusion of its opposite, and, lacking this power, cannot assert anything at all. Hence, the futility of logical conventionalism, for without the law of contradiction, the conventionalist's position lacks the minimum conditions for meaningfulness. Like the extreme skeptic, the conventionalist in logic wants the excitement of a general negative without paying any of the cost, but the generality of both positions traps their defenders in the very act of asserting them. As Blanshard puts it, "One cannot deny the law of contradiction without presupposing its validity in the act of denying it"(*RA, 276*).

The problem of what the scope of the law is remains, however. Only if it extends to reality as well as to thought can it be used to establish Bradley's claim that reality is rational. The following points seem relevant. First, the rationality of the real has never been "verified," for no comprehensive view of things exists that might have been so tested. Second, any direct attempt to prove that the law of contradiction holds of reality must fail, for it will be a circular proof. The proof would have to be in accord with the law of contradiction, but, because the proof is about reality, it must consider reality logically. This approach makes sense only on the assumption that reality is logical. But our assumption is just what we are trying to prove. Hence, the circularity. One might sum up the situation by saying that the law of contradiction is a fundamental assumption of all thinking, including any attempts to establish it.

Yet, one can approach the law from the negative way mentioned above.[1] The claim that the law of contradiction holds only of thought turns out not to be intelligible. Joseph has put the point most clearly:

> and the so-called necessity of thought is really the apprehension of a necessity in the being of things. This we may see if we ask what would follow, were it a necessity of thought only; for then, while e.g. I could not think at once that this page is and is not white. But to admit this is to admit that I can think the page to have and not to have the same character, in the very act of saying that I cannot think it; and this is self-contradictory. The Law of Contradiction then is metaphysical or ontological.[2]

Or one might say simply that when one tries to think of what it would mean for the law of contradiction to hold only of thought he sees that the result is nonsense. What meaning has the claim that something might both have and not have a quality at the same time and in the same way? I can find none. Yet, this is just what one is expected to believe is possible in the proposed view. If we can know anything at all, it seems clear that we can know that a contradictory state of affairs is impossible.

One might still argue that such an argument shows merely that the thinker cannot conceive of this possibility because thinking is under the control of the law of contradiction. But for all we know

1. See Blanshard, The Nature of Thought, 2, 422.

2. H. W. B. Joseph, An Introduction to Logic (Oxford, The Clarendon Press, 1957), p. 13.

we are imposing the manner of our thinking on a reality that does not respond to it.

It is worth noting that if our critic is correct about the scope of the law of contradiction he is forced into a complete skepticism. For no matter how persuasive any train of thought seems, it is always possible that the very opposite is also true. And, because our thinking follows rules that reality does not, no theory can ever be true of the real. And what if our critic is willing to accept this result? The next step is to remind him that such a complete skepticism must apply equally to his own theory about the scope of the law of contradiction. Thus, it may be as true that the law extends to things as it is that it does not, but, if so, it is hard to see how the critic's thesis can have been proved or even rendered probable.

We saw above the absurdity of attempting to deny the law of contradiction, and here we see the equal absurdity of denying the application of the law to things. Joseph's point is essentially the same, but it takes a somewhat different line. Once we have admitted that we cannot escape the law, the question arises of in what sense this law has authority over us. (No matter what view we take we shall be free to *say* contradictory things, for the law cannot limit our use of words.)

If the law applies only to our thinking, it must mean that we cannot, as a matter of fact, think two things that are contradictory, for the law is to be inescapable, something whose commands we must follow. And, if it applies to thought only, how can it assert this authority except by preventing certain ways of thinking? Two points follow immediately. First, the assertion is obviously false as it stands. People can and do make contradictory assertions. Second, even if it were true that we cannot think a contradiction, the view turns out to be self-defeating,[3] for its defender must claim that we cannot think a contradiction in the sense of finding it meaningful or of understanding how it could be true. The manner in which our thinking proceeds does not allow us to make sense of contradictions. But our critic claims that it is possible that in reality there are genuinely contradictory situations,

3. Blanshard, *Reason and Analysis,* pp. 424–25, is a valuable supplement to Joseph's analysis.

which is what he means when he limits the law of contradiction to thinking alone. But, as Joseph and Blanshard point out, when we assert that the real might be contradictory, we must be conceiving of such a situation. We must find the suggestion meaningful, for we assert it to be possible, and the possible is always that that might be the case but that we do not know to be the case. Indeed, if we are more bold, we may go further and assert that the real does contain contradictions.

But this is nonsense. By our own admission, a contradiction is that that we cannot find meaningful or true; yet, we claim that we can conceive of this possibility. There seems to be only one defensible sense in which we cannot think a contradiction: We cannot think in terms of contradictions if we are to think truly. And this is because reality is logical, and, if our thoughts are to be true, they must be true of reality. To do so, they must express the character of reality, and that character is defined as logically coherent.

It is important to see that the above argument is not a form of philosophical sleight of hand, an impression that arises, I think, from our democratic feeling that all views deserve at least a hearing and that no view can be ruled out until the last bit of evidence is in. There is much to be said for this feeling, both in philosophy and elsewhere, but as an absolute commitment it arises from a lack of understanding of the conditions under which any view can be meaningfully held.

This can be seen in the above argument. The claim that the law of contradiction holds only of thought implies that thinking may distort the real. But that implies some knowledge of reality that suggests this possibility. Yet, no matter how meager our knowledge of reality is, it is enough to establish that to this point thought is adequate to the way things are.

In our "negative" knowledge of reality, we have already passed over the gulf between thought and reality that is suggested by our critic. Either we do know something about reality, in which case there cannot be the kind of gap between thought and reality which our critic suggests, or we can know nothing about reality, in which case we cannot know even enough to suggest that it has a radically different structure. To know of a barrier between thought and reality is to have crossed that barrier, and any absolute difference would be out of sight and unknown. Those who want to limit the scope of the law of contradiction do not realize that in so doing they call into question the truth of every theory, including their own.

There may remain a feeling that we are somehow appealing to man's "logicocentric predicament." The situation seems comparable to Berkeley's proof that physical objects could not exist unless perceived (or conceived): He argued that, when we imagine a tree in a lonely forest, we forget that it is still being imagined or conceived—by us. Thus, we must accept his thesis that no physical objects can exist unperceived because we are unable to conceive of the opposite thesis, let alone prove it. Many philosophers have found this argument fallacious. Of course, we cannot conceive of anything without conceiving of it. This is the "egocentric predicament." But why should we conclude from this that things cannot exist unconceived? Berkeley is right in suggesting that realism cannot be verified by direct inspection, but if an analysis of physical objects reveals nothing that suggests mind-dependence, why should we not be realists?

However, there are important differences between Berkeley's argument and that supporting the ontological commitment of logic. First, though there is no difficulty in doubting Berkeley's thesis, we cannot doubt the law of contradiction. Thus, we feel that Berkeley is tricking us, for the opposite of his claim is not inconceivable; one does not need to do the impossible, to think of something without thinking of it, in order to question Berkeley's subjective idealism. Indeed, the mere fact of the "egocentric predicament" seems totally irrelevant to the issue between realism and subjective idealism. Of course, the fact that there is this predicament makes it hard to know what objects are like "outside" of the mind, but this uncertainty cuts both ways and affords no reason for the move to subjective idealism. It is as uncertain that there would be no physical objects without perception as it is that physical objects can exist unperceived, as long as one reasons solely from the egocentric predicament.

Philosophers have long doubted Berkeley's argument, and, when faced with a similar argument about logic, they have assumed that it is faulty for the same reasons. I question this assumption; owing to the generality of the claim regarding the laws of logic, there is no ground from which one might doubt the claim. Berkeley's argument has no such generality. It concerns objects and not our judgments about objects; therefore, one can make a judgment opposing Berkeley without contradicting oneself. Realism is not a self-contradictory doctrine; logical skepticism is.[4]

Further, there just is no "logicocentric predicament," as there is an "egocentric predicament." There is such an egocentric predicament precisely because we feel that unfair use is being made of the fact that we only know reality in perception and in conception. We try to draw an inference about things from the way we know them, though there seems to be no good reason for assuming that things must depend for their existence on human awareness. Perhaps things are "in" our minds when we are aware of them, and perhaps ideas can exist only "in" a mind, but what conclusions about things follow from these facts?

I believe these doubts to be valid, but I do not think they have any force in the case of Bradley's ontological claims for logic.

4. The reference to Berkeley is to A. A. Luce and T. E. Jessop, eds., *The Works of George Berkeley, Bishop of Cloyne* (London, Nelson, 1949), 2, 200. There Berkeley utters the challenge: "If you can conceive it possible for any mixture or combination of qualities, or any sensible object whatever, to exist without the mind, then I will grant it actually to be so." The evidence he offers to show that one cannot do this is that it is a "contradiction to talk of conceiving a thing which is unconceived" and that "all I can do is to frame ideas in my own mind." He concludes that the mere power to think of objects does not prove "that I can conceive them *existing out of the minds of all spirits.*" Perhaps not, but when I think of them and think that they are the kinds of things that have mind-independent existence, then I am meeting Berkeley's challenge. And in fact, this is very easy to do. It is not possible, as Berkeley says, to think of a thing that is not being thought about; nor is it possible to think of something that is, at that moment, totally "out of my mind." But though I must be thinking of something in order to think of it (true but harmlessly analytic), I can at the same time think that it could exist independently of any act of thought. I can think that the objects of my thought, as contrasted with the ideas by means of which I think, have a mind-independent existence. And in fact, later in the *Dialogues,* Berkeley renounces his earlier claim that he is willing to rest his entire case on the issue of conceivability. He says, "When I deny sensible things an existence out of the mind, I do not mean my mind in particular, but all minds. Now it is plain they have an existence exterior to my mind, since I find them by experience to be independent of it" (*WGB,* 2, 230). Berkeley does not explain how one might learn this from experience when it is supposed to be impossible to so much as conceive it to be possible.

There is a legitimate distinction between our awareness of things and things themselves that the subjective idealist denies. But we cannot believe in a similar division between thought and things to justify our doubts about the law of contradiction. Of course, there is a distinction between thoughts and things, but not the kind of difference that would help our critic. We can make a legitimate inference from the character of thought to the nature of things; we can assume that things conform to our desires for logical order, and this is because the attempt to divide thought and reality according to their structure is incoherent.

It is not as if we suffered from what Santayana called "cosmic impiety" when we view reality from the point of view of thought. Perhaps Bradley is right in insisting that the distinctions we make as thinkers have no exact counterpart in reality, but it is still true that there is no ground from which one might question the goal of thinking in relation to reality. We are not "trapped" within thought, for thought is co-extensive with reality in its scope and aim. The so-called "logicocentric predicament" is simply an expression of the fact that there is this kind of identity between the two. There is, in fact, no "predicament." [5]

Let us turn now to a brief discussion of Professor Nagel's attack on the above conception of logic in his famous essay, "Logic without Ontology." [6] For our purposes, we will consider his account of logic to be built around one negative and two positive theses. Negatively, Nagel claims that the law of contradiction can be interpreted as a necessary truth about the structure of things only by becoming trivially true. That is, the law is exceptionless only because "in specifying both the attribute and the conditions *the*

5. Blanshard sums up the case for the ontological character of logic when he says, "But is confinement really confinement when there is no desire or thought of escape? Is there really sense in saying we are 'in a predicament' if we can attach no sense to being out of it? Our situation, in short, seems to be this: We find it assumed in every judgment that the laws of logic are valid of the world with which thought is concerned, a world independent of present assertion. And this assumption is compulsory, since without it thought cannot take a step. Is it also true? That we cannot prove. But the contrary suggestion is meaningless. And thus the alternative actually before us is to accept these laws as independently valid or to cease thinking altogether" (*NT*, 2, 423).

6. Reprinted in Ernest Nagel, *Logic without Metaphysics* (Glencoe, The Free Press, 1956), pp. 55–92.

principle is employed as a criterion for deciding whether the specification of the attribute is suitable . . . In brief conformity to the principle is the condition for a respect being 'the same respect' " (*LWM*, 59). And the same is true of 'same attribute', 'belong', and 'not belong'.

Positively, Nagel urges, first, that logical laws "which are regarded as necessary in a given language, may be viewed as implicit definitions of the ways in which certain recurrent expressions are to be used, or as consequences of other postulates for such usages" (*LWM*, 80). Presumably, he is applying this thesis when he states that the impossibility of a penny having a diameter of both 11/16 of an inch and 12/16 of an inch arises from the fact that we use the expressions designating these lengths to refer to different results of measurement. Second, Nagel holds that our acceptance of "logical principles as canonical" is neither arbitrary nor based on their "allegedly inherent authority," but, rather, is grounded on pragmatic considerations. If the principles "achieve certain postulated ends," they are acceptable, and, if not, they must be set aside for other principles. The same instrumental standard applies, in Nagel's view, to the rules of inference. For him, both rules and principles are regulative in nature.

Does this view provide a viable alternative to the belief that logical principles are both necessary and ontological? I think not. All three theses presuppose the possibility of alternative logical principles, and I have argued that this is not a genuine possibility. If I am correct about this, the law of contradiction *is* necessary, cannot be interpreted primarily by its results, and cannot be interpreted primarily as *"prescriptive* for the use of language." Rather, it helps to achieve truth by forming the only conceivable basis for coherent thought, one based on an insight into the structure of things; it prescribes usage only because it so reflects the world that without such usage there would be no sense to our speech.

Thus, it is misleading to say that the law of contradiction is necessary "in a given language" and is an "implicit definition" of certain expressions, for these statements suggest that it is about words and derives its necessity only from linguistic considerations. But it is not about words; we know this as well as we know that any ordinary statement is about things rather than words. And its necessity holds beyond the structure of any linguistic system, for without it no coherent system is possible. Is it not clear that there is a reason why it is instrumental and prescriptive, a reason that explains the meaninglessness of attempts to deny it? To say that our expressions make certain measurements mutually exclusive surely reverses the natural order of precedence.

Nagel's claim that the law of contradiction is trivially true on the ontological interpretation appears to have described the situation precisely backward. We do not reject apparent exceptions to the law by defining "in the same respect" in terms of the law itself. That would indeed trivialize the exceptionless character of the law. Rather, we can see that apparent exceptions to it are merely apparent because we apprehend it as a necessary standard for reality. We continue to specify "same respect" because we know that we can and must rest on the law as our guide to the nature of things. Of course, there are cases in which an assertion is necessarily true merely because we so define our terms that nothing is allowed to count as an exception. That is why we regard "all bachelors are unmarried" as uninformative. But the mere fact that an assertion is exceptionless does not make it true by definition, and, in the case of the law of contradiction, there are good reasons for believing that it is both necessary and informative.

In short, if the law of contradiction is necessarily true in a non-trivial sense, then it should withstand the assaults of suggested exceptions. We do, in fact, see this to be the case when we recognize that the exceptions are only apparent and it is incorrect, therefore, to describe this insight as our refusal to allow genuine exceptions to count against the law. In this process, it is we who are under the constraint of things and not things that are being recast to meet our arbitrary demands.

II

Once the barriers to accepting Bradley's thesis—that the law of contradiction gives us absolute knowledge of the general character of reality—are removed, the view is still incomplete as it stands. Is it just a miracle that what satisfies us as thinkers also is true of the real, or can some rationale be provided for this fact? Two kinds of reasons might be given. We might assume that there must be a creator who is responsible for this "pre-established harmony." Leibniz's inference to God to explain the harmony among the monads, Berkeley's inference to God to explain the orderly character of our ideas, and the teleological argument for God's existence are all forms of this argument. Or, we might try to find the reason in the nature of things themselves, so conceiving of thought and reality that there is no need to go outside them to find the explanation for their "relation."

Bradley adopts the last kind of explanation, which is preferable to either no explanation at all or to an inference to a transcendent creator. We reject the denial that there is any explanation here at all, for our reason proceeds on the assumption that chance connections represent only our failure to see the logic of things.

Any explanation by means of God is also inadequate. Thought demands that a reason or ground not be external to the elements whose unity it is said to explain, and yet the traditional God is external to His world in just this way. The result is that it is equally a mystery why He, an independent and perfect being, would create any world at all as was the existence of the original regularities God was supposed to explain. And any attempt to link Him with necessity to His creation, while maintaining His independence, can only lead to the union of opposites without sufficient reason.

In seeing why the inference to God will not solve our problem, we begin to see what form a satisfactory account must take. There must be an internal reason for the identity of structure between thought and reality. Such a reason would be a whole in which "There is no point which is not itself internally the transition to its complement, and there is no unity which fails in internal diversity and ground of distinction" (AR, 507). In relation to its elements, this whole would be "at once their how and their why, their being, substance, and system, their reason, ground, and principle of diversity and unity." As for the parts themselves, "Each aspect would of itself be a transition to the other aspect, a transition intrinsic and natural at once to itself and to the intellect."

The whole or ground cannot stand "outside" of the parts. If it does, it cannot function as their reason, for only as expressed in the parts does it unite them intelligibly. When Bradley and other idealists spoke of the "concrete universal," they were expressing the demand of our intellect for a sufficient ground, one that is not separate from the facts to be explained. If thinking is something that goes on "in my head," and if reality is something "outside of my head" to which my thinking may or may not correspond, then any identity between the two must be a miracle. There is a problem of the relation of thought to reality, for the two are not merely the same, but such a "subjective" view of thinking precludes its solution.

In order to solve this problem, we must assume that, despite the obvious differences between thought and reality, we can look to reality for an explanation of the immanent ideal of thinking. We must assume that thinking is an "expression" of reality. The claim is not that our thoughts are caused by events in the world, but that thought is a "form" of reality and can only be understood in connection with reality.

What this means can be seen in Bradley's mature view of the nature of inference.

> Every inference is the ideal self-development of a given object taken as real. The inference is 'necessary' in the sense that the real object, and not something else, throughout developes its proper self, and so compels or repels whatever extraneous matter is hostile or irrelevant (*PL, 2, 598*).

This implies that when we reason the real connections that our initial fact has with other facts find expression in our thoughts. As we move out from our starting point, we form a more and more adequate concept of our "thing" in its connections with other things, and we do so under compulsion from the object itself.

On this view thought is not free from its object, but neither is it "compelled" by that object; for the end of thinking is to capture that object in ideas. Of course, not all thinking reflects things accurately. But all thinking does represent things to some degree, for there is nothing for thought to "embody" but the real. Thus, the assumption of the identity of thought and reality, an assumption needed to explain the possiblity of truth, supports and is supported by the doctrine of degrees.

The extreme objectivism implied in the identity thesis may seem extravagant, but the alternative is complete skepticism about the possibility of knowledge, a skepticism that cannot even be stated with consistency. We must believe in the possibility of truth, and Bradley's assertion that there is an identity between thought and reality is the only claim that makes our commitment to truth reasonable. If we think of thought as a form that reality takes, then reality will be the adequate ground for the identity in structure between the two.

Thought *is* reality, but only one form of reality. And because "that whole assuredly is not simply *one* of its aspects" (*AR*, 151), thought must be joined in reality with the other modes of experience, with feeling and will. As so joined, however, it must be "transformed and swallowed up." We cannot reduce the forms of experience to one another; feeling and thought simply are not the same. But we cannot accept their distinctness as final truth, for they are related, and relations are a "compromise between the plurality and the unity" of an "underlying identity" (*AR*, 159).

Two conclusions follow. First, the various forms of experience must lose their distinctive, separate character when properly understood, "For the result is a whole state which both includes and goes beyond each element" (*AR*, 151). Second, reality cannot be reduced to any one of these experiential forms. Rather, it is the ideal to which they point. Thus, it is misleading to speak of reality as thought, will, or feeling, and this means that the dream of some philosophers can never be fulfilled.

Those who have hoped to find one way of looking at things that would provide the key to understanding the world have often been criticized for ignoring the diversity of things. The facts are never (quite) what they should be if they are to fit easily into the philosopher's scheme. Bradley's philosophy explains this failure, which, by the very nature of things, cannot be avoided. To explain is to unify behind a single principle; philosophers are on solid ground here. But an all-inclusive concept obviously must be drawn from human experience, and because the various forms of experience are all limited, no concept drawn from any of them will serve as the one and only basic concept. Neither good, nor substance, nor duration, nor God, nor thought, will, or feeling will serve as *the* fundamental characteristic of the real. Perhaps all express the real to some degree, but none does so without distortion.

Thus, metaphysics is limited by its very nature to presenting the general structure of reality and to dispelling one-sided notions about the real. In a very real sense, Kant was right. An examination of knowledge reveals that the claims of knowledge have extended far beyond their capacities to succeed. Yet, Kant went wrong in thinking that metaphysics must try to "transcend" experience, in thinking that reality is an unknown of which man can say nothing, and in conceiving of thought as a form that man imposes on reality and that, therefore, prevents him from knowing of that reality. His experience with previous metaphysics and with Humean empiricism limited his perspective on the character and scope of thought in relation to reality. Though he rightly sensed that thought is limited, he misunderstood the nature of this limitation. In confining man within the circle of his sensible experience, he overlooked the possibility that this experience might contain the clues for a positive, albeit limited, theory about reality and was forced into a self-refuting skepticism. For all knowledge was to be found in mathematics and science, and, yet, the *Critiques* were neither of these.

Like Hume, Kant did not face up to the fact that he claims to give us knowledge—philosophical knowledge—and, as knowledge, it must be about the real. It must tell us what things are like, which can hardly be anything other than metaphysics. If we do not want to consign both the *Treatise* and the *Critique* to the flames, we must admit that the knowledge they deny is possible *is* possible. On the other hand, to avoid the one-sided character of much traditional metaphysics, we must incorporate into our philosophy some form of the skeptical message of Hume and Kant. It seems to me that Bradley has found the right blend of boldness and caution.

III

We have examined Bradley's claim that reality is logically coherent and his rationale for this union of thought's ideal and reality. But in order to see the full implication of this view, let us
consider the conditions under which thought can find satisfaction.
Specifically, does the notion of full logical coherence involve the
notion of value? Some philosophers have thought that value concepts are essential ingredients in any adequate metaphysical view.
Thus, Plato held that to understand anything is to grasp its function, first as an individual thing and then as an element performing a function as part of a whole, and for him the good of anything is its function. Ultimately, it is the job of the metaphysician
to see things as a whole in which each part plays a role, and this is
to see the whole under the form of the Good.

At this point, it is difficult to be certain how 'good' differs from
a purely logical notion, for if the function of a thing is simply the
place it has in reality, then 'good' need have no value connotation.
Leibniz claims that ours is the best of all possible worlds because
it is the most extensive in phenomena and the most restricted in
basic principles. But then our world is simply the most logical
world, that in which the intellect can find the greatest satisfaction. And Bosanquet explains that reality may be called purposeful or good, but not in the normal senses of these words
(*PIV*, 136).

If we are to understand these philosophers, we must keep such
qualifications in mind. Nevertheless, they cannot be saying *nothing* about value when they attribute goodness to the whole. We
may well admit, as Bradley does, that the standard for goodness is
the same as that for truth, that is, the perfect wholeness that we
assume characterizes reality. Still, moral fulfillment is not the
same as theoretical fulfillment, even for idealists. Perhaps a good
world must be logical, but without something besides logical coherence (pleasure, for example), it is hard to see how it could be
good in any sense. I conclude that Plato, Bosanquet, and others
meant that reality, properly understood, is morally ideal as well

as intellectually ideal; and this claim is justified in the same way that we justify the claim that reality is rational.

A recent philosopher in the Bradley-Bosanquet tradition, Brand Blanshard, has taken a far different view. According to him, it is a mistake to find either ethical or religious assurance in the argument that reality must be logical.

> First, between the rational as the logically necessary and the rational as the morally right, there is an abyss of difference. To show that the things and events of the world are necessarily interconnected is not to show that any of these things, or all of them together, are what they should be. To establish that, we should have to show that they are good, and this is a different matter, to be made out, if at all, on very different grounds (*RA,* 491).

Indeed, Blanshard asks, what could we mean by calling the events of nature good? And, "Secondly, to pass from 'everything is rational', in the sense of right, is to stultify one's moral perception."

Bradley's view on this matter, in which he sides with the Platonists, is an interesting example of his attempt to avoid extremes. To those who say that we can listen to our hopes and desires in metaphysics, Bradley answers that there is a confusion about the sense in which reality "satisfies" us.

> The whole question turns on the difference between the several impulses of our being. You may call the intellect, if you like, a mere tendency to movement, but you must remember that it is a movement of a very special kind (*AR,* 134).

Not all assumptions are practical, and the assumptions of metaphysics are those appropriate to theoretical activity. Thus, "It is only that which for thought is compulsory and irresistible—only that which thought must assert in attempting to deny it—which is a valid foundation for metaphysical truth" (*AR,* 133). Of course, as long as the world is morally unsatisfactory, we will be partially unsatisfied, for we are active beings who demand the complete realization of good for complete satisfaction. But then metaphysics is not a practical activity, and there is no reason to think that its conclusions are suspect as long as they do not demonstrate the moral perfection of the world. Again Bradley,

> We have no right to listen to morality when it rushes in blindly.
> . . . If I am theoretically not satisfied, then what appears must in
> reality be otherwise; but, if I am dissatisfied practically, the same
> conclusion does not hold (*AR*, 135).

As moral beings, we do want the just to be rewarded and the
crooked made straight. A belief in God may arise from a refusal
to accept the moral disorder of the world as final truth. Yet, how
can we justify the leap from feeling that things ought to be morally better to the claim that they are morally better? In metaphysics, we must appeal to the intellect, and we can find no reference
to morality there.

In fact, if the conclusions of Bradley's metaphysics are accepted,
there is an element of wishful thinking in all religious belief. The
concept of a God who is distinct from His creation and independent of it, though it is dependent on Him, is not a metaphysically
satisfactory notion. It combines the incompatible notions of relatedness and independence, and in so doing ignores the demand of
our intellect that reality be a coherent and comprehensive whole.
Because God is thought of as distinct from His creation, He can
"care" about it, but this reveals that a religious point of view involves some belief that reality responds to man's moral needs. In
religion, the will has a direct influence on the intellect. But does
not this influence induce us to claim to know more about the nature of things than we can rightly claim to know? And, if so, must
we not reject those religious claims that go beyond what metaphysics tells us must be the case?

Bradley's position here is equally opposed to William James'
brand of pragmatism. To say that "truth works," or "truths are
made," or "truth has positive value" is to confuse the theoretical
and practical in man's activity. Bradley agrees that ideas are true
because they "work," but the working of ideas, which is their
truth, lies not at all in their ability to satisfy us emotionally or to
provide a framework within which we can lead a more comforta-
ble, satisfying life. Ideas can do all of this and more and still be
quite false.

Ideas work theoretically, on the other hand, to the extent that
they express the nature of the real by being both comprehensive

and coherent. If a theory fits with other ideas we have, "leads" us to new ideas or facts, makes prediction possible, and is internally coherent, we say that it is true; but whether this theory is optimistic or pessimistic, can serve as a basis for action or not, seems beside the point. Pragmatism might be characterized as that philosophy in which the will has primacy over the intellect, but it is interesting to note that pragmatism does not apply this standard to itself. Are we to accept the arguments of the pragmatist because they are "instrumental" to practical success or because they accord with the nature of the real?

If the latter, then the standard of theory is implicitly accepted as the standard for the philosopher, despite what the pragmatist may say explicitly. And the former does not seem to be a real alternative. The pragmatist claims to *know* that his theory is true, and this knowledge seems to be of a different kind from that admitted within the theory. It seems inconsistent to say that we know that intelligence has a secondary place in determining truth. Bradley puts the matter nicely when he says, "Further the doctrine that the world and my nature are of such a kind that all truth must be practical, appears itself, so far, to be a truth which is theoretical and therefore is no truth" (*ETR*, 92–93).

Nevertheless, Bradley's theory that the intellect has primacy over the will in philosophy is not a mere denial of religious and pragmatic claims. For though he would agree with Blanshard that in metaphysics we are committed only to the intellectual perfection of reality, he does not separate the demands of the will and the intellect as sharply as does Blanshard. For Bradley, the will is to have no direct voice in theory, but it can and must have an indirect voice there. Bradley raises the question whether the intellect can remain satisfied if it ignores or contradicts the claims of the will.

First, man is, in part, a moral being; thus, a view of things that does not satisfy his moral aspirations cannot satisfy the whole man. Second, although "Philosophy like other things has a business of its own, and like other things it is bound, and it must be allowed, to go about its own business in its own way" (*ETR*, 15), it is also true that "A true philosophy must accept and must justify every side of human nature, including itself" (*ETR*, 14). Philosophy must "digest" all claims according to the dictates of the intellect. Thus, it may find it necessary to reinterpret the meaning and truth of any "postulates of conduct," and it may find it impossible to justify those postulates as they stand. Yet, it cannot simply contradict the claims of morality and religion, for the intellect is not all there is to man's nature, and it must respect the claims of the practical side of man. One might say that the form these claims will take must be determined by the intellect, but that some account must be taken of them.

Assume for a moment that freedom is a postulate for action, praise, and blame. Then a "true" philosophy will have to include free will. But what 'free will' means remains to be decided, within certain ill-defined limits, by the intellectual needs of the philosopher. For example, we cannot accept a sense of free will that conflicts with our belief in the coherence of the real. It follows that a mechanistic philosophy is ruled out by its denial of, or ignorance of, the demands of morality. On the other hand, 'free will' cannot mean an event for which there is no reason, for that is intellectually unsatisfactory. Similarly, we cannot accept a philosophy that simply denies the claims of religion, nor one that accepts these claims undigested and to the detriment of intellectual order. The belief in an independent God falls in this latter category.

But Bradley tries to show in detail that a lack of moral perfection must imply intellectual imperfection by pointing out that moral imperfection means unsatisfied desire, which in turn means a "discordance" between our idea of what ought to be and the presented facts. And whenever there is a distinction between fact and idea, there is appearance and not reality. This applies to all ideas, whether they be ideas of what is the case or of what ought to be the case. If the goal of thinking is to overcome the gulf between thought and thing, then it cannot accept a metaphysic that pictures the real as morally imperfect, for in such a world there is the very division of idea and object that we insist is made good in reality. Morality does not dictate directly to our intellect, but it does make its unrest felt as intellectual unrest and secures its end thereby.

What are we to say of a view that makes the moral perfection of things as logically necessary as the intellectual perfection of things? There does not seem to me to be any absolute knowledge that our ethical desires sre fulfilled in the world as it really is.

Bradley's belief that we can be certain about the goodness of things rests largely on his concept of thought, its goal, and its application to the moral sphere. For Bradley, there is contradiction and, therefore, appearance wherever there is a distinction between thought and thing. This is a difficult doctrine, but I believe it is sound. I also agree that where the will is unsatisfied there is a distinction between our idea of what ought to be and what seems to be the case. Without ideas, will would be bare impulse. Thus, I know that my intellect will not be satisfied until my ideas of the real are completely realized, and this can happen only when they have ceased to be mere ideas. In order for thought's ideal of an "experience entire containing all elements in harmony" to be realized, all ideas would have to be fundamentally transformed. Their larger context would necessitate a change of their meaning and truth, and thought as such would cease to exist as it would now be "present as a higher intuition."

Neither morality nor religion can gain any hope from this theory. For the moral ideal is an idea we do not predicate of the real. Though it is rejected by the facts, we continue to insist that it "ought" to be the case. At no time are we willing to say that the ideal has become fact. We do assert that the religious ideal is a fact, but not that it is now a fact for our world. The Kingdom of God is not yet here on earth, we think. In this sense, it is also true of the religious ideal that it is for us an ideal only. Yet, the conflict between idea and fact arises when the idea is held to be true of the fact, but there is no contradiction between the two when we withhold our assent from our ideal.[7]

Thus, though I see good reasons for accepting the view that reality must fulfill my theoretical demands, I do not see the same reason for believing that it must realize my moral or religious hopes. And it is important to remember the first sense, mentioned

7. Of course, in Bradley's view, *all* ideas are predicated; ideas do not "float." But even if we accept this claim, it is still true that our moral and religious ideals are not predicated as such by us. We deliberately hold them back; hence our surprise when we are told by Hegel and his followers in England that the ideal is not in the future.

above, in which our ideas must be changed as they become more adequate. Although my moral ideal may be said to "struggle" against the facts, and so cause "practical unrest," perhaps this ideal is only a confused way of conceiving of what we think are unrealized possibilities in the world. If we had a clearer grasp of the way things are, would we continue to hold on to the moral ideal as possible, or as an ideal at all? Perhaps our will "struggles" with fact only because we have a confused idea about the way things are and that, therefore, an adequate view would do away with this senseless struggle, without having to say that our moral ideal is ultimate fact. This, I take it, was the view of Spinoza, for whom a stoical view toward life emerges as the result of a metaphysics that does not picture the world as good in any sense. Bradley's case, as stated in *Appearance and Reality,* does not rule out such a metaphysics.

There are at least two points that Bradley draws on indirectly but that do not really support him. It is true, as he states, that one may be unsatisfied with any theory that does not respond to one's moral and religious aspirations, and a satisfactory philosophy must find some sense in one's religious hopes and some justification for the "postulates required for conduct." For example, Spinoza does not simply deny that man is free; he reinterprets the sense in which he is free so that it will accord with his intellectual demands.

But these admissions do not strengthen Bradley's case. One may be unsatisfied, but one's intellect may be satisfied, for philosophy is the work of the intellect alone. So much is admitted by Bradley himself. Of course, both religion and morality are partly the work of the intellect, and, to that extent, they must have a place in any comprehensive metaphysical view. But this recognition may take a form that does not satisfy my present desires while still satisfying my intellect. Spinoza's "philosophical" religion satisfies few if any of our normal religious yearnings, but it may for all that satisfy what a "true" religion is after. The intellect would then have satisfaction in full, whereas the will, not being fully rational, would remain partially unsatisfied.

Our intellect is not set off from our emotions and will in some philosopher's heaven. For this reason, the intellect must "account" for the will and its demands, and not by explaining away its demands in toto. But there is still a wide area for discretion in the handling of these demands. The "indirect" claims of the will require the intellect to justify only the rational in these claims. We may reject whatever claims we find to be theoretically unacceptable. If the latter elements include the idea of a personal God, a belief that this is the "best of all possible worlds," or a belief in undetermined choice, then so much the worse for religion and morality so conceived. If we sustain our belief in an ultimate reason for all that happens, or in man's freedom, it will be because such beliefs are essential to a coherent view of the world. I accept Bradley's claim that the will can have no direct voice in theory-making, but I believe he goes back on the substance of this view when he allows the same results to occur because of the indirect voice the will is supposed to have in our theories.

The following points seem to me to weigh against Bradley. First, to think of the moral ideal as fact seems contrary to the spirit of morality, whereas to think of the intellectual ideal as fact seems to be a necessary consequence of thinking itself. This seems to be a good reason for distinguishing the two ideals, rather than of thinking of morality in terms of metaphysics. Second, we are willing to explain away apparent exceptions to our belief in the logical character of reality, but we refuse to take the same attitude toward apparent exceptions to our faith that things happen for the best on the whole. We accept evil deeds as ultimate facts that cannot be explained as means to some greater good. Again, this difference is a good reason for treating the moral and the intellectual differently.

Third, even if truth, beauty, and goodness have a common standard, namely, reality, this common standard does not entail their common realization. And if the moral ideal is tied so closely to human nature that it makes no sense to speak of goodness apart from that nature, one obscures this fact and seems to give goodness a far greater role in the scheme of things than it deserves if he claims that the moral ideal is as certainly actual as is the intellectual ideal. Fourth, two theses that are important for Bradley's case have never been explained satisfactorily: In what sense is goodness necessary for intelligibility? In what sense do we contradict ourselves in denying the existence of the moral ideal? [8]

My conclusion is that, in this instance, Bradley was mistaken in trying to steer a middle course, or, at least, he was wrong in the manner in which he compromised between those who want to ignore religion in metaphysics and those who want to follow its dictates unthinkingly. The ideal of morality (and religion) should have no voice in the formulation of metaphysical theories. We know that our intellectual ideal is realized in reality, but we have not the slightest reason to believe, and good reasons for doubting, that our moral vision and religious hopes are similarly realized in the whole of things.

8. See Bradley, *Essays on Truth and Reality,* p. 219, n. 1, and Bosanquet, *The Principle of Individuality and Value,* pp. 48ff., for the claim that the denial of the moral ideal is contradictory.

1 0

Three Alternative
Accounts of 'Real'

The classical distinction between appearance and reality, and in particular Bradley's use of it, has been much criticized. Because it is undeniable that Bradley has used 'real' and 'unreal' in an unusual way, a defense of that usage against the more important criticisms is a necessity for anyone sympathetic with Bradley's views. In this chapter, I shall consider three accounts of 'real' that call into question Bradley's use of that concept. They are the argument from ordinary language (Austin and Moore), the argument from verifiability (Ducasse), and the argument from inconsistency (Stout).

The Argument from Ordinary Language
—Austin

In *Sense and Sensibilia,* J. L. Austin makes the following statement:

> Some meanings that have been assigned to 'know' and 'certain' have made it seem outrageous that we should use these terms as we actually do; but what this shows is that the meanings assigned by some philosophers are *wrong.*[1]

Taking 'real' as a test case, my intention is to criticize the view that philosophers are mistaken when they propose meanings for words that make our ordinary uses of such words seem outrageous.

Austin lists two central characteristics of 'real'. First, it is an "absolutely normal word, with nothing newfangled or technical

1. J. L. Austin, *Sense and Sensibilia* (Oxford, The Clarendon Press, 1962), p. 63.

or highly specialized about it." But, 'real' is not normal in that it lacks a "single, specifiable, always-the-same meaning," without at the same time having a number of different meanings (SS, 62, 64).

From the first feature of 'real', it follows that philosophers ought not to assign 'real' a meaning arbitrarily. From the second feature, it follows that the attempt to discover a single meaning for 'real' is to chase a will-o'-the-wisp. 'Real' performs a single, general function (as does 'good') without having a single, always-the-same meaning. The particular way in which we are to take 'real' will vary with the context and the intent of the speaker, although within a given context there are usually clues that tell us the meaning of 'real'. For example, 'real' does not have the same meaning when applied to a duck or to a piece of silk, but I can assume that, when applied to a piece of silk, it means that the fabric is not artificial.

Austin believes that our limited, overly simple approaches to language confuse us in our search for the meanings of words. For example, one may see immediately that 'real' does not have many meanings and may conclude that it must have a single, always-the-same meaning. Or, we may reach the same conclusion through paying too much attention to words that do have an always-the-same meaning. Not finding such a meaning for 'real', we may then conclude that 'real' designates some kind of 'nonnatural' property known only through intuition.

If we will only notice what uses 'real' does in fact have, the need to give a single meaning for 'real' disappears. Austin does not promise that this will happen in every case of philosophical perplexity, but at least in this one instance a philosophical dilemma could be overcome by the empirical study of language.

Austin lists four specific ways in which 'real' functions in ordinary discourse. (1) It is "substantive-hungry." That is, although one can attribute a color to an object without knowing what the object is, one cannot say of something that it is 'real' without knowing what it is. Unless you specify that the object you are referring to is a decoy duck, I just won't know what you mean when you say that it is real. (2) It is a "trouser word." That is, 'not real' is more basic to understanding 'real' than the other way around. As Austin says,

This, of course, is why the attempt to find a characteristic common to all things that are or could be called 'real' is doomed to failure; the function of 'real' is not to contribute positively to the characterization of anything, but to exclude possible ways of being *not* real—and these ways are both numerous for particular kinds of things, and liable to be quite different for things of different kinds (*SS*, 70).

(3) It is a "dimension word," that is, a general term in a group of more specific terms, all of which perform the same general function. The negative terms (artificial, fake, false) and the positive terms (natural, genuine, true) tend to fall into pairs so that one knows what is being excluded, for example, when he is told that something is "natural". (4) It is an "adjuster word." Experience provides us with exceptions to our normal categories, and when this happens we need a word to indicate that the thing before us is almost, but not quite, a something-or-other. Then we say that it is not a real whatever-it-is.

Austin draws three closely related conclusions from the "adjuster" feature of 'real'. First, we make the distinction between real and not real only when we suspect that things are not quite what they seem to be. And we cannot make the distinction when things could not be other than they seem. Thus, neither 'real' nor 'unreal' has any meaning when applied to after images. It follows, secondly, that we use 'real' only when there is some way of deciding whether a thing is or is not a 'real' something-or-other. Because our doubts about its 'reality' are aroused by something strange in the way it looks, behaves, and so forth, these doubts can be quieted only by looking at it more closely, touching it, and so forth.

Third, not only may we change our minds about whether a thing is a real so-and-so, but we may also change the criteria by which we decide whether a thing is henceforth to be called a real X. To use Austin's example, if we were to encounter talking cats, and if we felt that this was a new and important feature of cats, we might well decide to divide real cats from unreal cats along new lines.

Contrast Bradley's use of 'real' in *Appearance and Reality* with Austin's analysis. Bradley seeks a single definition for 'real' and thus seems to be pursuing Austin's will-o-the-wisp. Bradley uses 'real' in ways that violate all of the four characteristics Austin considers basic to the normal use of that word. There is a sense for Bradley in which I can say that something is unreal without knowing what the thing is and without having to answer the question, "A real what?" That is, for him I can just say of something that it is unreal, without qualification or specification. Austin's view seems to stem from his assertion that 'real' has no single, always-the-same meaning, whereas Bradley's view arises naturally from his belief that there is a single sense of 'unreal' that can be applied to all things.

Bradley has a positive notion of real, in terms of which he says that certain things are unreal. For him, 'real' does exclude certain possibilities, but it does so by virtue of its positive character. Hence, 'real' cannot be a "trouser word" for Bradley. In Bradley's view, 'real' cannot be a "dimension word" either. First, as he uses 'real' it does not fulfill the same function as 'genuine', 'natural', and the like and 'unreal' does not do the same work for him as 'fake', 'dummy', 'toy', and the like. And, second, there is no other set of less general terms that fulfill the same function as 'real'. As Bradley uses 'real', it is not at all an "adjuster word." He does not use it to differentiate things that are similar but not identical; instead he applies it to our most fundamental categories, such as 'thing', and to such fundamental features of experience as time and space.

And Bradley ignores the conditions that Austin cites as necessary for the application of 'real' in its role as an "adjuster word." He says that time is unreal, although there is no reason for thinking that time might not be what it seems to be. In fact, Bradley says that time is unreal precisely because of the character it exhibits. Nor does he use 'real' in a way that allows of an empirical test. Of course, he holds that there is some criterion by which one can decide that time is unreal, but it is not a criterion that would be of use in particular disputes about "unreality." Nor will Bradley admit that the criteria for reality may change, for he claims to know with certainty what reality is.

The meaning Bradley has "assigned" to 'real' *does* make our ordinary use of that word seem outrageous. Just as certain philo-

sophical senses of 'know' make it seem outrageous to say that in
the ordinary sense of 'know' I know that I am now speaking, so
Bradley's sense of 'real' makes it seem outrageous to say that the
paper from which I am reading is real paper. But does this feature of Bradley's concept of real show that his concept is wrong?
Looking beyond Austin for a moment, the general issue is
whether an appeal to "what we say" is relevant in evaluating
philosophical proposals. If so, then revisionary philosophy will
seem unjustified, its proposals "dissolved" by a careful examination of ordinary speech.

I believe the way to show that Bradley's use of 'real' and 'unreal' is justifiable is to make clear that there are genuine difficulties and legitimate arguments that lead to something like Bradley's concept of reality. If, indeed, Bradley's distinction of real
and unreal can play a fruitful role in philosophical inquiry, then
it cannot be ruled out of court by criteria that condemn the entire enterprise from the outset.

It may be, of course, that Bradley's concept of reality is faulty
because his analysis of time and relations is mistaken or because
he argues incorrectly from this analysis. But, if so, we can reject
his concept of reality only by an evaluation of its various steps
and not by any kind of wholesale judgment.

How, then, does Bradley arrive at his notion of 'real', that is, of
reality as a single, coherent whole whose unity is only dimly reflected by terms and relations? Consider once more what he says
about terms and relations. They must be taken together, for wherever there are terms there must be relations "between" the terms
and wherever there are relations there must be terms that stand
in those relations. However, if we take the two together we encounter logical difficulties. A relation is not a third thing alongside its terms; if it were, we would need a new relation to join
terms and the old relation. But in joining the terms, a relation
must make a difference to those terms. It follows that each term
has a double aspect. In part, it is what it is because of the relation
in which it stands, and, in part, it is independent of that relation,
for relations do not create terms. Somehow, the one term is the
two aspects taken together. And now each aspect has become a
term in need of a new relation to unite it with the other aspect

into a single whole. The terms both are something in themselves and are something because of the relation in which they stand, and how can these aspects be parts of a single whole?

When Bradley says that relations and terms are contradictory, he means that we cannot understand their union. Similarly, we cannot understand how a thing or a self is both one and many, both the same and different, with the result that such things must be "unreal" or "mere appearances." The basis for this characterization is his claim that we can know with certainty that reality is rational, for the mere attempt to doubt it leads to a self-defeating attempt to deny or limit the scope of logical laws. But then any general feature of experience that involves the joining of different elements without a sufficient ground or reason fails the test of rationality and, hence, must be not fully real as it stands. This infinite regress is a sign that we have failed to join terms and relations in a way that we find rational. And, of course, this is not the failure of a single philosopher, but has its roots in the very nature of understanding and judgment.

Bradley claims that an analysis of thinking and its origins reveals an implicit standard of rationality that alone defines what reality in its general outline is like. This same analysis reveals, however, that our intellectual products, of which term, relation, thing, and self are examples, cannot meet this standard of rationality. The conclusion is that they cannot be real. Besides having its source in experience, the theory provides a coherent, unified account of perception and judgment in relation to reality and supplies a rationale for two doctrines often associated with Bradley, the theory of internal relations and the coherence theory of truth.

Once the theory is understood in this way, one cannot dismiss it merely because it makes certain common usages seem outrageous. For example, why cannot the Bradleyean say that things across-the-board are 'unreal' if he offers reason for so speaking? Of course, his reasons are not the same kind as those we have for saying that a piece of silk is not real, but why may they not be legitimate reasons all the same? Why may not our suspicion about "reality" be aroused in a number of ways? And why must we agree with Austin that 'real' does not "contribute positively to the characterization of anything" if Bradley provides a plausible account of our commitment to reality as a noncontradictory whole?

This last question is important for Austin, I believe, because only if 'real' cannot be given a positive sense must it be tied to a specific thing that is said to be real, or be exhausted in its meaning by a series of specific ways in which individual things can be 'real', or function merely as an indicator for the different ways in which things can be almost like other things. That 'real' can only do these tasks can be shown, I think, only if 'real' has no positive content of its own. But because Bradley's account of that content cannot be dismissed out of hand, there is no reason to think that he has gone wrong when he makes the other ways in which we ordinarily use 'real' seem outrageous.

In trying to give a single meaning to 'real', Bradley did not intend that this meaning would cover all of the ordinary senses of 'real'. In no way is Bradley denying that 'real' has other uses than the one he suggests; he simply is not interested in those uses because of his particular purposes. Therefore, the fact that in its ordinary use 'real' is "substantive-hungry" or is an "adjuster word" seems beside the point when it comes to evaluating Bradley's attempt to define reality.

But, one might say, is Bradley doing anything more than arbitrarily assigning a meaning to 'real'? If he is not, then his strictures on the reality of things and relations do not in fact constitute a criticism of our ordinary claim that certain things are real, although they are misleadingly masquerading as just that. But this is not the case, as can be seen in two ways. In general, the fact that a philosophic use of a word conflicts sharply with the ordinary use does not make the former arbitrary or technical as long as the philosophical usage emerges from the ordinary usage and its differences from ordinary usage can be justified by argument or evidence. After all, our implicit convictions about knowledge, reality, and the like may only be dimly reflected in our ordinary use of words.

More particularly, Bradley has adopted no special meaning for 'real'. By 'real', he means 'logically consistent', and we would all accept logical consistency as a minimum requirement for reality. When we ordinarily distinguish appearance from reality, we do so in order to bring coherence into our experience, and Bradley is simply insisting that this endeavor be pursued with an unusual vigor. Of course, this leads him to use 'real' in a way that Austin would condemn, but then the issue resides in Bradley's reasons for finding contradictions where we usually do not. His philosophical proposals can be evaluated only by an examination of his reasons and not at all by noticing the manner in which his use of 'real' departs from ordinary usage.

Perhaps one might state the relation of philosophical and ordinary usage in the following way. In one sense, philosophical usage leaves ordinary usage alone and does not make it seem outrageous at all. The philosopher does not suggest that there is anything wrong with ordinary usage for ordinary purposes; he does not urge us to adopt his usage as our usual way of speaking. On the other hand, the metaphysician makes contact with ordinary usage in that he is correcting the view embodied in it and is suggesting that for philosophical purposes it will not do. Whether the word be 'real', 'perceive', or 'know', there is enough community between the philosophic use and the ordinary use so that the former cannot be viewed simply as made up, and there is enough distance between the two so that the philosopher is not encroaching on the legitimate interests of ordinary speech. All that the philosopher need insist on is that there are genuine contexts in which we can raise problems and offer solutions to them that are strange sounding if used in ordinary contexts and that this strangeness in no way calls the philosophical proposal into question. If anything, it reveals the different aims and needs characteristic of philosophy and ordinary language.

The quotation from *Sense and Sensibilia* with which we began yields at least two possible interpretations. Austin might mean that a philosopher goes wrong if he proposes a meaning for a word that seems to make ordinary use outrageous. If so, he is suggesting that certain kinds of departures from ordinary usage can be dismissed out of hand merely because they are such departures. I think this suggestion would be wrong, and I have tried to show that in a test case legitimate concerns and reasons can be provided for a very strange sense of 'real'.

Perhaps Austin only means that certain philosophical proposals are wrong because they are aimed at changing ordinary usage in an outrageous way. If so, he has misunderstood what metaphysicians do, and, in any case, his analysis of 'perceive' in *Sense and Sensibilia* suggests that he intends the former and stronger interpretation.

I suggest that philosophers are not trying to correct ordinary usage in any harmful way and that there are legitimate concerns that justify departures from the ordinary meanings of words even when these departures seem to make our ordinary assertions outrageous. And the legitimate character of these concerns means that our search for *the* meaning of 'real' does not originate with overly simple views about meaning that come from our attention to only certain kinds of words and that, therefore, the empirical study of language cannot make this search seem futile.[2]

The Argument from Ordinary Language—G. E. Moore

Moore was greatly interested in the meaning of 'real' and in Bradley's claims for the "unreality" of time, space, and the like. His views on these matters are to be found in two main places: (1) Chapters 11 and 12 of *Some Main Problems of Philosophy*,[3] and (2) his famous article, "A Defense of Common Sense." [4]

In his first discussion of 'real', Moore is concerned primarily with exposing the difficulty of explaining what we mean by 'real', rather than expounding his own view. The most common use of 'real', he claims, is equivalent to 'exists' and opposed to 'imaginary', which makes Bradley's assertion about time puzzling. But the distinction between 'real' and 'imaginary' is unclear, for imaginary things must *be* in some sense. One cannot say simply that the imaginary is not. As Moore says, "And philosophers have, I think, supposed that this which *seems* to be the right way out of

2. Of course, in another place, Austin presents a vastly different conception of the role ordinary language has in resolving philosophical disputes. (See J. L. Austin, *Philosophical Papers* (Oxford, The Clarendon Press, 1961), pp. 129–33.) However, the view present in *Sense and Sensibilia* most closely reflects the theory and practice of current linguistic philosophy and so deserves special attention.

3. G. E. Moore, *Some Main Problems of Philosophy* (London, Allen & Unwin, 1953).

4. G. E. Moore, *Philosophical Papers* (New York, Collier, 1962), pp. 32–59.

the difficulty *is* the right way out. They have held that there really *is* such a distinction" (*SMPP*, 215).

We might ask, then, how are we to distinguish between the imaginary and the real. We cannot say that the imaginary is either in the mind or dependent on the mind for its existence, for the former criterion would make mental acts imaginary and the latter would make sense-data imaginary. We cannot distinguish them by naming the property that we actually use to decide whether a thing is real or not (having causes and resulting in effects), for this procedure presupposes the notion of 'real' and results in circularity. Nor can the property that real things have be something they can have in degree, despite Bradley's claim to the contrary. For though this notion would help us to understand Bradley's claim that both appearances and the absolute are real and might help us with the distinction between the real and the imaginary, introspection reveals that 'real' does not stand for a property that has degrees.

Moore draws no conclusion from his failure to come to a definite solution to this problem, but his references to what philosophers "suppose" suggest a possible conclusion. Perhaps the philosopher's assumption that imaginary things have a certain property (being) and lack another property (that which real things have), and that his job is to grasp the difference between these two properties, is misleading and creates its own needless difficulties. Moore, however, does not quite take this line.

He concludes that particulars exist, facts (or truths) and universals have being, and all are real. Imaginary things do not have being in any sense at all. Though there may be some property of particulars that gives them existence instead of the mere being that truths and universals have, the important distinction is between things that have being and those that do not. This distinction is "fundamental," for truth and falsity and cannot be glossed over without serious consequences.

How does this conclusion apply to Moore's discussion of 'real'? We question the distinction between 'real', 'exists', and 'being', on the one hand, and 'imaginary', on the other, for it seems that if we can speak and think of the imaginary it must have being—and if being, then existence and reality. Thus, we are forced to say that in some sense the imaginary *is* and in another sense it *is not*. We then view it as our task to define the sense in which some things *are* but *are not real*. So we set out in search of a property that unreal things lack and that real things have, remembering that this property cannot be being, for this is shared by both the real and the imaginary. And we just do not find this property.

But perhaps we were wrong to admit that unreal things have being. Once we are clear about the status of the unreal, we see that it has no being at all. The ordinary use of 'real' as opposed to 'imaginary' is vindicated, and the distinction between the two remains clear.

Moore offers two reasons for the origin of the mistaken assumption that the unreal has being. We can think and speak about the unreal, which leads one to believe that words used are names of unreal things. But the fact that I may entertain false beliefs about what exists shows that I can speak of what is not, of that which has "no being at all." If the fact referred to in my belief had being, my belief would be true. And there must be an object for my false belief, call it a proposition, and that *this* is in some sense, still it "remains a fact that *one* thing, which those words *would* stand for, if his belief were true, certainly *is not*" (*SMPP,* 290).

The second reason for our assumption reveals the heart of the difficulty. Because (it seems) I must think about something when I think of the unreal, one is tempted to think that such acts involve a certain relation (belief) that holds between the assertor and what is asserted. We then think of the "that" clause, or of the word, as the name of the fact believed in. But such phrases or words only seem to be names; thus, a statement about a chimera cannot be analyzed into a thing named by 'chimera' and something said about it. This "seeming," however, makes us believe that we contradict ourselves in saying that the unreal is not, for we seem to speak of a thing named by a word or phrase and at the same time say that it is not. Yet, this contradiction is merely verbal if the word or phrase is not a name at all. Moore does not claim to know how to analyze statements about the unreal, but he thinks that they cannot be analyzed in any way that assumes that the unreal thing is a subject named by a part of our sentence.[5]

The ultimate conclusion of Moore's analysis, although he does not state it outright, seems to be that, when Bradley said that time was unreal-but-existent, he made no sense whatsoever. Of course, Bradley thought that he was saying something meaningful, for he thought that he meant something different by 'exist' and 'real', even if this difference was only one of degree. But Moore's analysis shows that he could not have meant something different by these terms; and this is not very surprising, for 'real' is a term whose meaning is unclear, and whose meaning cannot be made clear by an appeal to introspection. Thus, Bradley, despite himself, contradicted himself in his assertions about space and time. Bradley's distinction between appearance and reality fails if one sees that 'real' and 'exist' mean the same thing.

I am not concerned with evaluating Moore's attempt to show that the unreal doesn't have being in any sense as a theory in its own right, although one does wonder what propositions "have" if it is not being. My concern is, rather, with whether he has been able to show that there is something basically wrong with Bradley's distinction of appearance and reality. Moore has failed to show this for three reasons. First, he is mistaken when he identifies the source of Bradley's distinction as his failure to see that some terms are not names (SMPP, 290). Bradley is careful to recognize that the grammatical subject of a sentence may not be the real subject of the judgment expressed by the sentence, and his evidence for this view is that certain phrases, such as 'four-cornered circle', do not name anything in the world. It seems unlikely to me that Bradley somehow forgot this distinction when he came to his metaphysics, especially when this metaphysics emerges from his theory of judgment.

The source of the distinction between appearance and reality lies in the notion of contradiction. Moore does mention that Bradley thinks he has proved time to be "unreal" because of its contradictory character, and he claims that this proof is unsuccess-

5. As Moore says, "We aren't in fact really even mentioning a chimaera when we talk of one; we are using a word which isn't, by itself, a name for anything whatever" (SMPP, 291).

ful; but Moore defines 'contradictory' as meaning that two contradictory propositions could be derived from the assertion "Time is
unreal," and this is not at all what Bradley means by contradiction. For him, time is contradictory because its character (before
and after combined into one) is not rational. Therefore, Moore
has not offered a good reason for denying that the source of Bradley's concept of appearance lies in the notion of contradiction.

Second, Moore's proof that Bradley's assertion, "Appearances
exist but are not real," is a contradiction is mistaken in two ways.
The proof throughout uses 'real' as opposed to 'imaginary'. But if
Bradley uses 'real' in some other sense, then it is possible that in
his sense 'real' and 'exist' may differ in some important way, and
he does use 'real' in another sense as shown by the fact that for
him 'contradiction' is a matter of degree. In fact, Moore has so
much trouble with Bradley precisely because for Moore 'real' excludes the very possibility of degrees.

Moore's proof that 'real' and 'exist' cover the same ground is
unconvincing, for it proceeds by showing that the imaginary and
the false have no being and, therefore, that the unreal has no
being. But, for Bradley, the unreal is equivalent to neither the
imaginary nor the false. Appearances are not imaginary, and they
are not brought in to supply a subject for false statements, for
they are the subject of many true assertions. Thus, appearances
may exist in a sense that the imaginary and the false do not, without being fully real.

In addition, there seems to be working throughout Moore's
presentation a feeling that the vital distinction between truth and
falsity is that between "what is or has been or will be, and what
neither is nor has been nor will be" (*SMPP*, 373). But is Moore's
assumption about the nature of truth and falsity correct? He acts
as if either he had no such commitments (this is obviously false)
or that they need no defense, and Bradley might well accuse
Moore of begging the question by assuming points that must be
cleared up before considering the distinction of 'real' and 'exists'.

Third, the uncritical way in which Moore employs his own metaphysical predilections can be seen in his criticism of Bradley's
notion that appearance and reality differ only in degree. Moore
claims that when he "looks into his mind" he finds that the prop-

erty one says elephants have when one says they are real is "merely positive" and "not the highest possible degree of any property whatever" (*SMPP*, 233). But if one did not already hold that things either are or are not, would he be impressed with this appeal to introspection? I confess that, when I try to perform Moore's mental experiment, I find that I do intend to say something about elephants that makes them unalterably different from anything that I say is "unreal." A thing is real or it is not, I want to say. But am I correct in thinking of 'real' or 'true' in this way? Does not my attitude on this matter stem from a metaphysical view that I uncritically hold and that further analysis may show to be untenable? Introspection in this case can reveal only the metaphysical view that I hold and not anything about the truth of this view.

And I am perplexed by Moore's insistence that a philosopher may be mistaken when he reports what he means by a term. When anyone says that he means so-and-so by 'real', "It only proves that it is what he thinks he means; and what he *thinks* he means may be very different from what he does mean" (*SMPP*, 220). But surely part of what he means by 'real' must be whether or not it is a property that a thing can have in the highest degree. Yet, Moore thinks he can know by introspection that it is not such a property. My difficulty is that I can see no reason why Moore's claim is not as problematical as is its opposite and why, therefore, one cannot say that Moore merely thinks that 'real' has no degrees. Perhaps he would change his introspective report if an analysis of 'real' showed that reality can have degrees. If so, Moore's point against Bradley represents at best a commonly held but not philosophically binding view about 'real'.

Moore's own position is stated most clearly in his famous article, "A Defense of Common Sense." (1) We know certain propositions, those that make up the "common sense view of the world," to be wholly and without question true, although one does not know how, that is, on what evidence, he knows them (*PP*, 44). Moore does not argue the point, perhaps because there is nothing more certain in terms of which he might prove his contention; he merely states it as a fact. (2) If anyone claims that we cannot be certain of the meaning of such commonsense statements, he must be confusing understanding the meaning of an assertion with being able to give an analysis of the assertion. Moore does not pretend to offer an analysis of "The earth has existed for many years," for he regards this as a "profoundly difficult question"; but he does claim that the meaning of such expressions is perfectly clear.

(3) Commonsense propositions could not be true unless space, time, material objects, and selves were real. Thus, in knowing that commonsense propositions are true, we by implication claim to know that propositions asserting the existence of time, space, and so forth are true. Similarly, to deny that time is "real" is to deny that any proposition involving a temporal reference is true. (4) Nevertheless, some philosophers have denied the reality of time and so forth. Moore finds this puzzling, for, in his view, such denials are inconsistent with propositions that everyone knows to be true. The way to argue against such claims is to point out either that they are openly contradictory in that they imply the very knowledge they deny (example: "We *believe* in the existence of material things but cannot say we *know* that they exist." But the use of 'we' indicates that the assertor does have the knowledge he claims no one has); or they are, at the very least, inconsistent with other things the philosopher says (example: Frequent references to "other philosophers" betray a certainty in the existence of physical objects that the philosopher denies is possible); or they are peculiarly self-denying (example: In knowing that philosophers have denied the reality of space and time, I know that they are wrong, for their denial is possible only if space and time exist and are real).

First, Moore's claim that the reality of space and time follows from the truth of propositions involving spatial or temporal concepts does not follow. 'Exist' does not entail 'real' as Bradley uses those terms. And Bradley's distinction of 'real' and 'exist' undercuts Moore's criticism that philosophers who deny the reality of time assert propositions that conflict with other propositions they know to be true. For even if I admit that "The earth has existed for many years" is absolutely true, I am not committed to the view that time is real. The proposition necessarily implies that there is such a thing as time, but not that time is a coherent and fundamental feature of the world.

The sense in which I must believe in time in order to make assertions about it is far different from the sense in which I must believe in time in order to think that it is real. These senses would be the same only if 'unreal' meant the same as 'imaginary', and because it does not, Moore's criticism fails to be effective against Bradley. Moore has lumped together all sorts of positions that might be called 'skeptical'. And though it is certainly worth pointing out to the Cartesian skeptic and to the solipsist that their philosophic beliefs are not in accord with the commonsense certainties that we all share, Bradley does not, like Descartes, hold that we know the existence of the self with certainty and can doubt only the existence of the external world; he does not hold, like the extreme skeptic, that we can be certain of the existence of neither the self nor of material things. When Bradley speaks of the "unreality" of time, or when he questions the truth of ordinary temporal assertions, it is not that he thinks that time does not exist, but that it lacks the comprehensiveness that absolute truth must have. It follows that Bradley's metaphysical skepticism is not self-refuting as Moore claims; it may ask questions that common sense does not ask, but it does not directly question the ordinary truths that Moore mentions.

Moore's second claim, that we know certain common assertions to be wholly true, seems to be vulnerable on at least two important counts. Moore admits that the truths he lists are not known "directly," but only by means of evidence, and he adds that he does not know precisely what that evidence is. Now it is possible that Moore is not saying what he seems to say because he uses 'certain' in a particular way. (Is "This assertion is certainly true" one of those claims that Moore says is unambiguous?) Perhaps he only means that in ordinary speech it is all right to say that we know a proposition to be true and are certain of it even when we do not know why we know it or have inferred it from something else. If so, then I have no quarrel with him here, as I am not concerned with what we ordinarily say.

But if Moore is using 'certain' as roughly equivalent to 'necessarily true', or 'logically true', then it seems to me that the circumstances he mentions do detract from the certainty of commonsense assertions. If one is told that a claim rests on unknown evidence, why is it not proper to doubt its certainty? Moore plainly does not mean that commonsense truths are self-evident, true by the very meaning of the terms. If not, then the fact that they are inferences from evidence indicates that they may possibly be in error.

Consider, for example, the belief in other minds, a certain belief for Moore. Is there no possibility that this belief is false? I would agree with Moore that not knowing what my evidence for a judgment is does not reduce the likelihood that it is true, but, as long as that judgment is an inference, it needs to be tested; and such testing can never establish the assertion beyond the realm of probability.

Remarks of a similar nature are relevant to Moore's claim that certain propositions have a commonsense meaning we all understand, even though we cannot give a conceptual analysis of the ideas used in these propositions. Such propositions are known to be wholly true because they are unambiguous. Now, even if this be so, it does not bear on Bradley's assertion "Time is not real," for, as Moore himself says, such an expression *is* ambiguous (*PP*, 39). Therefore, we cannot be certain of its truth or falsity until we know what 'real' means, that is, give an analysis of 'real'. This is shown by Moore's own misplaced criticism of Bradley, a criticism based on the assumption that Bradley must have meant by 'real' something completely opposed to 'imaginary'.

Most important, however, is Moore's claim as it stands that there is a clear and sharp distinction between the ambiguous and the unambiguous. It seems to me that this distinction is one of degree and is not so clear as Moore believes. Consider Blanshard's example of the proposition "Napoleon lost at Waterloo" (*NT*, 2, 307). Moore would want to say that this is an unambiguous and wholly true assertion. But even granting that these words are to be taken in their ordinary sense, does each one have a single meaning? Is not the meaning they have a function of what we *can* mean by them? If these words were spoken by an historian and an ordinary person, would they have the same meaning? Blanshard thinks not, and I agree.

If the meaning of an expression varies with what one can put into it, then will not a proposition be more true the more its meaning approximates the character of the thing to which it refers? And if so, the truth of propositions will be more hidden than we ordinarily think, for we will not know how true an assertion is until we learn what meaning a given person has been able to "pack" into the words he is using. In everyday life, we assume that we all mean roughly the same things by the same words; but if we conclude from this practical attitude that when words are used in an ordinary way the propositions they express are wholly true or false, I think we have made a mistake. Truth, like meaning, is a matter of degree.

Consider "The French Revolution began in 1789" and "The earth has existed for many years past." How can I be certain of the former without knowing what the assertor conceives of as the French Revolution, or how philosophical he is about 'began'? And how can I be certain of the latter until I have a satisfactory analysis of the concept, earth? If Hume is right and there is nothing continuous to which 'earth' could refer, the assertion is false. The important point is that there is not such a sharp division between our commonsense meaning and the philosophical analysis of concepts. The latter, I suggest, is a necessary element in estimating the truth of ordinary assertions.

Moore is right, I would agree, that we understand the terms used in ordinary speech well enough to have some idea of what we are saying; we can identify the objects spoken of and have a (good) sense of what is said about them. Because of this situation, we often feel that we can commit ourselves to a proposition even if we cannot say why we think it is true. But still the evidence may not be so demonstrative as we think, and it is entirely possible that a more precise determination of the meaning of certain terms could induce us to modify our truth claim. Moore says that he is certain that he has had dreams, but if this is a judgment based on memory, and if memory is fallible, is his certainty justified?

If I am correct, it makes sense to speak of the "real" meaning of a concept, a meaning that is present in a distorted form in our ordinary usage and somewhat better in our philosophical analyses. But as there is just one adequate meaning for the philosopher, so only with that meaning will our assertion be fully true. Despite what Moore says, we do not understand what a term means without an analysis of it, but we do have a strong enough sense of its meaning to be able to say that some judgments are true and others false. My conclusion is that there is, in a sense, an ambiguity in even our ordinary assertions, which is owing to the different meanings that identical sentences can express and not solely to philosophers' strange usages. We do not notice this ambiguity in our daily speech, for it is unimportant for ordinary communication, but it is there, and it affects the truth of the proposition that our words express.

The Argument from Verifiability—Ducasse

C. J. Ducasse presents an argument about the meaning of 'real' in his Howison Lecture for 1944. Like Austin, Ducasse appeals to ordinary usage to demonstrate the inadequacy of certain metaphysical accounts of 'real'. The difference between the two is one of emphasis. For Austin, it is the diversity of uses of 'real' that makes a general account impossible, whereas Ducasse argues that for any theory to be capable of truth or falsity it must be empirically testable and thus it must have some data with which it can be confronted.

In the case of theories about 'real', our data must be of a special kind. For example, if we want to know what the nature of chalk is, we would compare "real" chalk with apparent chalk; and we may be led by an easy analogy to think that the way to solve the problem of the nature of reality is to compare "real" being with "unreal" being. However, no impartial selection of "real" being is possible, for philosophers are already Idealists, Materialists, and so forth and would, therefore, select as something "real" just what other philosophers would condemn as "unreal." This fact makes one realize that the two questions are of different logical types and that the data relevant to each will likewise have to be different.

Ducasse insists that, if we are interested in the nature of reality, our data

> can consist only of concrete examples of the manner (or manners) in which the word "real" or its cognates, "really" and "reality," are used predicatively. That is, our data will have to consist

of *statements* such as that a certain substance, which seems to be paper, is really asbestos, or that mermaids do not really exist, or that trees far away appear blue but in reality are green, and so on.[6]

Because our hypotheses must fit this kind of data if they are to be valid, the problem of the nature of reality becomes the problem of what 'real' means "as applied in the given examples," and our examples should "illustrate commonly accepted usage."

The ability to test our definitions of 'real' against certain specific usages distinguishes objective definitions from merely verbal definitions. Without the method of empirical verification, philosophical theories contribute nothing to our knowledge of the world. It is only because philosophers have tended to employ a different method in their work that we think that all philosophical questions are incapable of solution.

Ducasse proceeds to run through several ways in which 'real' is used. (1) There is the technical use of 'real' as in "real property," or "real numbers." We can dismiss this from consideration, for "It is clear that no problem involving the distinction between reality and appearance arises in connection with these or possible other equally technical uses of the word 'real' " [7] (2) There is the descriptive sense of 'real', as in "a stone looks like glass but really is a diamond." In such cases, the thing in question displays some but not all the characteristics of the kind of thing it seems to be. If it had all these characteristics, it actually would be what it only seems to be, and the features it does display are the same as those that a "real" example would display.

Ducasse concludes that the term 'real' here does not qualify the kind the thing is said to (really) be because there are not two kinds of diamonds, real and unreal. If something is not a real diamond it is not a diamond at all. What function does 'real' perform then? Ducasse says,

Rather, what is qualified is the descriptive proposition "This is paper," and the effect of inserting the word "really" into it is simply to assert that *that proposition is true:* to say "this is really

6. C. J. Ducasse, "The Method of Knowledge in Philosophy," *University of California Publications in Philosophy, 16* (February 1945), 147.

7. Ibid., pp. 148–49.

paper" is exactly the same as to say, "truly, this is paper," or "that this is paper is true." [8]

To stress that something is of a certain kind, despite some evidence to the contrary, we say, "This *really* is an X."

(3) There is the *existential* sense of 'real', as in "Spain is a real country, but Utopia is not" or "Mermaids are not real." In such assertions either 'is real' means the same as 'exists' or its meaning is additional to 'exist'. If the meaning is additional to 'exist', it is to be understood as in case 2. That is, 'really' qualifies the whole assertion and has the effect that 'truly' would have in the same context. If 'real' means the same as 'exists', the question resolves itself into what 'exists' means, and Ducasse suggests that, when used about physical objects, it means that the thing is in some place at some time.

(4) There is the sense in which 'real' means "to be relevant to the purposes or interests which rule at the time." Thus, when we say that water is really a compound of hydrogen and oxygen, we do not mean that it only seems to be water. We mean that, for certain chemical purposes, it is important to treat water as characterized in this way. In this sense, 'unreal' means the same as 'insignificant'. Statements such as "Nothing is more real than an idea" employ 'real' in this sense, and when one speaks of the real color of an object, he means that he will treat the way the object looks from a certain distance as indicating its color.

The four ways of using 'real' share the characteristic that they form hypotheses that can be tested by empirical means. In this regard, they contrast sharply with a fifth class that Ducasse calls "ontological positions" and that he defines as "essentially of the nature of an exclusive or basic interest in the things which have a certain character; it is a rule one adopts as to what things one will regard as alone of interest, or will rank as basic or primary." [9]

It follows that an ontological position cannot be true or false, for because it is not an hypothesis about empirical properties, there are no facts that can establish it one way or the other. Thus, to use Ducasse's example, when a scientist assumes that 'real' means "publicly observable or implied in what is observable," he

8. Ibid., p. 150.
9. Ibid., p. 155.

merely indicates the character of the things in which he is interested. There is no suggestion that it is a character that real things have that unreal things do not, a character whose presence we might verify by investigation.

The implications for metaphysics are obvious. When the idealist says that reality is mental, or when the materialist says that reality is matter in motion, we may interpret them in two ways. Perhaps their claims are ontological, in which case they merely present their preferences. Or, if 'reality' is being used denotatively, their claims may mean that everything that exists is mental or material. But though these are meaningful claims, they are, Ducasse insists, both obviously false. 'Mental' applies to emotions and thoughts, whereas 'material' applies to tables and chairs.

We only think that such claims are true because we arbitrarily change the meaning of either 'exist' or of 'mental' and 'material' by qualifying them with the word 'really'. Thus, we say that only the mental has "real" existence, but in so doing merely express the preference that we began with. Or, we say that what exists is "really" mental. Are we then claiming that physical objects have properties that when noticed show that they are mental after all? Not at all. As Ducasse says, we have merely chosen to call material things by the term 'mental'. And, he continues:

> To do this, however, would be exactly the same logically, and just as futile, as proposing to say henceforth that white men are really negroes, or that negroes are really white men. This would not be revealing any hitherto hidden fact as to the color of their skins, but only tampering wantonly with language.[10]

The only genuine problem about mind and matter is what these words mean when they are applied to things in the world; there is "no doubt at all" that some things have and some do not have the properties that we mean when we use the words 'mental' and 'material'.

Ducasse feels that his is the only way that the problem of reality can be solved and that his method has applications to other philosophical dilemmas. Yet, I question the relevance of his concern with language to the philosophic claim he makes. His analy-

10. Ibid., p. 157.

sis of 'real' may well be correct, but what does it have to do with the philosopher's attempt to get at the nature of reality?

First, I think Ducasse is trying to impose a method on philosophy that is foreign to it. There are no facts that will refute or establish the claim that reality is rational. Rather, we accept this claim because it is needed to make sense of assertions of any kind, including those that oppose it. In Bosanquet's words, it is a genuine case of "this or nothing." We interpret the facts as we do because we already accept the claim about reality, and we accept it because we have no alternative. Metaphysical theses can be suggested by facts, but they cannot be verified by them in any simple way. I have argued that philosophy establishes its claims differently than does science and is not, as Ducasse suggests, in need of a new approach to its problems.

Second, Ducasse is working with the sharp division between ordinary usage and illegitimate usage that seems to be so popular today. But can ordinary usage supply the philosopher's data when he is not interested in word usage and when he may reject ordinary usage as inadequate for philosophical problems? The philosopher may want to develop a philosophical usage, one that cannot be called "tampering" with language if the philosopher can show that his subject demands such usage. It may be necessary for philosophical purposes to use words in unordinary ways, and Ducasse offers no proof that such usage must be illegitimate.

Consider Ducasse's comparison of 'mental-material' with 'white-negro'. If someone said that Negroes were white men and meant simply that in the future he was going to use 'white' in this expanded way, we might well say that this change in usage was arbitrary. But neither the idealist nor the materialist is making such a proposal. Both argue that the distinction between mental and physical does not fit the facts. The materialist argues that references to the mental should be translated into physical talk, for he finds the arguments for the existence of mind to be obscure and inadequate. He questions the dualism of ordinary speech, and I cannot see that he is refuted either by pointing to our common usage, or by saying that the existence of the mental is obvious. His arguments may not be good ones, but they cannot be dismissed because they do not reflect ordinary usage.

I add the following comments. (1) If I say "Reality is mental," I may mean that everything that exists is mental; but if I say "Reality is logical," I do not mean that everything that exists is logical. Ducasse's analysis of "Reality is rational" simply ignores Bradley's reasons for distinguishing between existence and reality. (2) It seems to me that Ducasse's analysis of the "ontological position" is precisely the opposite of the correct account. He first analyzes scientific claims about theoretical entities as merely expressing an interest in regarding things from this point of view and then treats ontological claims on the same basis. But this is a mistake. To understand ontological claims, one needs to ask: What do I mean when I say that reality is changeless, free from contradiction, and so forth? I mean that these are characteristics of reality, and this introspective report is my ground for rejecting any theory that tells me otherwise.

Of course, metaphysicians are primarily interested in the nature of reality, but this is not at all what they mean when they make statements about reality. If anything, their interest is stimulated by what they know of the real, and so assertions about reality cannot be reduced to mere expressions of interest. Ducasse says that ontological assertions cannot be true or false, but he offers no argument to show that this is so. In claiming that there are no such things as ideas, wishes, and the like, is not the materialist making a claim about the nature of things, and one that is not obviously false? And if he suggests a certain philosophical usage for 'material', isn't this because he thinks that such a usage is more in accord with the facts than is our ordinary distinction between mental and material?

My conclusion is that Ducasse has failed to show that there is a sharp distinction between hypotheses, which are verifiable and, therefore, genuine assertions, and ontological statements, which are not verifiable and, therefore, are not genuine assertions. He assumes the truth of the verifiability theory of meaning, and this is the fatal weakness in his case. If the distinction between empirical hypotheses and ontological claims is not as Ducasse conceives it to be, Bradley's attempt to distinguish between appearance and reality can be what it seems to be. There will remain a legitimate philosophical way of speaking about appearance and reality, a

way that is strikingly different from that which we ordinarily encounter.

The Argument from Inconsistency—Stout

In the course of defending the existence of a "universal mind"
as an "individual really distinct from the world of finite existence," which "determines the whole course of nature," G. F.
Stout attacks the notion that "all reality is a single individual, ex-
cluding from its eternal unity all real distinctness of parts." [11] In
this view, there is "really" only the one changeless reality, and the
world of multiplicity and change is cast aside as "unreal."

Stout contends that such a theory cannot account for appearance satisfactorily. We must admit the world of change as real in
its own right and find our changeless reality in a distinct and perfect Being. First, he argues that in the natural sense of 'appearance', "What exists as mere appearance merely appears to exist,
and does not really exist. But there is no difference between saying that something does not really exist and saying simply that it
does not exist" (*GN*, 224). It follows that, in the monistic view,
"Thirst never really preceded the quenching of it; it cannot, because there really is no preceding or succeeding, because there
really is no thirst and no quenching of it either in our experience
of it or as physical fact" (*GN*, 224). And, he insists, we must have
this natural sense of 'appearance' and 'reality' in mind when we
deny the reality of time, for only such a sense will support our denial of a separate God and world that are both "real." This is so,
apparently, because only if the world of finite things does not
exist can we assume that reality is a single, changeless whole; if
the ordinary world does exist, it is real and must be recognized as
such. If there is some metaphysical need for a changeless reality, it
will have to be separate from the ordinary world.

Stout's second point is an ingenious argument I call "the argument from inconsistency." He charges that a theory of reality such
as Bradley's assumes and depends on the reality of the appearances in the very act of saying that they are not real. If something

11. G. F. Stout, *God and Nature*, ed. A. K. Stout (Cambridge, Cambridge University Press, 1952), pp. 222–28.

appears to be so-and-so, there must be something real that directly and simply appears. Stout calls the latter a "direct apparition," and he might well have used the term "sense-datum." In the case of such a direct appearance, "What appears must be real in so far as it appears. Its reality and its appearance are coincident" (GN, 225). For we err only when we interpret this datum as the appearance of something else, and all appearing things presuppose such data.

Now either these data must be identified with the "particular contents of sense-experience," in which case the real will be many, will change, and so forth, or these contents are not the same as the "real" given, in which case there is something still more basic that is given and that we (mistakenly) take for a plurality of successive sense-data. Presumably, this would be Bradley's changeless reality.

This escape from plurality leads to an internal inconsistency. We mistake the changeless reality for a changing plurality. Mistakes are possible only when there are finite minds to make them. Thus, there really must be a plurality of finite entities if we are to account for the fact that reality "appears" plural. Yet, the position is that all plurality is appearance. Therefore, it must be to appearances that it appears that there are many finite minds, and what sense does this make? As Stout says, "How can the imperfect apprehension which is to account for the distinction between what merely appears to be and what is real, be itself merely apparent?" (GN, 226).

Stout sees one possible escape from this dilemma. Perhaps 'appear' is not being used to imply that there must be (finite) minds to which reality appears. But he insists that only this sense of 'appear' is relevant to denying the existence of a supreme being distinct from the world of change. For if the appearance cannot be explained by the "imperfection of our knowledge" (thus involving the doctrine in a self-defeating inconsistency), the distinction between appearance and reality will have to be made differently, perhaps between the dependent and self-existent or between the adjectival and the substantial. Yet, neither of these distinctions allows us to conclude that reality is changeless and that the ordinary world is a mere appearance. Whatever is derived from something must be distinct from that source, and, if derived from the real, it must also be real (GN, 227). And finite selves are not adjectives of anything. Stout adds that we express ourselves poorly if, in saying that reality is the "substance" of finite things, we mean only that such things are parts of some greater whole. No doubt they are parts of the universe, but they are neither adjectives nor "unreal" because of it.

It seems clear that Bradley is not denying the common facts mentioned by Stout, for he uses 'real' in a very unusual sense. Nor do I see the force behind Stout's claim that a philosopher *must* use 'real' and 'appear' in the usual sense if he is to make out his case for a single, changeless reality. He seems to assume that either appearance must not exist, which is absurd, or it does exist, in which case it is real and distinct from any changeless reality. But Bradley's philosophy is built on the denial of any such "either-or." He thinks that there are arguments that force us to conclude that (1) appearance must "belong" to reality, whereas (2) reality and appearance cannot be simply identified. But, then, appearance and reality must be both the same and different, which is what Bradley means in saying that appearances express reality partially and inadequately. We can deny neither the consistency of reality nor the existence of appearances, and though this is difficult, one-sided views seem even more inadequate.

We may, like mystics, try to deny the existence of our ordinary world; or, we may deny the need for anything but the world of change; but then can our intellects accept such a world as final, and, if not, can we accept it as "real?" Finally, we might, like Stout, try to have both worlds by keeping them quite distinct from each other. But then the same arguments that led Bradley to monism come into play. The universal mind determines the course of nature, and so a relation exists between the two. But an analysis of relations reveals that they are the expression of an underlying unity between the terms. Thus, appearance and God become aspects of a whole that includes them both in an intellectually satisfactory manner. Relatedness and real independence are contradictory notions.

Hence, Stout's claim that, if appearance is "derivative" from reality, it must be both real and distinct from reality, is true enough, but it is not the whole truth. Bradley refuses to accept such conclusions without qualification. Appearance is distinct from reality, and appearances are real; but, equally, appearance is not distinct from reality, and appearances are not real.[12]

Second, when Stout identifies the real with the given (thus proving that the real is plural), Bradley tries to modify and enlarge his claim, rather than simply to deny it. The given does have an aspect that makes it a prime candidate for what we mean by reality. As Bradley says,

> And the 'this', secondly, has a genuine feature of ultimate reality. With however great imperfection and inconsistency its owns an individual character. The 'this' is real for us in a sense in which nothing else is real (*AR*, 198).

But the immediately given cannot be simply identified with reality, for "Its elements are but conjoined, and are not connected" (*AR*, 199). In feeling, we are close to reality, for we have not yet destroyed the unity found there in an attempt to explain the connection of its parts, but without this explanation one must have less than the fully real. Thus, we must go beyond the given to find reality, always hoping to re-establish the immediacy of the given in a whole that "includes and is superior to mediation."

Thus, when Stout asserts that individual minds are not adjectives of a single reality, Bradley questions the grounds of this denial. Granting that the distinction of substantive and adjective is inadequate to describe the way things stand to one another, he insists that we cannot verify the organic character of reality. But he insists equally that one's metaphysics cannot be based on a simple appeal to the "facts" of experience,[13] for there are conclusive reasons that call these "facts" into question. And if we cannot doubt that reality is one, then it must be one. For Bradley, finite things are "unreal" because the whole is present in every part in such a way that one takes an "abstract" view of anything if he considers it apart from this larger context. In this sense, finite

12. In Bradley's words, "Every partial truth is but partly true, and its opposite also has truth" (*ETR*, 232).

13. Quoting Bradley, "It is a mere superstition to suppose that an appeal to experience can prove reality" (*AR*, 182).

things are "adjectives," and I can find nothing misleading about this use of the term 'adjective'.

The above clarification of Bradley's views goes a long way toward answering Stout's main contention, that Bradley's view of appearance results in a vital inconsistency, although I must admit that I find the objection a vital one and the answer less than fully satisfactory. Stout's point is vitiated by an interpretation of 'appearance' that is far too subjective to capture Bradley's meaning. He does not imagine that we, as finite, distort a coherent and unified reality that stands over against us. Rather, we take the world as plural, temporal, and so on because reality takes that form in us. Perhaps it is best to say that, for Bradley, there is not the kind of division in judgment between thinker and thought-of that is assumed by Stout's criticism. In Bradley's words:

> We must view the Reality in its unbroken connection with finite centres. We must take it as, within and with these centres, making itself an object to itself and carrying out them and itself at once ideally and practically. The activity of the process is throughout the undivided activity of the Reality and of the centres in one (*ETR*, 327).

The distinction between appearance and reality is not made by the "imperfection of our knowledge," although out knowledge is imperfect in that it must make use of this distinction.

In short, though perhaps there could not be appearances without finite minds, this does not prove that such minds are "real." It only proves that reality must appear in a plurality of finite minds if there is to be a world of appearance. But then all appearances exist; none is imaginary or merely appears to exist.

Stout seems to feel that, if pluralism is not the final truth about finite minds, then the rest of appearance must be built on shifting, even nonexistent, sand. But this is because he thinks that whatever is not real cannot exist, that this is the natural sense of 'unreal,' and that no other sense is relevant to Bradley's case. Because we know that there is another sense that is relevant, there is no need to be bound by the natural sense of 'unreal'. Perhaps finite minds are necessary for there to be appearances, but such minds need not be real for all that. Of course, there are notorious difficulties in Bradley's notions of appearance and its relation to reality. Thus, when he says,

> There really is within the Absolute a diversity of finite centres. There really is within finite centres a world of objects. . . . These things are realities, and yet, because imperfect, they are but appearances which differ in degree . . . (*ETR,* 412),

our credulity is taxed beyond reason. Nevertheless, the difficulty arises, I believe, not from confusion or perversity, but because Bradley is determined to do justice to the ordinary world without, at the same time, giving it a metaphysical preeminence that it cannot sustain. Unless pluralism can be shown to be a consistent view of things, I can see no other choice than to follow Bradley down this difficult path.

In this chapter, I have tried to show that the most important criticisms of Bradley's use of 'real' do not prove that this use is arbitrary because it violates the standard by which usage must be judged. I have argued, further, that Bradley's defense of his concept of reality is legitimate and compelling. The claim that Bradley denies certain obvious facts about the world is based on the mistaken assumption that Bradley must use 'unreal' in its normal sense of 'nonexistent'. Nor is the assertion convincing that Bradley's theory is arbitrary because it cannot be proved as we prove assertions in science. Most important, his theory need not be written off either because it ignores the many senses in which we ordinarily use 'real' or because it employs 'real' in an unusual way. In short, there is no argument known to me that shows that Bradley's theory of reality must fail because of the general kind of position that it represents. There is no alternative to evaluating the specific arguments that Bradley uses.

Part II

The Self

Introductory Remarks

In the preceding chapters, I attempted to elucidate and defend Bradley's conception of reality and to shed some light on the connection between reality and its appearances. Bradley has been accused of claiming that the elements of our commonsense world —space, time, things, and relations—just do not exist, are imaginary, or something of the kind. This accusation has created the false impression that Bradley is an other-worldly philosopher and a prime exponent of "news from nowhere."

Yet, the charge is not without foundation, for after all the appropriate reservations have been made, Bradley is committed to the view that our commonsense world lacks the ultimacy with which we credit it in our speech, our actions, and our thoughts. Normally, we feel that we know the world as it is in perception and reflection and that, though the details of our knowledge of this world are subject to correction, there is no possibility that the framework that contains these details might somehow be called into question. The peculiarity of metaphysics, in Bradley's view, is that it compels us to regard as untenable theories precisely those things common sense regards as final, ultimate facts. Bradley practices a thoroughgoing doubt that goes far deeper than Descartes', and he does so in the name of reason.

The general reasons in favor of such a wholesale re-evaluation of our ordinary categories and experience have been given in the previous chapters. But such abstract arguments rarely carry much weight in philosophy—we are more certain that space and time are real than we are of any proof to the contrary, even though we cannot say precisely what we mean by 'real'; we tend to agree with Moore that we can know the meaning of a term without being able to give an analysis of it. And (ignoring for the moment the absolute character of metaphysical claims for Bradley), we might even claim that Bradley should be sympathetic to such doubts, for he has said many times that theories must be tested by their ability to work. In the case of philosophical theories, 'working' does not mean making prediction possible, as it does in science, nor does it mean making life more satisfactory, as James seemed to think, but rather fitting the facts to be explained into a framework in a way that we find theoretically satisfactory.

Using this measuring stick, the most obvious way to test Bradley's conception of reality would be to find a fact that seems most unlikely to fit the theory and then, by what Bradley called an "ideal experiment," to see how the theory can cope with it. There is no better candidate than the self for something that is "real" and yet part of the commonsense world. Nothing is more clear than that I am an absolutely unique, particular existent, and that I am quite real—perhaps even the foundation for the very existence of things about me. Nothing could make one question his own reality! Still, that the self exists is certain enough, but can one be certain about the ultimacy, the reality of the self until one is able to say what a self is? Perhaps the self exists—as undoubtedly things do—but are there reasons that will make us wonder whether the self is, in addition, "real"? Descartes perhaps moved too quickly from the discovery of the existence of the self to the claim that the self was of a certain character, one that guaranteed it a fundamental place in the world. There are many questions to be answered before one can be sure that our natural picture of the world as a plurality of related-yet-individual selves is also metaphysically warranted.

By placing his discussion of the self at the close of the section on "appearance" in *Appearance and Reality*, Bradley gives it a special importance. As he himself says, we expect to find reality in the self if we are to find it anywhere. Yet, he finds the notion of selfhood as inadequate and as "contradictory" as he had previously found the notions of space, thing, and relation. Here, Bradley highlights two elements in his philosophy that have been generally ignored or underrated by recent critics: his empiricism and his negativism.[1]

1. A striking exception to this is Richard Wollheim's *F. H. Bradley*.

Bradley's empiricism—present in his insistence that metaphysics cannot transcend the data given in feeling—leads him to reject two ways in which philosophers have spoken about the self. On the one hand, Bradley rejects moves to a transexperiential entity called an ego, insisting that what a self is, and what it can do, can be explained without entities that transcend experience and that bring additional troubles in their wake.

Second, he criticizes the idealists, who have looked to the self as an "ultimate concept." By this they mean that the self (and our experience of selfhood) is a paradigm in terms of which we must understand reality, for they think that its organic character is our best clue to the nature of reality. Bradley is willing to grant that selfhood is the "highest" kind of experience we have—it comes the closest to embodying the kind of unity we demand of reality. But he insists that, if we stick to what we actually experience of ourselves, there is no warrant for believing either that the self experiences itself as a perfect, complete organic whole or even that such experience "provides us with a type, by the aid of which we may go on to comprehend the world" (AR, 64). It is not a perfect whole because our actual self-consciousness turns out not to reveal the whole self in the way that is claimed; it is not the ideal type because the experience of the self is too defective, too replete with the kinds of difficulties that plague our experience of relations, to allow us to think of reality in such terms. To find the real, we must look beyond the unity present in a self to a unity that, in transcending the unity of relations, implies the extinction of the subject-object relation so essential to selfhood.

This leads us directly into Bradley's negativism, an attitude that leads him to question the vague certainty that common sense has regarding the reality of the self. The category of 'self' is no more immune from his searching criticism than are any of the other categories used in everyday life and taken by one philosopher or another as "fundamental." As a critical thinker, Bradley seeks out the vagueness and inconsistencies in notions that philosophers have taken uncritically from our commonsense life and have used to characterize the real.

He suggests that such philosophers are using our ordinary concepts in a way never intended by common sense. Metaphysicians speak constantly of the real world as something transcending our ordinary world of perception, but because common sense knows nothing of the metaphysician's reality, its concepts could not have been intended for his use. Far too often, however, the metaphysician proceeds as if this extended use of ordinary notions were no problem and called for no special reflection on his part. Bradley insists that, precisely because of the special character and interests of metaphysics and its distance from the claims of ordinary life, the metaphysician must critically examine the concepts he has taken from common usage to see if they will satisfy the demands of his own discipline. The fault of speculative philosophers—whether empiricists or rationalists—is that they are not critically enough aware of what they are doing. They misjudge the gap that separates them from common sense and allows them to build systems with concepts suitable for ordinary use but containing unobserved faults that make them inadequate for metaphysics.

Another serious error Bradley sees in both types of philosophy, and particularly in empiricism, is that the actual facts of experience are distorted so that they will fit into the pattern demanded by highly speculative and arbitrary a priori views about the real. Here again, he criticizes the lack of awareness of the influence an arbitrary theory can have on the point of view, method, and goal of philosophers. Perhaps having underestimated the distance between philosophy and common sense, metaphysicians have been led illicitly to transfer the certainty that common sense has about its concepts to the attitude that, as metaphysicians, we can be sure that these concepts will work in metaphysics. But if the certainty of common sense is not transferable to metaphysics, we may draw on the certainty illicitly in our philosophizing. We need not, however, if we will examine what we are doing, what end we seek, and how we must seek it.

Bradley believes that from this critical self-awareness will emerge a view of the world that will have its own justification and be far different from that of common sense. Bradley's view is distinguished from contemporary insistence that we must become more aware of the extent to which philosophers distort ordinary usage, at the same time relying on that usage to give their theories plausibility. For the contemporary view suggests to many that when this illicit propping up of philosophical views is exposed, it will be seen that there is no other, legitimate support for them.

Bradley, on the other hand, tries to provide just such support. Yet, one might argue that the meager character of Bradley's positive philosophy suggests that he was a metaphysician in spite of himself. Once his critical task was completed, it was obvious that metaphysics on any basis is impossible, but (so it might be argued) Bradley continued to do metaphysics because of the tradition in which he was nurtured. I do not think that this is correct, but Bradley's emphasis on critical self-investigation does place him far closer to contemporary views than is generally realized.

Bradley's fidelity to experience has a role to play in his negative attitude toward the self. He does not find in experience the kind of unity or substantiality that has been attributed to the self, and he rejects attempts to salvage this substantiality by placing the self wholly or in part "out of time." But this leaves the self of experience a mere "construction" whose conflicting elements refuse to combine into a logically acceptable whole. And this is what Bradley insists we mean by appearance.

Bradley's empirical approach to the self, largely influenced by his interest in psychology and its limitations, results in an interesting contrast between the kinds of criticisms that seem most weighty here and those that were most formidable in relation to his metaphysics. The apparent transcendence and ignoring of ordinary fact and use in his metaphysical speculations drew the fire of empirically minded critics. When it comes to the self, I believe that the situation is almost the reverse. Bradley's attempt to account for the self, its identity and activities, solely in terms of the self's contents—what is given in introspection—is an attempt to reduce the self to its presentations. And, as Ward said, does not this omit the very elements that need to be assumed if the notion of 'content' or 'presentation' is to make any sense at all? It seems to me that the defenders of the ego—those who argue that the self must be conceived in terms beyond what is given in experience—offer the greatest challenge to any view such as Bradley's. The concept of a substantive self is not much in favor among contemporary philosophers, but it seems to me that there are serious and important arguments in its favor.

One might state the issue more generally as follows. In order to account for what the self is as revealed in experience, must we assume any entities, powers, dispositions, and so forth that are not in that experience but that are presupposed by it? If so, what is the nature and extent of these elements? Is such transcendentalism necessarily empty or is it unavoidable? If the latter, how can we distinguish between a "real" and a merely verbal explanation? On these questions, Bradley seems far closer to Hume than to more speculative philosophers. But this is not surprising, for though, in Bradley's view, reality does "transcend" our common sense world in one sense, it does so not as another world set alongside or "above" our ordinary world, but simply as the world of common sense shorn of the interpretation of the data given in feeling, an interpretation present in perception and more explicitly in thinking. Reality is that world more properly experienced. Bradley's refusal to admit transcendent elements into his conception of the self follows his general principle that transcendent entities are never admissible for the metaphysician.

I have divided what follows into seven chapters: "The Discrete Self," a discussion of Hume and Ayer; "The Continuous Self," a discussion of the views of Alexander, Sartre, and James; "The Self as Ego," a survey of the major arguments in favor of this view; "Bradley's Conclusions about the Self," a presentation of Bradley's conclusions about the self and a defense of these conclusions against various objections; "Three Contemporary Views of the Self or Mind," a discussion of the identity thesis of Smart, the behavioral thesis of Ryle, and Strawson's concept of a person; "Personal Identity and Its Criteria," a discussion centering on Locke and Bradley; "Bradley's Theory of Personal Identity."

I shall next consider several major theories of the self, hoping that the apparently paradoxical character of Bradley's attitude toward the self will be lessened by placing it in a context of these theories and that the reasons for the success or failure of these theories will provide a basis from which Bradley's claims can be evaluated. If we find these claims to be correct, this would seem to be strong support for the metaphysical base from which they spring. Conversely, if Bradley's criticisms of the self seem incorrect, and, particularly, if they seem so because we find the self to be substantial, then a serious objection will have been raised to Bradley's metaphysics.

II

The Discrete Self

The title of this chapter calls attention to two aspects of Hume's theory. First, the elements comprising a self have no internal reference to one another. This does not imply that Hume does not think of them as related; he does. It means only that these relations are external to their terms. Second, a self is composed only of such elements. There is no "center" for such a self that could in any way be said to unify its contents. In short, 'discrete' means merely the thoroughly atomic character of the self as Hume conceives it.

According to Hume, one can trace back to their original impressions the concepts of unity and number (plurality), and thereby justify them. The concept of unity is "conveyed" by the contemplation of a single object, whereas the idea of number is "conveyed" by a series of objects.

The problem with identity is that it seems to be "incompatible" with both unity and number, leading us to think that it must fall between them; whereas "Betwixt unity and number there can be no medium; no more than betwixt existence and non-existence" (*THN,* 200). We seem trapped with two mutually exclusive and exhaustive alternatives. Given one object, either we have a second object existing after it, which implies no identity between the two objects, or we have the same object still existing, which involves the continued existence of a single object, not the identity of this object with itself. To say that A is identical with B creates a dilemma. Either A and B are the same object or they are not. If they are, then we assert only that A is A; if they are not, then we falsely identify two things that are different. How, then, can we account for our notion of identity?

The clue lies with our notion of time. Earlier, Hume tells us that identity is a relation and that it can only be applied "in its strictest sense to constant and unchangeable objects" (*THN,* 14). Now he observes that time involves succession and, therefore, gives one the concept of plurality. This effect occurs not only with moments of time, but also for an object imagined to exist at different moments of time, for we must imagine the object twice in order to think of it occupying first one moment and then another. On the other hand, the same facts can give rise to the idea of unity. If we think of our object first at one moment and then at another, all the while imagining that it is the same and continuously existing, we have the notion of the unity of one object. But an object that is one object, because there are no breaks in its existence, no changes in its character, and that still exists at many points in time, is just what we mean by an identical object in the "strictest" sense. Clearly, this "strict" notion of identity is modeled on what Hume imagines to be the basic elements of things—his simple impressions. For if we take a colored patch, we would say, I think, that if it "changed" color then, strictly speaking, there was another patch before us; and if it ceased to exist and another patch appeared of exactly the same shade, we would say that this was a second patch identical in shade with the first.

Because this is Hume's model of identity, and because he thinks of things as mere complexes of simple impressions, it follows that he must explain the identity of things in terms of the identity of basic elements. His conclusion is that a thing cannot be identically the same if it undergoes even the slightest change, something we would not say under ordinary circumstances, for we do not ordinarily use 'identical' in only the strict sense given by Hume. Of course, Hume allows that we do speak of the identity of things other than in the strict sense, but he believes this sense to be "fictitious" or "Pickwickean" and thinks that by using 'identity' in the two senses we may think that things have a kind of identity they do not have.[1]

In the strict sense of 'identity', what is different are the moments of time, whereas the identical thing is merely one at each

1. For a discussion of these two senses in relation to the self, see Norman Kemp Smith, *The Philosophy of David Hume* (London, Macmillan, 1949), pp. 499–502.

moment. Hume adds, " 'tis only by a fiction of the imagination, by which the unchangeable object is suppos'd to participate of the changes of the co-existent objects" (*THN*, 200–01). And, although I am going beyond Hume here, it seems to me that even this strict sense of identity should be suspect for him. One thing is said to exist at two moments of time. But this seems to be a change of the one thing, whereas our "thing" is a perfectly simple impression. One wonders how such an entity can sustain even such a simple change. Wouldn't it be better to say that impressions are momentary existences and that what seems to be one impression over a period of time must really be a series of impressions precisely similar to one another? If so, then Hume's position would be that there is no such thing as identity at all, that there is only unity and plurality, and that under certain special circumstances (when "seeing" an impression for several moments) we are led to combine the two notions inconsistently into a single idea. On analysis, the unity falls only to the impression and the plurality only to the series of impressions. Hume does not say this, but it seems to be the logical outcome of his belief in atomic impressions.

But, of course, Hume admits, we do ascribe identity to an object usually on the basis of far less than our twin criteria of invariance and uninterruptedness. We say, for example, that my watch is the same watch I had yesterday, although I was unaware of it for long periods, merely because of its invariable appearance. According to Hume, we have no reason to believe in the continuous existence of the watch; therefore, our reason tells us that we must be confusing two distinct but similar entities. Yet, the tendency of our imagination to unite two such similar appearances, a process that feels much the same as does the contemplation of a single unchanging object, leads us to believe that the object is one and not many (*THN*, 204). Our common belief is that our two "perceptions" must be the same because of their likeness.

How can we overcome the conflict between what our reason tells us is the case and what our imagination encourages us to belive? We make a distinction between our perceptions and the objects we perceive, a distinction, Hume claims, unknown to man in his ordinary, unreflective state. Then we attribute the interruption to our perceptions and the continued existence to the objects of our awareness (*THN*, 215). Like Ryle, Hume brands this "solution" as a "monstrous offspring" of two conflicting and irreducible principles. It is a mistake that philosophers have foisted on us to explain how what is interrupted can still be the same. And, although Hume does not continue his analysis at this point, one can see how it would apply to other identity claims. We often say that a thing is the same as before even when its "appearances" differ. Using our same principle, we must say either that our perception of the thing is different, though the thing is the same (in which case we no longer see things and, apparently, cannot know what our "things" are like), or say that though the qualities of the thing have changed (these are what we perceive), the thing itself has been invariable and uninterrupted (in which case the "thing" becomes Locke's unknowable substratum). Either way, our "things" become unobservable, when all along we thought that we perceived things.

Thus, the notion of identity is twice condemned. It may be a self-contradictory combination of unity and plurality, a contradiction hidden from us by a "fiction" of the imagination. Second, ignoring this fatal defect, when we apply the strict notion of identity to our experience, we find that there is nothing corresponding to one of the criteria of identity, namely, continuous existence. Therefore, we are forced into a mistaken distinction between perceptions and things perceived, a distinction that leads to an enormous number of unnecessary philosophical puzzles.

We shall see below how this applies to Hume's theory of the self. For the moment, let me mention two related difficulties with Hume's view of identity.[2] When Hume agrees to speak with the vulgar, he makes his task seem much easier than it in fact is. For, at such times, he allows himself to speak of "surveying the furniture of my chamber" and then trying to explain why I think the objects are the same when I return to my chamber. But the original survey presupposes the notion of an object that is the same

2. I am following here the masterly analysis of Hume by T. H. Green in his introduction to Hume's *Treatise*, *The Works of T. H. Green*, ed. R. L. Nettleship (3 vols. New York, Longmans, Green, 1894), *1*, 253–58.

throughout my changing awareness of it, and, of course, this notion employs the very "Pickwickean" concept of identity that is condemned in the case of "discontinuous" existence.

Furthermore, Hume cannot explain his tendencies to "feign" without reintroducing the very notion of identity he is trying to expose as fictitious. For Hume, we cannot "really" have the idea of an identical object because no impression or set of impressions could be its source. Thus, Hume must explain why we think we have this idea. He does this by introducing our tendency to think that a series of resembling impressions are the impressions of one and the same object, because such a series feels to us exactly like the contemplation of one and the same impression. But one might argue with at least equal plausibility that the presence of my idea of an identical object explains my habit of thinking of my impressions as the impression of one object. This is particularly clear when one considers that I do so even when my impressions do not resemble one another at all and so should not "feel" the same as the contemplation of a single impression. And one still seems to have the idea of an identical object, an idea that seems underivable from Hume's elements.

Hume's theory of the self centers around his famous introspective report:

> For my part, when I enter most intimately into what I call *myself*, I always stumble on some particular perception or other, of heat or cold, light or shade, love or hatred, pain or pleasure. I never catch myself at any time without a perception, and never can observe any thing but the perception (*THN*, 252).

Because, for Hume, all ideas must be derived from impressions, such an introspective report leads him to the following conclusions about the self. (1) We have no idea of a self that is simple and identical through time (in the strict sense of identity), for there are no impressions that are "constant and invariable" and, even if there were, the "Self or person is not any one impression, but that to which our several impressions and ideas are suppos'd to have a reference" (*THN*, 251). That is, the self is supposed to be a subject, but in fact it must be fictitious because it is not the kind of thing of which we could have an impression. Furthermore, the qualities attributed to it are not the kind that characterize impressions.

(2) The idea we do gain of ourselves through introspection, and that represents what we are, is that of a "bundle or collection of different perceptions, which succeed each other with an inconceivable rapidity, and are in a perpetual flux and movement" (*THN*, 252). As Hume says, there is neither simplicity at one moment nor identity in different moments in the self, despite "whatever natural propension we may have to imagine that simplicity and identity" (*THN*, 253). Rather, the mind is only a theater across which our perceptions pass, although Hume hurriedly adds that the metaphor is misleading in suggesting that there is something more to the mind than its perceptions.

Why do we have a "natural propension" to believe in the identity of what we call the self? The answer is that in certain circumstances contemplating two different objects feels much the same as contemplating a single object, and this allows our imagination to confound what our reason tells us are two distinct notions. Even without these circumstances our tendency to "feign" gathers a kind of momentum that runs roughshod over more accurate methods of thinking. Hume names two sets of circumstances that encourage our imagination. If a change is small in proportion to the whole, or if it occurs gradually and insensibly, we are apt to consider the object to be the same after the change as it was before, although such change "absolutely destroys the identity of the whole, strictly speaking" (*THN*, 256). Hume adds that even sudden changes can be allowed for, as in the case of a river, if we consider them natural and, therefore, expect them as a matter of course.

Faced with changes of greater magnitude, however, we resort to fictions that make us believe that identity is preserved. For example, we conceive a "common end or purpose" that makes the object the same, no matter what change, so long as it is able to perform this purpose. Further, if the shape and material of the thing have totally changed, as when a child grows into a man, we add the notion of "mutual dependence" or "sympathy" among the parts. As long as this stays the same, our thing can be thought of as identical throughout all of its changes. Thus Hume condemns both the notions of mechanism and of organism as fictions that help us to overlook the disrupting changes things undergo. Or, faced with extreme change, we may fall back on the notions of "soul, and self, and substance," which are thought to be the same while only their properties change. And if all these fail, we may continue to believe in the identity through the time of a complex thing merely because of the power that our imagination has over us.

When it is a question not of change but of an interruption in our awareness of the thing, we merely postulate the "continu'd existence of the perceptions of our senses." And we may even say that a sound that is intermittent is the same sound, thus confusing numerical and specific identity, or that a church rebuilt of different materials in a different style is still the same church because it has the same relations to its congregation as the old one did. All such things can be said without the slightest "breach of the propriety of language," but then common language and thought lack the precision and rigor of philosophic thought.

Because the self is, like other things, merely a "bundle," in the strict sense it can have no more identity than they. We believe in self-identity only because of the "fictions" discussed above. This is obvious, Hume thinks, if we keep in mind two certain and fundamental principles: All our distinct perceptions are distinct existences; the mind has no power to observe any real connection between such existences (a "real" connection being one that binds distinct perceptions together into a whole whose unity is more than that of a collection). For Hume, the individual impression is a substance, and it has no intrinsic relation to any other substance (*THN*, 244). The relations that the perceptions constituting our minds do have lead us to believe that they also have the relation of identity, and this is false.

Memory, by reproducing images that resemble the impressions from which they are derived, produces for us the relation of resemblance, and this relation encourages us to think that what we call one state of our mind is the same, that is, is a state of the same mind, as a previous state. Second, the causal relation existing among our perceptions allows us to see some continuity in our various states and, thus, to believe that we are one self; just as a republic is considered to be "the same" if its stages follow with causal regularity one from the other. In this case, memory makes us aware of the causal relation, but once in possession of it we can extend our identity far beyond the reach of our memory. Thus, we have the sense that in memory we discover, rather than produce, our identity. Hume concludes that self-identity is fundamentally a "grammatical" problem, meaning that identity is a matter of degree; thus, "We have no just standard, by which we can decide any dispute concerning the time, when they acquire or lose a title to the name of identity" (*THN*, 262).

It is well known that in the Appendix to his *Treatise*, Hume expressed dissatisfaction with the two principles mentioned above. He says that they are not "consistent," but I do not think he means that they are logically incompatible. Rather, he means that taken together they lead to a view of self-identity based on a principle of which, Hume says, "Nothing but the seeming evidence of the precedent reasonings cou'd have induc'd me to receive it." For if distinct perceptions are distinct existences (Hume's atomism), then a thing can be one only by some interconnection; yet, because the mind can find no such bond (Hume's thesis that reasoning must work with the elements furnished by the senses), we must be seduced into thinking that the elements of things have a real togetherness. If the former were false, the various impressions could form one self by inhering in some simple subject; if the latter were false, the self might be one by being a whole of parts that entailed one another. But because both principles seem to be true to Hume, he can accept neither way out of his dilemma—we find it impossible to believe that we merely "feign" self-identity because we sense the paradoxes involved in Hume's concept of the self as a bundle of atomic units.[3]

Let me here mention a few of the paradoxes in Hume's theory. (1) Insofar as our concept of moral responsibility is based on a belief in self-identity, it would have to be abandoned in Hume's

3. Thus, the incompatibility is between our feeling or belief that the self is one (in some "strong" sense of one) and the conclusion that it is not one (in any "strong" sense) to which our two principles, discovered by reason, lead us. See J. N. Wright, "Hume on Self-Identity," *Aristotelian Society Proceedings, 18,* supp. (1939), 3–4, for this interpretation.

theory. (2) Because nothing about me can be essential to me, in the sense of being more important than any other element, there is a sense in which every perception is essential to the self I am: without any of my perceptions, I would be a different person. (3) What I call *my* pain could just as well have been *your* pain and if impressions can be strictly identical, might well become what you call *your* pain, just as a brick in a pile of bricks could have been in another pile and could remain the same while becoming a member of another pile. Yet, though I might have a pain of the same quality, duration, and so forth as yours, what would it mean to say that *my* pain had become *your* pain? Whatever the relation between me and my pain, it is not the same as that between me and my coat. (4) As Hume admits, in his view, an idea might sever "all its relations, with that connected mass of perceptions, which constitute a thinking being" (*THN*, 207). Because ideas or impressions are substantial, according to Hume, this must be true for him. But can there be ideas that are not the ideas of some person or self?

It certainly looks as if both points 3 and 4 form an effective *reductio ad absurdum* of Hume's view. The difficulty—one philosophers are apt to ignore—is that it is hard to be certain either which part of Hume's view is thereby shown to be absurd or what conclusion we are to draw about the self from our insight that something in Hume's view will not do. It is all too easy to think that Hume's failure implies that the opposite of his view—a version of the pure ego theory—must be correct, just as some philosophers seem to think that difficulties in the pure ego theory must mean that a nonegoistic theory will give us an adequate view of the self. One point that concerns Bradley is what meaning or significance one should give to the failures of theories of the self, and it is a point to which we shall return.

One could say that, in the very statement of his view, Hume lets the cat out of the bag. When he says that "I" look into myself and find only discrete perceptions, he implies in spite of himself that there is a part of the self, an "I", that is not part of the bundle and that observes it. But, as so stated, the argument is less than conclusive. For example, the divisions in our language suggest a distinction between "thing" and "property of a thing," and important philosophic views have been based on this linguistic suggestion. Yet, other philosophers have thought that, when this view's logical implications are explored, the distinction is seen to be philosophically unacceptable, and they have, therefore, developed views in which there is no such distinction. In turn, they say, we must think of language as misleading in our search for the way things are. And because there are other languages in which nouns and adjectives do not function as they do in English, one might be reluctant to read too much into the particular structure of our language. We can choose between views only *after* we can see which one explains more of the facts in a way that we find convincing. The same remarks apply equally to the self. The mere fact that the statement of Hume's theory violates what Hume is explicitly saying may be a commentary on the worth of English for philosophical purposes, although Hume is still obliged to give some account of what we mean when we use such words as 'I' and 'me'.[4]

Nevertheless, the bare appeal to the structure of our language could be supported in ways that make the successful working out of Hume's view rather doubtful. As Broad points out, our self does seem to have the unity of a center. That is, when I see or hear or introspect, there does seem to be a relation between the object of these states and some one thing that perceives and that I call "I." Because there seems to be an "I," we find it very hard to accept a view that insists that "the relation of 'himself' to 'his toothache' is the same relation as that of the British Army to Private John Smith" (*MIPN*, 585). And even if there is no center of reference to the self, we have seen that Hume himself was unable to accept his own explanation of why there seems to be a systematic unity to the self. How much harder to explain why there seems to be a center to the self, which is called "I" by the perceiver!

Now some philosophers have suggested that the certainty that there is a center of awareness is momentary, so that the "subjective referent" in awareness may or may not be a permanent "I"

4. See C. D. Broad, *The Mind and Its Place in Nature* (London, Routledge & Kegan Paul, 1925), pp. 569–70 and 584–85, for a discussion of what account might be given for the meaning of these words by a philosopher such as Hume.

around which we might unify the experiences that make up 'our' biography.[5] This is a topic for later discussion. Here it is enough to point out that, even if our "subjective referent" be as momentary as the experience whose subject it is, that is enough to refute Hume's theory of the self. For, in his view, there is nothing to the self except the particular perceptions, and whatever the "subjective referent" may be, it cannot be one of the introspected perceptions.

Of course, Hume would deny that he could find any such subjective ingredient in the experience of himself, but I think a rather simple distinction shows his doubt to be misplaced. We want to distinguish between what one might "stumble on" in a moment of introspection and what would be listed in a complete inventory of the elements that go to make up an introspective situation.[6] Granting that a careful listing of elements-stumbled-on would contain only particular sensations and ideas (and, perhaps, other elements), one might insist that a complete inventory would have to contain an item corresponding to our "subjective referent," and it is correct to insist on the inclusion of such an item. It is very hard to say what one means by a subject of experience, and it is even harder to describe the experience of it. Yet, it seems to me certain that we are aware of something like such an element in introspection, that we are sometimes aware of it in perception, and that we may become aware of it by a shift of attention even when we are immersed in the perceived object. And what if one objects that no such awareness of a subject seems to be a certain, indisputable datum of introspective experience, because a philosopher as capable as Russell has decided on reflection that he was mistaken in thinking that he was acquainted with a subject? This is a serious objection, but I think that we might make two replies to it.

Even if the experience in question is as much of an item in in-

5. See J. R. Jones, "The Self in Sensory Cognition," *Mind*, n.s., *58* (January 1949), 42–43, and Bertrand Russell, *The Problems of Philosophy* (London, Oxford University Press, 1950), p. 19, for this view. Interestingly, Russell retracted even this momentary certainty in *The Analysis of Mind* (London, Allen & Unwin, 1921), pp. 17–18, where he adopts a bundle theory of the self.

6. For an excellent brief discussion of Hume's introspective reports, see Roderick M. Chisholm, "The Concept of a Person," *The Monist*, *49* (January 1965), 29–32.

trospection as is the impression introspected, it is not claimed that the experience of a subject is like that of the object, nor that it is easily separable from that of the object. On the contrary, it has been stressed that the awareness of a subject seems to defy description. Thus, it is not surprising that some philosophers have wavered in their certainty that they could always, or even sometimes, find a "subjective referent" in their experience. In fact, it is exactly the reaction that one might expect in the case of an experience whose "object" is itself and of a "subject" to which we are too "close" to make the kind of observations that we make of ordinary objects. Just as some philosophers have said that certain propositions were self-evidently true without (necessarily) implying that this was easy to see or that it was disproved when someone failed to see it, so here one need only claim that there is a "subjective referent" in all experience, that any description of experiences that omits it will at least be *felt* to be incomplete, and that, if a person approaches experience without too many preformed conclusions, he can distinguish the sense of a subject from his awareness of an object. One wishes that there were some other means of arguing the point, for introspective reports are notoriously vague and shifting, but this particular reply to Hume arises from an analysis of our experience and can only appeal to that experience if its claims are questioned.

It may be said that this reply comes close to question-begging. In a similar case, G. E. Moore claimed that one could discern in things a nonnatural property of goodness, though presumably this could not be done by the means of the five senses and required some kind of special awareness. Failure to find such a quality could always be blamed on the difficulty of the awareness and the difference of the property from normal properties. But if one doubts the existence of nonnatural properties and thinks that ascriptions of goodness can be explained perfectly well without assuming them (and this has been the position of philosophers espousing doctrines as different as emotivism and self-realization), one is likely to feel that all the talk about the difficulty of perceiving nonnatural properties is simply a means of disguising the fact that there are no such things. As applied to the self, this argument may seem to throw us back on the rival claims of what is given in experience. And one reply to it is simply to ask the questioner to go to his own experience. Though there is nothing wrong with this reply, it will not convince the person who says that he "stumbles on" only various particular impressions.

We could further point to the extreme implausibility of views that try to do without a "subjective referent." It is not that such views are not completely satisfactory; they lack all plausibility whatever. Even without good reasons for doubting such views, we continue to feel that they are fundamentally wrong. Of course, Hume would not be convinced by this point, but it does help to highlight the very peculiar nature of his view.

There are at least two other ways to answer Hume's introspective claims. One might try to show that there must be some elements other than what one "stumbles on," or one might argue that Hume's failure to "stumble on" a subject is not relevant to the existence of the subject. When I perceive or introspect, there must be something in addition to the "impressions" perceived, if, indeed, the "impressions" are ever "parts" of me at all. Unless there are acts of perception, unless there is consciousness or awareness, it is impossible to see how there could be thinking, perceiving, desiring, and so forth. Without consciousness, there might be things, but there could not be the truth or falsity, the confusion or clarity that consciousness makes possible. Yet, the acts of perceiving or of thinking cannot be observed in the same way as the objects of these acts, and they might easily be missed if one was prepared only to notice the objects of awareness. Because there must be such elements in a mind, there may be another element, also not to be "stumbled on," which is a constituent of a mind, namely, our "subjective referent." I have not shown that there must be such an element; but I have shown, I believe, that Hume's analysis of the self is necessarily incomplete. What comprises a mind or self is then at least an open question.

Second, Hume's argument is at best a non sequitur and thus leaves the question of the existence of our "subjective referent" completely open. If there were such things as subjects or mental acts, they could not be "stumbled on" when we introspect. Therefore, the fact that they are not found in this manner leaves open the possibility that there are such things and that they are experienced in a different way from a sense impression.[7]

Hume might then fall back on his claim that we can have no such "experience," because all our ideas are derived from sense impressions, but how could one know that all knowledge is derived from sense impressions? This claim is not itself based on sense impressions, surely, and if it were it would be useless. How can our sense experience testify to the fact that all knowledge is derived from it? Said otherwise, a being who knew Hume's general empirical thesis to be true would already have the very kind of knowledge that the thesis claims is impossible. It is just no use arguing that there could be no such thing as a "self" and that we can have no idea of such a thing because it is by general admission not the kind of thing that could be an impression. The general assertion on which this claim is based is incoherent, using knowledge not derivable from the senses while declaring that such knowledge is impossible.

Bradley uses a second way of showing that Hume's theory will not do as a complete account of the self. Whereas the previous argument showed that Hume without justification restricted the elements of which a self is comprised, the present argument is designed to show that Hume's theory cannot account for the facts of mental life that even Hume is constrained to recognize. Bradley's central contentions against Hume are that his theory of the self is nonempirical; cannot account for the common or "vulgar" notions we have about the self; cannot explain admitted facts about the self, and when it tries to do so lapses into nonsense.

Hume's theory suggests, by its very language, that an appropriate model for the mind is a collection of atomic particles in space. Yet, if we deny the appropriateness of this model, it is hard to understand exactly how we are to take Hume's theory. More important, Hume's theory is not at all based on experience. As Bradley says,

> What is immediately experienced is not a collection of pellets or a
> 'cluster', as it used to be called, of things like grapes, together

7. See Broad, *The Mind and Its Place in Nature,* pp. 308–10, and Wright, "Hume on Self-Identity," p. 9.

with other things called relations that serve as a kind of stalk to
the cluster. On the contrary, what at any time is experienced is a
whole with certain aspects which can be distinguished but, as so
distinguished, are abstractions (*CE, 2, 376*).

Atomism must be abandoned simply because the given is "a continuous mass of presentation in which the separation of a single
element from all context is never observed" (*CE, 1, 209*). It seems
to me that an impartial reading of one's self-experience reveals
the self to be a "whole" as described by Bradley. Whatever else a
self may or may not be, experience gives no warrant to the view
that it is merely discrete.

As an explanatory device, Hume's theory fares little better. It is
surely not the task of the philosopher to justify all our commonsense notions; but if it is the philosopher's task to provide reasons
for certain deep-seated feelings that we have about things, then
Hume's theory must be judged a failure. Bradley maintains that
it cannot, for example, account at all for our belief that human
beings are generally responsible for their actions because it ignores "the abiding personality which is the same throughout all
its acts, and *by which alone* imputation gets a meaning" (*ES, 33*).
In Hume's view, "A criminal is as 'responsible' for his acts of last
year as the Thames at London is responsible for an accident on
the Isis at Oxford, and he is no more responsible" (*ES, 40*).

Hume cannot account for either desire or self-consiousness.
What are the elements of desire? Here Bradley departs radically
from the whole "composition" theory of desire, a view made plausible by treating the self as if it were a physical thing and its desires
the directions such a thing takes. In the case of the physical thing,
its "action" can be understood as the result of the forces operating
on it; as applied to the self, this results in the theory that desire is
to be explained by "certain 'forces' called motives, acting within a
given space called self, and, by their 'composition,' resulting in no
movement at all or in a movement called 'will' . . ." (*ES, 35*).

Bradley turns to our experience of desire to test the accuracy of
such a metaphor. It fails miserably, for the things we want to say
about desire have no physical analogy. As Bradley points out, in
desire the self is divided against itself, for the desires are all *its* desires; the self can "distinguish" itself from all of its desires; and the

self expresses itself entirely in the desire it finally takes as its own. Thus, the will of man *is* himself, not "a certain disposition of elements not *in* a self, but the whole self expressing itself in a particular way, manifesting itself as will *in* this or that utterance" (*ES*, 33). In general, the composition theory fails because it ignores the "I," the element of unity that is expressed as a whole in all of my volitions.

Will the Humean claim that common sense is deluded in thinking that the above really are the characteristics of will? If so, we are confronted again with the problem of responsibility. Something I "do" is not an "act" for which I am responsible unless the "act" is the result of or expresses my will. But when an act does express my will, it is I, the whole self, that am responsible. How could this be so unless my will is myself, that is, unless I am as a whole my will? Because, in the composition view, there is no one person who can be said to will, it is hard to see how any one person can be held responsible for acts issuing from his will. Thus, we can be reasonably assured that something on the order of Bradley's description of desire and will must be correct, for a theory that denies this involves, ultimately, rejecting a belief about persons that is stronger than any theory.

The problem of self-consciousness involves Hume in even deeper troubles. As Broad pointed out, the mind does *appear* to have what he called the "unity of a center," and Hume is forced to explain this appearance as an illusion. For him, we are not simple, although we do speak of ourselves as if we were simple. This can only mean for Hume that a "collection" claims that it is not a "collection," and the problem is as to what sense we can give this "explanation," regardless of the principles Hume invokes to explain our tendency to "feign." If the self be merely discrete, then how can "it" ever come to believe otherwise? There is nothing to the self, no element in it, that is such that it would come to be deceived in this way. If I so much as think that I am more than a collection, then I must be more, for how can a collection be deceived? Must *I* not be deceived into thinking that I am merely a collection instead of a collection being deceived into thinking that it is an "I?" I have the idea that I am more than a collection; but this idea is not itself an impression, not a member

of the collection, for it is a fantasy. Hume claims that this belief is
generated by the similarity between a rapid succession and a single thing. But how is it generated? There must be something that
mistakes the one for the other, to which the one "feels" the same as
the other, and this something cannot be a part of the collection or
even all of the collection. Similarly, Hume's explanation of how I
come to believe in the necessity of the causal relation presupposes
a constant self that, after a while, comes to take mere regularity
for necessity. A mere collection could not even be aware of itself
as a collection, much less come to think that it is something else
and only later realize the error of its ways. Just as the solipsist in
claiming to know that solipsism is true claims, despite himself, to
know more than one in a truly solipsistic position could know, so
the bundle theorist in claiming to know even so much as the truth
of his own theory proclaims that he is more than a bundle. No
collection can be self-aware.[8]

But, Bradley warns, such criticisms should not lead us to embrace an ego theory of the self, for though our "consciousness of
self-sameness" shows that the self is not merely discrete and that
such a doctrine "contradicts itself in principle," we are not entitled by "some wonderful alternative" to conclude that the self
must be a single, absolutely-the-same entity (*AR,* 97). All we
have shown is that some kind of unity and continuity is necessary
to explain self-consciousness, but we have left open what kind of
unity and how much continuity are needed. (Of course such extreme leaps are not unknown in philosophy.)

My last important criticism of Hume is the claim that his
theory involves a vicious circle. It has been obvious to many philosophers that Hume cannot explain how the elements of a single
bundle are differentiated from those of another bundle with the
relations at his command. What relation do the impressions that
constitute my mind have to one another, which they do not have
to the impressions that constitute another mind? The relation
cannot be spatial, because my mind is not made up of spatial elements, despite Hume's misleading analogy; nor can it be coexist-

8. See John Stuart Mill, *An Examination of Sir William Hamilton's Philosophy*
(London, Longmans, Green, Reader, & Dyer, 1878), p. 248, for this admission. Also
stated by Bradley, *Ethical Studies,* p. 39.

ence at a moment of time, for "my" impressions share this relation with "your" impressions. For the same reason, succession will
not do. Causation, which Hume says forms the basis of the "true
idea of the human mind," fares no better, for "my" ideas are at
least indirectly causally influenced by "your" ideas. Resemblance
will not do either, for my present impressions may bear far less resemblance to one another or to "my" past impressions than they
do to the impressions now in "your" mind.

For this reason it has been suggested that if one takes a "relational" view of the self, perhaps he should claim that the relation
among the elements of a single self is "unique and indefinable" [9]
or that "Perhaps nothing more illuminating can be said than that
it is the relation that holds between experiences when they are
constituents of the same consciousness." [10] But the fact that one
can find no relation suitable to the task seems to indicate that
there is something wrong with the relational conception of the
self, unless one either has an independent argument proving that
the self must be relational or has independent evidence that the
relation in question exists and is indefinable. Otherwise, one is
open to the charge that he is hiding the failure of his concept of
the self behind the term 'indefinable'.[11]

More important for our immediate purposes, it is clear that this
move will not help Hume. As both Ewing and Ayer point out, the
relation between the elements of a single self, even if indefinable,
would have to unite those elements in a far more intimate manner than that that holds between any such element and the elements of other minds. (Ayer uses the phrase "logically necessary.") As Ewing says,

> The relation between different experiences of what we call the
> same self is in any case radically different from the relation be-
> tween members of a mere aggregate like a heap of stones. It is so
> close that they could not conceivably be what they are without be-

9. A. C. Ewing, *The Fundamental Questions of Philosophy* (London, Routledge & Kegan Paul, 1951), p. 115.

10. A. J. Ayer, *The Problem of Knowledge* (Harmondsworth, Penguin Books, 1956), p. 199.

11. Ayer concedes this point in his later book, *The Concept of a Person* (London, Macmillan, 1963), p. 115.

longing to a whole of this particular kind, i.e. a self, while a stone might quite well not belong to a heap at all (*FQP,* 115).

But because Hume denies the existence of such relations and of such involvement in his two theses discussed above, and because his theory of the self is a logical result of these theses, it follows that he cannot fall back on any such relation. Yet, the relations he does admit cannot account for the unity of a single self at any moment, or its identity through time.

One might add a further logical difficulty. In Hume's view, we are to analyze a self into a collection of elements. But how are we to identify the elements that make up a single self except by indicating that they are the impressions of a given self or person? It is obvious that we are involved in a circle. We wish to analyze the concept "self" and the identity of that self into a series of related elements, but we find that the elements themselves can be named only if we re-introduce the supposedly banished concept of self or person. We say the experiences in question (which constitute me) are those that are mine. Such considerations suggest that the concept of self or person is primitive in that all discussion of the self presupposes the concept, with the result that it cannot be defined in other terms.

Let us ask whether this circle is vicious as regards Hume's theory. When writing *The Problem of Knowledge,* Ayer was inclined to think not. He admitted that we can make no sense of speaking of experiences unless we imply that they are the experiences of a person, that is, that they are "owned." In order to understand the term 'experience', you must already understand the term 'person'. But, he argued, the analysis of person and personal identity into a "factual relation between experiences" does not result in a vicious circle because one can know the meaning of 'person' without being able to give an analysis of it. Therefore, Ayer concludes, our *analysis* into experiences can be "informative" even if the meaning of 'experience' seems to derive from that of 'person' (*PK,* 197). Something might have to be an element of a person in order to be an experience, and I might have to know what you mean by 'person' in order to know what you mean by 'experience', whereas it still might turn out that a person can be analyzed into a whole of mutually entailed parts. This is not very convincing, and Ayer himself seems to have had different thoughts in his later work.[12] The circularity occurs because, in the analysis of 'person' in terms of 'experiences', we are forced to employ the very notion of 'person' we claim to be analyzing. It is not merely that we must understand 'person' in order to understand 'experience', for this fact does seem to leave open the question as to what a self is. It might be, for all we know, a whole of mutually entailing experiences. Rather, in trying to say that a person is some grouping of experiences, we find that this notion illicitly implies the notion of person.

It follows that a person cannot be defined in terms of a whole of experiences, for such a whole itself can only be defined in terms of the person whose experiences they are. Thus, Hume's theory of the self does involve a vicious circle, because it tries to define the whole self in terms of one of its "parts." The problem that will concern us later is precisely what Hume's theory does omit that causes the circularity.

In the light of these remarks about Hume, let us consider Ayer's theory of the self in *Language, Truth and Logic*. There he follows Hume's rejection of the substantive ego, his argument being that such an ego is not given in self-consciousness, and if not there then nowhere.[13] It follows that such an ego is a metaphysical entity and that "The considerations which make it necessary, as Berkeley saw, to give a phenomenalist account of material things, make it necessary also, as Berkeley did not see, to give a phenomenalist account of the self" (*LTL*, 126). The self is a "logical construction out of sense experiences."

In addition, Ayer believes his theory to be an improvement on that of Hume. For, whereas Hume could not find the relation that forged a group of perceptions into a single self, Ayer claims to have found the connection "by defining personal identity in terms of bodily identity, and bodily identity is to be defined in terms of the resemblance and continuity of sense-contents" (*LTL*,

---

12. "In the ordinary way, we identify experiences in terms of the persons whose experiences they are; but clearly this will lead to a vicious circle if persons themselves are to be analysed in terms of their experiences" (*CP*, 84).

13. "For all that is involved in self-consciousness is the ability of a self to remember some of its earlier states" (*LTL*, 126).

127). Whose sense-contents? Those of a perceiver or self to whose "sense" history they belong; that is, the sense-experiences that "constitute" a body and, thereby, a self, are not parts of that self but of the self that perceives. To assert anything about a self is simply to "say something about sense experiences" (*LTL,* 128). This does not mean that we must regard others as robots, for in speaking of the consciousness of a person I refer to what I can or might observe, namely, his behavior. As he says, "If I know that an object behaves in every way as a conscious being must, by definition, behave, then I know that it is really conscious. And this is an analytical proposition" (*LTL,* 130). Ayer looks to language to support his theory, for according to him it is self-contradictory in our language to say that a person survived the annihilation of his body.

One wonders if this theory would seem plausible to anyone not committed to defending strict verifiability at all costs. Consider the case of A and B seeing each other. A is to be a logical construction out of sense-data *for B* and B a logical construction *for A*. Are A and B then nothing but logical constructions? If so, who constructs A when B is not around? (Is A a logical construction for himself? If so, who or what is the A who "constructs" the A who is constructed?) If not, then B is something over and above what he is for A, who is limited to his sense-experiences of B for his information about him. But what is this "additional" B, and is it something unobservable? If the sense-experiences that A has of B do not constitute B, what then does constitute B? Are these experiences to be the same as B's body or not? If so, then they constitute B; if not, then who or what is B?

Does A believe that B or B's experiences can be reduced to his own experiences of B? (*LTL,* 130). The suggestion makes no sense at all. B is *what* A experiences and is not something private to A as his experiences are. How could there be sense-experiences in the first place unless there was experience, that is, consciousness? But then it is absurd to say that a self *is* its sense-contents. If it is even so much, it must be something more.

In saying that someone is conscious, I do not mean to refer to any actual or possible behavior on his part, and I know this beyond the strength of any theory to convince me otherwise. Nor is it an analytic proposition that someone acting in a certain way is conscious. I can perfectly well doubt its truth and would do so if confronted with a mechanical man who could act like a human being. Ayer says nothing to show that such doubt is impossible, and we shall see, he stresses this possibility in his criticism of Strawson.

Why is the survival of the body said to be self-contradictory in our language? Ayer himself considered in *The Concept of a Person* that one of the weaknesses of physicalism is that it leads to a necessary denial of immortality, and I think his later view is correct. Man may not survive bodily death, but no one has yet shown that the idea is logically absurd. Ayer holds that the fact that A perceives a certain sense-content is to be "analyzed in terms of the relationship of sense contents to one another, and not in terms of a substantival ego and its mysterious acts" (*LTL*, 122). But has he shown that these are the only alternatives? And, even if they are, what relation does he suggest between my pain and my tickle, which will be the same as what I call *my* awareness of my pain? Any such attempt must presuppose the awareness that it is trying to explain away.

I conclude that Ayer's theory of the self, combining solipsism and phenomenalism in the name of strict verifiability, is a maze of puzzles arising from the confusion of meaning and verification. It solves Hume's problem only at the cost of creating a host of additional ones.

There are two criticisms of Hume that fail to hit the mark. The first might be stated in the way G. E. Moore dealt with Descartes's argument that, for example, you can't know that the object before you is a hand, because you may be dreaming and there may be no physical object before you at all. Moore replied that one might just as easily say, "Because I *know* that this is a hand before me I can be certain that I am not dreaming." His certainty that this thing before him was a hand seemed much stronger than whatever doubts he may have had about whether he was awake. Similarly, why could one not say of Hume's concept of "strict" identity that, because I know that I am the same self I was yesterday and because I am also different from the way I was then, I also know that his concept of strict identity is inadequate to "actual" identity? One would thus simply reverse Hume's contention that because "real" identity must be strict identity, therefore, our sense of our own identity-through-difference must be misleading.

C. A. Campbell has stated just such a position. He says that "Self-consciousness, it must be insisted, is a *fact*, a datum from which we have to *start*" (*SG*, 81). And what is the testimony of self-consciousness? "The self of which we are conscious in self-con-sciousness *is* a subject which in some sense has, rather than is, its different experiences, and is identical with itself throughout them" (*SG*, 82–83). Campbell concludes that "It can hardly be accepted as an irrefutable principle of philosophic criticism that sameness excludes all difference, when it is a datum of self-con-scious experience that it does not" (*SG*, 83). We might agree that we have a sense of self-sameness and that the existence of this sense disproves any theory of the self as merely discrete, not by its mere existence, but by the fact that the discrete theory cannot explain the existence of this sense.

But how does this "sense" either refute Hume's claim that strict identity gives us the "real" sense of 'identical', or give us another standard in its place? After all, this sense of self-sameness must fully be understood before we can rest on it as a datum. And it turns out that Campbell employs the very notion of identity to which he thinks self-consciousness "gives the lie direct." For, he claims, one is aware of oneself as a subject, and this subject is known to be identical in the many experiences it "has." But what does this mean if not that I, the subject, remains the same in Hume's strict sense, although the experiences I have are many and change constantly? The disagreement between Hume and Campbell, then, is over the nature of the self and not over the na-ture of identity. What if, for example, Campbell were willing to admit that there was no element in the self, neither subject nor introspected content, which, over a period of time, remained iden-tical in Hume's strict sense? What would we say then about our sense of self-sameness? If the change of some elements had been slight, we might say something like "Well, I am close enough to being the same so that it seems all right to speak of myself as being the same." I do not think that our reply would be "Despite my total lack of sameness in the strict sense, my self-awareness tells

me that I am the same, and so I must be the same." For what warrant is there that our sense of self-sameness can discern between a
slight change and no change at all? If there is none, I do not see
how we can avoid asking, "How can I truly be the same if nothing at all in the self is exempt from change?"

Hume's concept of identity, then, is not an arbitrary standard
imposed on an experience that rejects it. Rather, it is the standard
we use to understand this experience when we are interested in
the theoretical or philosophical problem of identity. The question
might be put as follows. Once you abandon the strict sense of
identity, what is going to be your standard of identity? By what
principle will you decide when a change is a "change" *to* another
thing and when it is only a change *of* that thing? And if you continue to say that a thing is the same to the extent that it has not
changed, are you not, in fact, still using the strict sense of identity
as your criterion?

A second criticism of Hume, which I find unconvincing, I will
call the "argument from the way we speak." Hume was right in
criticizing those philosophers who created a thing called the "self"
to explain the unity which a mind has despite the changes it undergoes. He was wrong, however, in thinking that out attribution
of identity to things that have changed is a mistake that depends
on the fiction of an underlying "thing," which preserves the identity of the observable thing by not itself changing. As Terence Penelhum points out,[14] Hume really agrees with the basic premise
of the substantialist, namely, that identity is to be found only in
an unchanging thing. Because he finds no substance or unchangeable impression in complex things, he concludes that they cannot
really be identical through time.

But if we go to the way we ordinarily speak of things, a very different picture of identity arises. First, we notice that "Whether we
get one or not depends entirely on what nouns we choose to work
with, and not on the concepts of identity and diversity." [15] Invariance is our standard of identity only with a few kinds of things
(a single note, for example), whereas with other kinds of things

14. Terrence Penelhum, "Hume on Personal Identity," *Philosophical Review, 64*
(October 1955).
15. Ibid., p. 582.

"The words we use to talk about them are words the meanings of which allow us or require us to continue to use them throughout certain changes, though not of course *any* change." [16] There just is no mistake, in most cases, in saying that a thing that has changed is the same thing. For the kind of thing our object is determines the sense of identity appropriate to it, rather than a special sense of identity that in all cases determines whether a thing is one or "really" many. Some things, such as tunes, for example, may be one thing even though they are composed of a succession of distinct notes.

The conclusion is that Hume's theory is said to be the result "of a linguistic error, of a misdescription of the way in which certain words in the language are in fact used." [17] What Hume in fact has done is to give us "The factors governing the use of substantives, and not the *mis*use of the adjective 'same.' " [18] There simply is no paradox in our ordinary ascription of identity to things that change, even if we take an "accurate" view of what we are doing instead of a general or pragmatic view. Therefore, both the "cure" offered by the substantialist and Hume's conclusion that the failure of this cure leaves us saddled with a paradoxical skepticism are wrong, for the "ordinary language user" was in no need of a cure in the first place.

The difficulty with Penelhum's case against Hume is not simply that his argument is unconvincing; I suggest that he has not presented any argument at all. He practices a kind of "linguistic phenomenology," according to which Hume's theory can be refuted by merely pointing out that it is not in accord with ordinary usage. Thus, Penelhum seems to "argue" along the following lines. (1) Hume's theory of identity entails that ordinary usage is paradoxical; (2) but it is not paradoxical; (3) therefore, Hume's theory is wrongheaded. Or, perhaps (1) in Hume's view all ascriptions of identity must be judged according to a single, strict standard; (2) but an analysis of when we actually ascribe identity to things reveals that the standards of identity vary with the thing spoken of; (3) therefore, Hume is wrong.

16. Ibid., pp. 580–81.
17. Ibid., p. 586.
18. Ibid., p. 587.

In general, this approach is not promising. If one wanted to know whether consciousness continues after death, I do not see that the issue could be resolved by referring to what we ordinarily say—even if what we say about immortality had important implications for the very structure of our language. At most, our ordinary speech might be considered a starting point for reflection; it might embody one or more points of view. Similarly, the fact that Hume's theory of identity "would require a complete overhaul of the concepts and syntax of our language" does not prove anything at all about Hume's theory.[19] It does mean that Hume has to produce good reasons for our thinking that there is something fundamentally wrong with ordinary usage, but it does not at all show that such reasons may not be forthcoming.

One suspects that Penelhum reveals his true feelings when he says that he finds it "hard to believe that a mistake lies at the root of so much of our language." [20] Because I do not find this hard to believe, I am not shocked at the distance between Hume and ordinary usage; and unless one can show that our ordinary usage is justified, it is no argument at all to refer to it. (Penelhum seems to assume that it is because he argues from it, but he makes no attempt to show this.)

We commonsensically believe that a thing or person is one at any moment while also being many, but our justification for such beliefs may be confused and logically incoherent. If so, what do we mean when we say that something is the same? Can we find a meaning for 'identity', other than the strict sense, which will allow us to see how a thing can be the same while still being different? If not, then by what principle will we justify our ascriptions of 'same' to that which is different? And if by no principle, is there any way to justify these ascriptions other than by employing our ordinary criteria? Could one be mistaken in one's ascription of identity other than in the sense that he has misapplied one of our ordinary criteria?

There are important issues involved in identity claims. If I am really not the same, no matter what I say, then I am not responsible for my past acts, despite what a law court may rule. Similarly,

19. Ibid., p. 579.
20. Ibid.

if I am really not free, no matter what we ordinarily believe, then I am wrongly punished for my actions. Saying so cannot make it so when it comes to identity, and it may be that all actual ascriptions of identity are arbitrary, because nothing complex is actually identical. They may be just a matter of point of view, or interest, that is, of "saying." In any case, ordinary language embodies a point of view about identity, and I am under no compulsion to accept it until and unless it can be shown to be consistent and convincing.

Consider one example. Penelhum denies that there is anything paradoxical about our ordinary use of 'same'. But how does he know this? Of course, we do not feel that this usage is paradoxical —this is why it is common. Similarly, we do not feel that there is anything peculiar about our use of 'thing'. But then, common sense is not very philosophical. It is perfectly possible that both usages may contain, for reflection, fundamental problems or paradoxes we normally ignore. We ignore them because ordinary usage does well enough by us without having to worry about theoretical problems. We cannot decide the matter simply by applying our ordinary standards of paradox to our ordinary usage, for this is merely to justify one ordinary practice in terms of another, whereas one needs a justification of both practices.

It seems to me that we ascribe oneness or identity to a thing because there is something about the thing that warrants the ascription. A corporation is one entity because there is a certain unity among its parts. But when we come to things in the literal sense, and especially to persons, we feel that "something more" is involved. We feel not only that there is some warrant for calling them one, but that they "really" are identical. It is not just convenience; we so speak because they are one and identical in some literal sense of those words.

The difficulty comes in trying to say what about things and persons makes them one and identical in a way that is radically different from that demanded by our looser uses of these terms. Because Hume could find nothing about things and persons to justify our belief in their identity, he judged identity assertions to be mistaken. He challenges us to find a sense of 'thing' and/or 'person' that will sustain our belief in their unity and identity. Until we do, we are not justified in saying that they are identical merely because we ordinarily say this and, indeed, must say this within the confines of our language. I say this because I cannot rid myself of the question *"How* is it possible that the things we say are the "same" really are so?"

It might be said, finally, that Hume's theory of the self fails because it treats the self as a thing, whereas the self is sui generis and must, therefore, be treated on its own terms. Presumably Hegel's dictum that the self is a subject and not a substance was meant as a warning against this error. And Berkeley echoed this sentiment when he claimed that 'soul' does not stand for an idea but for "The subject of the aforesaid powers . . . which being an agent cannot be like unto, or represented by, any idea whatsoever" (*WGB*, 2, 52–53).

Now it is obvious that selves and things are different in important ways and that, therefore, one must not treat them exactly alike. Bradley's criticism of the use of mechanical concepts in discussing the self illustrates this abhorrence of a "physical" approach to the self. Nevertheless, the ways philosophers have conceived of 'thing', in order to give a coherent account of their identity, are much the same as the approaches to 'self'. It seems also that the problems that continue to crop up in our theories about 'thing' are those we face in our concepts of 'self'.[21] If this be so, Hume's theory of the self may fail not merely because it treats the self as a thing, but, rather, because the concept of 'thing' that he used is inadequate to both 'thing' and 'self'.

How, then have philosophers conceived of things, and what can we say about these theories? I will attempt to summarize Bradley's discussion of this problem in *Appearance and Reality*. We might conceive of things as groups of related sense-data. And as Bradley says,

> Against its opponents Phenomenalism would urge, What else exists? 'Show me anything real,' it would argue, 'and I will show you

21. Because of my awareness that a thought is *mine* and that, in memory, it was *I* who once liked the Yankees, it seems reasonable initially to say that there are better reasons for believing in an ego that is more than it states than there are for believing in a thing that is more than its qualities. Whether this is actually the case is something we shall discuss later on.

mere presentation; more is not to be discovered, and really more is meaningless. Things and selves are not unities in any sense whatever, except as given collections or arrangements of such presented elements' (*AR*, 105).

But such a view must answer the following objections. How do the relations and the elements come "together" to form a single thing? How will phenomenalism account for the reality of the past and future? How can it account for change? Change involves identity; there must be something that changes. Yet, what could this "something" be for phenomenalism, this thing that is the "same throughout diversity"? If phenomenalism is to be a complete account of things, how will it account for its own existence or for that of theories that introduce other kinds of unity? Phenomenalism itself is a unity in a sense not allowed for within the theory.

So we give up the "empirical" approach to things and try the "metaphysical." The "thing" is to be "other" than its qualities, and "out of time," to give "unity" to those qualities and to form an identical core throughout change. The qualities are the mere appearance of the thing, whereas the thing-in-itself is the unknowable reality, beyond the corrosive touch of change. Such a view is hopeless. First, it cannot account for change any more than phenomenalism can, for, in its view, things never change. Yet, change is the change of things. If one admits a relation between the "thing" and its "qualities," the thing must be affected by the alteration of the qualities. But if there be no relation, how can these be the qualities *of* the thing? Second, it is as internally inconsistent as phenomenalism, for we claim to know about the unknowable. As Bradley says, "It would be much as if we said, 'since all my faculties are totally confined to my garden, I cannot tell if the roses next door are in flower' " (*AR*, 111).

Will the distinction of primary and secondary qualities give us a coherent view of things? It hardly seems so. The arguments that show that secondary qualities exist only as effects in us—as Berkeley has shown—show the same for primary qualities. If the extended is to be the same as the real, then how will we explain the existence of the secondary qualities? The primary qualities are never given by themselves and, in fact, "Without secondary quality extension is not conceivable—it is the violent abstraction of one aspect from the rest—a fiction which, forgetting itself, takes a ghost for solid reality" (*AR*, 13–14).

We conclude that to be a thing at all, something must exist for more than the present moment, although Bradley points out that we are unclear whether rainbows, waterfalls, and flashes of lightning should be called "things" or even whether something must be spatial in order to be a "thing." This means that a thing "to be at all, must be the same after change, and the change must, to some extent, be predicated of the thing" (*AR*, 62). Succession is essential to 'thing', and succession involves both permanence and change. And the identity of a thing lies in its character. If a "thing" changes, there is something that is the same before and after the change. And what is the same is some character, some content to which we appeal if there is doubt about the sameness of the thing.

The fact that the sameness of a thing lies in its character has two important results for Bradley. First, it means that a thing is "ideal," not "real," and that the identity of a thing is a matter of one's point of view and not of some inherent feature or quality of the thing itself. To be real, a thing must be a unity of content and existence, of "what" and "that." But "Existence is given only in presentation" (*AR*, 62), whereas what we call "one thing" necessarily extends beyond presentation. Thus, a "thing" cannot be real, for it lacks (in part) one of the elements of reality—existence. A "thing" is a theory, an interpretation, we make about what is given, and as such it is an abstraction, by which we extend part of what is given (the content) into the past, constructing something we ordinarily take to be a real element in the world. But, Bradley argues, abstractions of whatever kind and however useful are not "real"; only the concrete is "real." Thing-ness is a category, and reality is not a "ballet of bloodless categories." There is no theme more pervasive in Bradley's philosophy than that in ordinary life we mistake our interpretations of experience for experience itself.

Second, what identical character of a thing guarantees its identity? One might reply, "Whatever is essential to the thing." But "essences" are relative to one's point of view: "It is often impossible to reply when we are asked if an object is really the same—You must go on to mention the point or the particular respect of which you are thinking" (*AR*, 63). In general, to be the same a thing must continually exist and have some "qualitative sameness." We may find this sameness in shape, size, color, material substance, purpose, and so on, and there are cases, such as Sir John Cutler's silk stockings, in which we have no principle at all of sameness. If Cimabue's *Crucifixion,* severely damaged in the flooding of Florence, were restored, would it be the same picture or not? We are free to say what we like because our ordinary notion of a thing is worthless in this case. Bradley insists that the arbitrariness by which we decide that something is one thing, and the abstractions implied in relying on the character of a thing to guarantee its identity, yield the conclusion that "things" are appearance and not reality.

A Possible Compromise with Hume

Before proceeding to our second group of theories of the self, there is an intermediate stage that is worth mentioning. Imagine someone who is sympathetic with Hume's attempt to define the self in terms of what he could "stumble on," perhaps because he thinks that any other view will involve the introduction of obnoxious metaphysical entities. Yet, at the same time, he thinks of the self in a more commonsense way than Hume does and shares no belief in atomic impressions. Such a person might say,

> When I wonder what kind of a person I am, or when a friend feels that he knows me, we both seem to be concerned with whatever makes me the person I am. It is natural to interpret this "something" as those features of my mind that "comprise" me. I must then identify precisely which features of my mind *are me*. If we take the self in this commonsense way, perhaps we shall be able to find my "self" within that "stream" of experiences we say are my experiences.

On a commonsense level, is that not how we think of the self? Our friend is the person with the bad temper, conservative political views, an interest in sports, and so forth. Without these characteristics, he would not be the person he is, and, therefore, he *is* those very features. And this is not merely the view of the common man. Philosophers have taken it over, formalized it, and presented it as a true account of the self. For example, C. J. Ducasse states that "a mind, thus, is literally a society of semi-independent, semi-interdependent role-selves." [22] He compares the self to a symphony or a rope, that is, to a whole of "intuitions" that are distinguishable but that interpenetrate with one another. The self "has" its experiences only in the sense that a chariot "has" its parts; the whole, which is nothing more than the parts "in a certain relation to one another," "has" the parts (*NMD*, 414). Alternatively, the self is said to be the "cumulative total" of its experiences, or to be its experiences and activities.[23]

Can such views give us what we mean by the term 'self'? Consider the alternatives. In wondering what my friend is really like, I might want to identify him with the totality of what is "in his mind" at the moment I am concerned about him. (John is the person who is now feeling pain, wishing he were in a warmer place, and so forth.) Clearly, this is not what we mean by John's self, even if we have correctly described the "contents" of his mind, for the self we "mean" exists beyond the present moment. Perhaps, then, the self is the totality of experiences that Bradley calls "the man's mere history." But, if so, why should we call this the history of *one* self? What is there about the experiences so different at different times that makes them the elements of *one* self? It is hopeless to seek a relation between the elements that will unify them, and we see that in speaking of the history of a person we presuppose a notion of selfhood not reducible to any set of elements. The circularity involved in the quoted passages above is obvious and destructive.

As another alternative, 'self' could mean the "constant average mass," those features that are usual or ordinary about a person. (When we name John's tendencies or dispositions, we have said what John is.) The self will then include a man's regular behav-

22. C. J. Ducasse, *Nature, Mind and Death* (LaSalle, Open Court, 1951), p. 413.

23. These views are expressed, respectively, in Duane H. Whittier, "Causality and the Self," *The Monist*, 49 (April 1965), 291, and Rem B. Edwards, "Agency without a Substantive Self," *The Monist*, 49 (April 1965), 274.

ior and even those elements of the environment essential to a man's average self. Bradley raises two objections to this view. It makes the self dependent on a changing world, whereas "A man's true self . . . cannot depend on his relations to that which fluctuates" (AR, 67). As Bradley had said earlier,

> "We assume that a thing must be self-consistent and self-dependent. It either has a quality or has not got it. And, if it has it, it cannot have it only sometimes, and merely in this or that relation" (AR, 9).

We have not yet found the "me," that "thing" that remains the same throughout change and that is not a mere result of his environment. Second, there may be no average self over all, and we have no way of combining the average selves of different periods, into a single self. Perhaps the unified self lies in some essential content. But either the essential elements change, and, Bradley urges, it seems impossible to find anything within the self that time and environment will not alter, or the essence remains the same no matter what happens. But Bradley scornfully replies, "this wretched fraction and poor atom, too mean to be in danger —do you mean to tell me that this bare remnant is really the self?" (AR, 69). If in desperation one tries to find the self in a simple, unchanging monad, he may find an unchanging element, but it "will be the man's self about as much as his star (if he has one) which looks down from above and cares not when *he* perishes" (AR, 74).

In sum, this way of defining the self seems unable to escape from either of two extremes. If we locate the self in any observable content, it will change; and if it changes it cannot be one self. But if we locate the self in something unchanging, we also seem to have missed the self, for our monad will have no connection with what we take to be ourselves. Unhappily, the possible compromises fail to avoid these extremes. This suggests that a new approach to the self is required.

12

The Continuous Self

The theories grouped under this heading share two features that differentiate them from Hume's view of the self. First, there is a common feeling against Hume's atomism, partly because it does not seem to be based on introspective data and partly because it leads to insoluble difficulties about personal identity. A self composed of discrete units is to be replaced by a self that is more or less continuous. Second, there is agreement that Hume's attempt to reduce the self to an object, known in introspection, is fundamentally mistaken. The self, at least, must be conceived as a subject as well as an object if we are to explain the role of the self as knower. Third, there is general agreement that both continuity and the subject must be provided for within the bounds of experience. There must be no appeal to entities incapable of being observed, for talk about such entities is meaningless, and we have no need for them in an adequate theory of the self. But here the basis of agreement ends. What kind of continuity does the self require? How are we to provide for it? What kind of a subject is the self? Can the self ever be an object? The answers to these questions are what distinguish from one another the specific theories of the group I call the "continuous self."

I

Samuel Alexander distinguishes three meanings of 'self': the self as embodied, the inner self, and the personality. The first I refer to when I make a direct reference to my own body ("I have a cold" is Alexander's example); the second is referred to when I speak primarily of my consciousness, although even here I cannot

avoid, Alexander claims, an indirect reference to my body ("I dislike grading exams"); the third is the "persistent, stable, orga-
nized set of habits of action and thought and feeling by which I
am to be judged." [1] I speak of my self as personality when I say, "I
was not myself when I told that lie."

Now we can say that the inner self is a subject, and we can say
that it is not an ego "to which objects are presented," for it is not
an "unknown something." Rather, it is "empirical through and
through." Why do we refer to this self as a subject? "The subject
itself . . . is rightly called 'I' because it is not an object experienced, but an experiencing experienced." [2] And Alexander identifies this subject with "consciousness." As to how we know or experience this subject, which is never an object, never a "presentation," "It is enjoyed or suffered, but it is not revealed to itself, it
is not contemplated." [3] This consciousness-as-subject consists of
"certain conscious acts, which become the subject-matter of
psychology." [4] The subject is complex at any one moment, but "it
is also continuous from moment to moment of its life. As such, it
has substantial existence, for like other substances it is continuous
in its changes." [5] And, Alexander adds, "We are aware of ourselves as the continuity of our changing selves," and beyond this
continuous stream "there is for us no other self of which we can
say anything whatever." [6] Last, a mental act is the act of a certain
mind "because that act is continuous . . . with contemporaneous
acts and with preceding and succeeding ones." [7]

As an account of the self-as-subject, this theory has its inadequacies, although, in stressing the self as "that which experiences"
rather than as a mere object of awareness, Alexander has ad-
vanced beyond Hume's account. This advance is facilitated by Alexander's distinction between "enjoying" and "contemplating," a
distinction that makes it reasonable that a subject can be known

1. Samuel Alexander, "Self as Subject and as Person," *Aristotelian Society Proceedings*, n.s., *10* (1910–11), 3.
2. Ibid., p. 9.
3. Ibid., p. 9.
4. Ibid., p. 6.
5. Ibid., p. 6.
6. Ibid., pp. 17–18 and 25, respectively.
7. Ibid., p. 6.

without being "stumbled on" introspectively. Alexander rejects
the ego because it is an unobservable, but this rejection raises
four questions in relation to his own theory: Is the ego unobservable? If it is, is this a sound reason for rejecting it? Are Alexander's
acts any more observable than the ego he rejects? Are there good
reasons for thinking that Alexander's theory requires him to believe in an ego?

As Ewing has said, "It is at least arguable that we are immediately aware in introspection of a pure Ego over and above its experiences . . ." (*FQP*, 131). It is hard to argue about self-reports,
but it seems as reasonable to claim that I "enjoy" an "I" that
wishes, hopes, and thinks as it is to claim that I "enjoy" these activities themselves. Certainly, the matter is not clearly in Alexander's favor. Nor has Alexander avoided Hume's inability to show
that the ego does not exist, for the lack of immediate awareness or
"enjoyment" of an ego does not prove that there is no such thing.
An ego is not an act and, therefore, need not be known as acts are
known. Certainly, no observation can decide the question, and Alexander provides no proof that the two must be known in the
same way. Indeed, how could he do so without in the very act
transcending the data provided in "enjoyment?" His decision to
limit himself to these data is, therefore, arbitrary and proves nothing about the unreality of the ego.

It might well be argued that, despite his claims to the contrary,
Alexander's theory is as unempirical as any ego-theory and that
his mental acts are theoretical entities introduced to explain the
fact that we can err, know, and so on. A defender of mental acts
has gone so far as to say that they are inferred through their effects and not immediately known.[8] Are mental acts given? The
following description by Blanshard is reasonably close to what
one feels when desiring something: "I seem to catch faint stirrings
in the contemplation, and an unmistakable feeling of longing.
But I cannot identify, as distinct from these, any *act* of desire"
(*NT, 1,* 397). What can be named always seems to fall on the
side of some content, and soon one wonders if one has missed

8. James Ward, *Psychological Principles* (Cambridge, The University Press, 1920),
p. 58.

something or if there was nothing there to miss. But if mental acts are known only by inference, if they are theoretical entities that one needs in order to make sense of the given facts, then they have no observational advantage over the ego. Alexander's claim reduces to the assertion that whereas we need mental acts to give a satisfactory account of a self and its experiences, we need nothing more to do so.

It seems clear to me that Alexander's theory of the self is incomplete unless he introduces something to play the role of an ego. Consider the following points. When I experience myself desiring something, what I "enjoy" is that I am desiring something. And what do we mean when we say that an act is *my* act? According to Alexander we mean that the "act is continuous . . . with contemporaneous acts and with preceding and succeeding ones." This will not do for reasons we have discussed before. With *which* contemporaneous and succeeding acts is my present act continuous? With mine, of course. But then to say that an act is mine cannot mean that it is continuous with other acts (my acts?), for to make sense of this claim we must reintroduce the "I" that we are supposedly explaining. And, second, what kind of continuity must any act have with these others in order that they be parts of the same self? Neither spatial, nor temporal, nor causal continuity will do, and one awaits in vain a kind of continuity that will suffice.

In any case, continuity is not enough for self-identity. What we call the history of a single self could just as well be called the history of many selves continuously evolving from one another. Continuity may be necessary for self-identity, but it is not sufficient for it.

According to Alexander, "We are aware of ourselves as the continuity of our changing selves." How are we to explain this awareness of a "continuous stream"? Only, it seems, if there is something over and above the stream that watches it "pass by," and this something seems to be an ego. Alexander must face Ewing's question: "Thoughts are only events, but could a mere series of events know anything?" (*FQP*, 112). Then he must explain how a merely continuous stream could be aware of itself as such. It appears that to introduce the concepts of 'subject' and 'continuity' into our account of the self does not answer many basic questions that arise with Hume's theory.

II

If one is quite serious about the sharp distinction between consciousness and object (the mind or self being identified with consciousness) and limiting one's conception of the self to what is immediately given, the results can be very startling indeed. In *The Transcendence of the Ego,* Sartre develops a theory of the self based on both attitudes.[9]

At the risk of oversimplifying what is an obscure work, let me summarize his view. There is no ego "in" or "behind" consciousness, for two reasons: If we re-create our state of mind when we are absorbed in some object, "There is no doubt about the result: while I was reading, there was consciousness *of* the book, *of* the heroes of the novel, but the I was not inhabiting this consciousness" (*TE,* 46–47). The ego is not needed to provide either unity or individuality to our self. Unity is provided by consciousness itself. Sartre says, "The object is transcendent to the consciousnesses which grasp it, and it is in the object that the unity of the consciousnesses is found" (*TE,* 38). And, he adds, "It is consciousness which unifies itself concretely, by a play of 'transversal' intentionalities which are concrete and real retentions of past consciousnesses. Thus consciousness refers perpetually to itself" (*TE,* 39). Individuality is also provided by consciousness. In Sartre's words,

> Consciousness (like Spinoza's substance) can be limited only by itself. Thus, it constitutes a synthetic and individual totality entirely isolated from other totalities of the same type, and the I can evidently be only an *expression* (rather than a condition) of this incommunicability and inwardness of consciousnesses (*TE,* 39–40).

If there were an ego, it would change the character of consciousness as it is given to itself. Consciousness knows itself unre-

9. Jean Paul Sartre, *The Transcendence of the Ego,* trans. Forrest Williams and Robert Kirkpatrick (New York, The Noonday Press, 1957).

flectively or with an "absolute inwardness." That is, when I am aware of my consciousness in reading a book, I am not an object to myself as the book is. In self-awareness, I find consciousness to be "clear and lucid, all lightness, all translucence." An ego would divide self-consciousness into a subject and an object and would be like an "opaque blade" in our self-awareness (*TE*, 40–42). It follows that our unreflected consciousness is impersonal (without an "I"), is "nothing" (being "transparent," it can have no content), and is an "impersonal spontaneity." [10]

Because consciousness is an "impersonal spontaneity"—is not restricted to the capacities of an ego—it is the continual "cause of itself." Nothing can affect it, and it is, therefore, not bound in any way by its past. As Sartre says, "Thus each instant of our conscious life reveals to us a creation *ex nihilo*. Not a new *arrangement*, but a new *existence*" (*TE*, 98–99). When we realize the limitless possibilities before consciousness, we may experience the "vertigo of possibility" before us and develop a "dread" of ourselves. Sartre describes the "genuine" spontaneity of consciousness, in contrast to the "bastard" spontaneity of the ego (so-called because the ego is an object and must, therefore, in part be passive) as "beyond freedom"; and he clearly intends to imply that "genuine" spontaneity guarantees "absolute" freedom. All that one can say, apparently, is that consciousness "is what it produces and can be nothing else" (*TE*, 79) and that it is "beyond contemplation" because it cannot be an object of awareness.

An ego, then, is an object apprehended and constituted by reflective consciousness, a "locus of unity" constituted *"in a direction contrary* to that actually taken by the production: *really* consciousnesses are first" (*TE*, 81). Sartre adds that the ego is not something that "underlies" and "supports" its states. Rather, it is the "spontaneous, transcendent unification of our states and our actions" and "the infinite totality of states and of actions which is never reducible to *an* action or to *a* state" (*TE*, 76, 74). Thus,

10. Because consciousness is a contentless intentionality, Sartre concludes that any fact about me is as directly observable and knowable as are physical objects. Sartre rejects the privacy of mental states and the argument from analogy when he says, "Peter's *me* is accessible to my intuition as well as to Peter's intuition . . ." (*TE*, 96).

the predicates we affirm of ourselves are merely qualities considered apart from the totality that is ourself. When we reflect on
our consciousness, the ego appears to be inseparable from, and
presupposed in, every mental act. Sartre expresses this by saying
that the ego appears at the "horizon" of its states. We never see it
directly, but only as that that is "beyond" any state or states
where we reflect on ourselves. As Sartre places the ego, it is "to
psychical objects what the World is to things," which is another
way of saying that the ego "is not the owner of consciousness; it
is the object of consciousness" (*TE*, 75, 97).

This theory is designed to fit a certain general philosophical
stance, and, thus, although filled with interesting insights, it is not
much stronger than apologetics usually are. I would question the
method, the claims made for consciousness and the ego, and the
implications of the theory.

Consider Sartre's method. Why does he think that, because I can
find no ego in my awareness of a moment ago when I was absorbed in reading, I am entitled to conclude that there is no ego
there? If I am absorbed in my thoughts and do not notice you
passing me on the street, I do not feel obliged to deny that you
were there. In fact, here is precisely a case in which I can infer
nothing from my lack of awareness. Conversely, if I consciously
look for something and cannot find it, in some circumstances I
may conclude that it is not there. Why is not the same thing true
of my awareness of an ego? Why is it said that when I reflect I distort the true character of my unreflective consciousness, thus priz-
ing inattention over attention? The only reason I can find is that
Sartre is wedded to the so-called phenomenological method.
But, then, the above examples show the absurdity of the method,
thus freeing us from the assumption that reflective consciousness
is "creative."

Regarding consciousness, I can make no sense of Sartre's claim
of something that is a "nothing" because everything is "outside"
it, or an "absolute spontaneity." What Sartre calls the "transcendental field," that is, consciousness "purified of all ego-logical
structures," is by necessity without quality. But if something has
no qualities, is it not exactly nothing, not a special kind of "something" referred to metaphysically as nothing, but literally nothing

at all? It seems to me that, in order to be spontaneous, consciousness must be something more. It must be some kind of entity that
is spontaneous, as persons or events are sometimes said to be. Similarly, it is just a contradiction to say that consciousness, because
of its "genuine" spontaneity, *"is* what it produces." To be able to
"produce" anything it must be more than the result, and as this
"something more," it must have a structure, a nature, a character.

It can be said that Sartre has made a rather simple error in describing consciousness. Because he finds it impossible to speak of
intending apart from the thing intended, he thinks that he is onto
some special, characterless kind of thing. But if you try to isolate
consciousness in this way, it is not surprising that your residue
seems to have wonderful powers and to be absolutely transparent,
for you have nothing at all. You have tried to contemplate in isolation that that cannot be isolated, and the result is that your
claims about it make no sense. The existentialist discussion of
existence presents a similar case. *It* is thought to be mysterious
and beyond reason, but one wonders if the "that" simply is not
abstractable from the "what." [11]

Sartre's remarks about the ego fall prey to the same objections
that ruin Hume's and Alexander's approaches to the self. Many
thoughts about one thing may in some sense bring unity to them,
but they in no way provide the unity we assert when we say that
these are the thoughts of the same self. Similarly, which past consciousnesses are unified when consciousness refers to itself? Presumably those that were *mine* when they occurred. If we accept
these criticisms, we can dispense with two very difficult Sartrean
notions, that of an impersonal consciousness and that of consciousness unifying itself. If *"really* consciousnesses are first," then
we are confronted again with Hume's problems of unowned ideas
and a plurality that can come to have an awareness of itself as
unified. Concerning privacy, one can only boggle at Sartre's
claims. Does he merely mean that Paul may know as well as Peter
(or better) that Peter hates some person? If so, who denies it? But
how can Paul's knowledge of Peter's consciousness be said to be
"intuitional?" And is everything about Peter known with as much
certainty by Paul as by Peter himself? Is Peter's pain, for in-

11. See Bradley's remarks on the 'this' in relation to content (*AR*, 203–05).

stance? It seems that Sartre's radical separation between consciousness and its objects compels him to hold that even sensations are not mental and that all "mental content" is as common property as physical objects are ordinarily thought to be.

Finally, the theory leads to unacceptable results. If at each moment I was (and not merely appeared to myself to be) a creation from nothing, then responsibility seems doubly condemned. On the one hand, there is no reason for my present self to be considered as identical with my past self. As a new creation, I am new and not involved in "my" past. But then I can hardly be held responsible for what "I" have done in the past. On the other hand, whatever I now do comes from nowhere, has no roots in "my" character. It is merely a fortuitous twist of fate that I am now characterized by a certain mental state, and I cannot be responsible for acts that are not mine. Sartre has pushed freedom so far that it is indistinguishable from chance, and, in an Heglian way, chance removes responsibility as surely as does the hardest determinism. Yet, I have argued, no theory can win our assent that fails to do justice to our belief that a man is responsible for his actions, once certain obvious exceptions have been noted.

III

Assume now that one were sympathetic with Alexander's attempt to keep his concept of the self within the bounds of observation and that, as with Alexander, this implied a rejection of both Humean atomism and the belief in a pure ego. Assume at the same time, however, that the arguments against Hume and Alexander, based on the claim that there must be a center, an "owner," for the elements that comprise a self, are convincing. The problem for such a position would remain: How can one provide for the unity, identity, and self-consciousness of a self without postulating meaningless, metaphysical souls or egos? How can one find a center for the self within experience?

When William James came to write about the self in his *Principles of Psychology*,[12] he was faced with just this problem. He begins with what seem to him to be two indisputable facts. When we are conscious of our "empirical self," what we are conscious of

12. William James, *The Principles of Psychology* (2 vols. New York, Dover, 1950).

can best be described as a "stream" because its fundamental characteristic is continuous change (*PP, 1,* 239). "Absolute insulation, irreducible pluralism, is the law. It seems as if the elementary psychic fact were not *thought* or *this thought* or *that thought,* but *my thought,* every thought being owned" (*PP,* 226). James's problem is to define the ownership of each "stream" and the self-identity that goes with it within the limitations his empiricist outlook permits. This last requirement means that he must explain "ownership" within the data the stream of consciousness provides.

James notes that we can distinguish within the stream a central core that is "felt by all men as a sort of innermost centre within the circle . . . constituted by the subjective life as a whole." Compared with the rest of consciousness, this central core seems permanent, the "active element in all consciousness," that which "presides" over our sensations and which "disowns" them and to which pleasure and pain "speak" (*PP,* 297–98). In short, "It is something with which we also have direct sensible acquaintance, and which is as fully present at any moment of consciousness in which it *is* present, as in a whole lifetime of such moments" (*PP,* 299). This sounds very like the subject that seems an essential part of selfhood. And, James continues, when one tries to describe what this center feels like, all he can say is that it "is found to consist mainly of the collection of these peculiar motions in the head or between the head and throat" (*PP,* 301). Thus, he ties our self-awareness to our awareness of our body in a strikingly intimate manner. Is there anything else that we can observe about ourselves, asks James? No, there are just the two parts of the subjective stream, the "inner" self and the "outer" not-self.

How, then, are we to account for the fact that these elements of the stream are "owned" as parts of a single self? James's answer is that the thinker, or "I," can be found within the stream itself. For things to be related, as they are at any moment of consciousness, there must be a unity of consciousness, which James calls a pulse of thought, or merely the thought. The unity of this thought is said to be "indecomposable" because it is not "composed of parts" (*PP,* 371, 363), but the thought ceases to exist after a moment and is replaced by another thought and so on. This thought is our thinker, our "owner."

This view attracts James for at least three reasons. First, the thought so conceived is a genuine subject in that it "is never an object in its own hands" (*PP*, 340). James agrees with Comte that the knower and the known can never be identical. Second, the subject, although unknown as long as it is a subject, is eminently knowable, for the immediately subsequent thought can make it an object of reflection and does so in introspection and memory. James's subject is no mysterious entity that is always behind the scenes, never in front of the camera. Third, we have not been forced to admit that our subject is a substantial entity that never changes and, perhaps, is immortal. In effect, we have allowed our "thought" to have just the kind and length of existence required by the facts. Hypotheses about the soul are said to explain nothing, and Kant's transcendental subject is only a " 'cheap and nasty' edition of the soul," whereas "the Ego is simply *nothing*: as ineffectual and windy an abortion as Philosophy can show" (*PP*, 365).

With such a concept of the self, how will James handle the problem of self-identity? It is obvious that there can be no substantial identity between the elements of any given stream of thought, but, James argues, we do not need this to account for personal identity. What, he asks, distinguishes for me a thought of mine from a thought of yours? My thoughts have a "warmth and intimacy" for me that your thoughts do not. Similarly, "Remembrance is like direct feeling; its object is suffused with a warmth and intimacy to which no object of mere conception ever attains" (*PP*, 239). Thus, I can be certain that what has warmth and intimacy now is mine and what I recall with the same feeling was a state of mine. For, as James says, the only past selves that can be felt warmly by me are those that were felt warmly by me when they existed. This feeling makes us claim a certain past as ours, and James adds that the continuity of the past self with the present self and the similarity of our past and present encourages us even more to call "one" what dissimilarity and discontinuity respectively might lead us to think of as many. James is quite clear that self-identity so conceived is very limited:

> The past and present selves compared are the same just so far as they *are* the same, and no farther . . . And if from the one point

of view they are one self, from others they are as truly not one but many selves (*PP, 335*).

How does this apply to James's notion that the thought is the thinker? Each thought passes away as another begins. Because there is no break in continuity, the present thought "appropriates" the thoughts that have preceded it; it inherits its "title" and "owns" it. In James's words, "Each Thought is thus born an owner, and dies owned, transmitting whatever it realized as its Self to its own later proprietor" (*PP, 339*). Each pulse is distinct from every other pulse, but they are so arranged that they form a single self.

James explains his theory with the aid of two analogies, whose meaning it is important to grasp if we are to understand his claims. He says that the present thought "is the actual focus of accretion; the hook from which the chain of past selves dangles, planted firmly in the Present, which alone passes for real, and thus keeping the chain from being a purely ideal thing" (*PP,* 340–41). The present "hook" will soon become an object of awareness for another hook, and so on. Alternatively, the present pulse of thought is said to be a "herdsman" and the feeling of warmth the "herd mark." Our past selves play the role of the cattle, and it is said that we assimilate our past selves to one another and to our present self "much as out of a herd of cattle let loose for the winter on some wide western prairie the owner picks out and sorts together when the time for the round-up comes in the spring, all the beasts on which he finds his own particular brand" (*PP, 333–34*). James adds that

> Each brand, so far, is the mark, or cause of our knowing, that certain things belong together. But if the brand is the *ratio cognoscendi* of the belonging, the belonging, in the case of the herd, is in turn the *ratio existendi* of the brand. No beast would be so branded unless he belonged to the owner of the herd. They are not his because they are branded; they are branded because they are his (*PP, 337*).

James rightly says that common sense demands that self-identity be based on a "real belonging to a real Owner" and not merely on a grouping of similar or continuous parts. In fact, the strength of his theory, he believes, as against Hume's theory, is that in it "the medium is fully assigned" in terms of the present thought, which is "not among the things collected, but superior to them all" (*PP*, 338). There is a real "I" and not the imaginary center of a herd. To complete the analogy, as many consecutive herdsmen may inherit the title to the same cattle, so each thought inherits the title to the selves which are past.

Before commenting on James's theory, I must make an initial point. James does not rule out the possibility that we might want to accept an ego "on *general speculative grounds*" (*PP*, 370 n.), because his theory is intended merely for the psychologist, to give him a model for his investigations. Thus, when I criticize James on general grounds, it may be said that I am ignoring the explicit intent of the theory. But although James says that he is only attempting this limited task, he, in fact, does more. He claims that the facts require no thinker beyond his thought, and this seems to mean that his theory is adequate to the facts. Yet, is that not the "general speculative" criterion for theoretical adequacy? Nobody would believe in the soul or the ego if he felt it explained nothing. So the question is: Does James's theory account for all the facts? I take it that this is what we want to know about any theory.

My fundamental criticism of James's theory is that it is an unstable compromise between two conflicting desires: the desire to limit a theory strictly to observables and the desire to account for all the facts. On the one hand, James's theory is impossible to verify, for it introduces an entity, the passing thought, which in its function as subject can never be observed. Of course, James says, I can be introspectively aware of my state of mind of a moment ago, but not of my immediate state of mind. Therefore, the hypothesis that it has an "indecomposable unity" now can never be established by observation. Similarly, the realist's claim that a chair exists unperceived in the room now cannot be proved by walking in and looking at the chair. Nor does my retrospective awareness show by itself that it is probable that my present self has no other unity than that of the thought.

On the other hand, if James is willing to introduce the passing thought to unify one's experiences, why not introduce an ego? In fact, the incoherence of James's doctrine suggests that what called for a thinker initially calls for more of a thinker than James has provided. The doctrine is incoherent in several ways. It makes no sense to speak of a thought being a thinker. Thoughts are activities of thinkers; perhaps they are manifestations of a thinker, but they are not the thinker himself. And, of course, James constantly reveals this by unknowingly appealing to a sense of self far different from that allowed in his theory. He says that "The past thought of Peter is appropriated by the present Peter alone" (*PP*, 238) and that the only past selves that can now be felt with warmth and intimacy are those that were felt this way in the past.

James's notion of appropriating makes no sense unless the present Peter is identical with the past Peter and unless this identity forms the reason for my appropriating just these experiences as mine. In fact, James nowhere attempts to explain what keeps one stream of consciousness within its banks and makes it impossible for it to "overflow" into another "stream," and his theory provides no reason why this should not happen. We must ask: Felt warmly by whom? Every experience is owned, every experience is (or can be) felt warmly by someone, but I remember only certain experiences. Which ones? Those that *I* felt warmly. But then there must be an identity between the present and past "I," and this is impossible in James's theory. James uses our ordinary ways of speaking of the self alongside his very unordinary theory of the self. The result is that his theory may seem less absurd than it is unless we notice the illicit reference to a sense of self for which the theory cannot account.

James appeals to common sense to support his claim that all experiences must be "owned," in opposition to a Humean, nonownership view. But such an appeal cuts two ways. Commonsense also holds that my present and past selves are identical, that I am an "indecomposable unity," at least throughout my life. It holds, further, that I am that that thinks and desires, and *not* a pulse of thought. From the point of view of common sense, James fails to provide either an owner for my present experiences or even the semblance of an owner for my past states, because for common sense I do not "own" my past as I might own an object whose title I have inherited. Such an object becomes mine now, whereas my past was mine then. Nor can James's theory give a meaning to the commonsense belief that I change as well as remain the same. If I am the present thought, then I do not change. One self continuously succeeds another, but no self changes because there is nothing in James's "stream" that could change. Perhaps most importantly, James's theory completely fails to explain our common notions about responsibility. Pulses of thought cannot act; only I can act, and because each pulse of thought is distinct from every other pulse, there is no "self" that now could be responsible for what a past self has done.[13]

What of James's account of personal identity? His analogies with the hook and the herder seem to show that there is no single self. We may feel that we are the same as some past, remembered self, but in James's theory, this feeling must be false. The hook is distinct from the chain it supports, and each successive herder is another being who inherits the title to his herd. Certainly, a herder would realize his distinctness from his inheritance, but, apparently, for James the present pulse of thought cannot see its difference from the past it owns. It is cruelly deceived. James admits willingly that, in his theory, it is a matter of one's point of view whether one calls the series of thoughts one or many. But such latitude is certainly not in accord with common sense, and, in addition, one looks in vain for any significant sense in which my present and past selves can be said to be the same.[14]

Second, James's discussion of "warmth and intimacy" is most confusing. He speaks, at times, as if they were a criterion of self-identity (when he says that it is a "herd mark"), whereas, at other times, he speaks as if such criteria were the "glue" that make a series of discrete thoughts into one self. Neither view is adequate. The same examples show equally that our warm feelings cannot be our test of self-identity and that self-identity cannot consist in them. Of course, as James points out, we lose the feeling of self-

13. Interestingly, James mentions responsibility as an argument for a soul substance, but he passes over it rather quickly (*PP,* 349).

14. It has been said that James "replaced the atoms of Hume, Taine, and Mach by his own psychical molecules, which, though having a larger temporal span, remained essentially as external to each other as the elements of the associationistic 'bundle theory.' " Milic Capek, "The Reappearance of the Self in the Last Philosophy of William James," *Philosophical Review, 62* (October 1953), 535.

identity when we cannot read ourselves back into our past, but this is irrelevant to the judgments we make about self-identity. Warmth and intimacy are too restricted to define self-identity or to serve as its criteria. Sometimes, we can remember with no warmth, and sometimes, we cannot remember at all, yet we assert self-identity all the same. At other times, we can feel warmly about what was not ours at all.[15] But no one claims that this makes us the same or even that it is a discovery of our real past. Instead, we say the person is mad or has a very lively imagination. It seems to me that James was wrong both in claiming that warm feelings tell us unerringly about self-identity and that being self-identical was a necessary condition for feeling warmly about a past self.

Finally, James speaks of continuity and similarity as the two features that *"constitute(s) the real and verifiable personal identity which we feel"* (*PP*, *1*, 336). But as we have seen, such features simply cannot constitute self-identity. The French Revolution may be indirectly continuous with the Russian Revolution, but for all that they are not the same thing; events may be strikingly similar and still not be the same.

In summary, James has tried to bring unity and identity to the self through the concept of a single subject that is not part of what is known. However, his concept of this subject simply will not do the work it is supposed to do. Because theories of the self that do without a subject have failed because of this omission, one is tempted to think that one must push ahead to a fuller, more complete concept of the subject if one is to have a satisfactory theory of the self. More specifically, this seems to suggest that we need to introduce the self-as-ego if we are to overcome the failures of the theories we have discussed so far.

15. James himself gives an example of this in *The Principles of Psychology*, *1*, 379.

13

The Self as Ego

Although our criticisms of other theories of the self seem to point to some conception of the self as ego as the answer, this view is not widely accepted by contemporary philosophers. Their antispeculative orientation causes many philosophers to accept uncritically some version of the Humean view and reject any form of the ego view. Yet, there are (at least) two kinds of reasons that show that the ego view of the self is a viable alternative.

As we have shown above, there are fundamental difficulties with any form of the "no-ownership" theory, which, I believe, are strong enough to prevent our accepting it. On the other hand, the ego view is not obviously saddled with all the difficulties of the physical-substance theory of things, a view with which it is naturally associated by philosophers. For example, some claim that the ego is experienced in memory and even in present awareness, and there are arguments, based on the nature of experience, that claim to establish the need for an ego and that have no parallel in the arguments for an underlying physical substance. We must, then, consider the case for the ego on its own merits and not reject it because it shares something with a position we already reject. Our concern is with the question: Do any of the arguments establish either that the self *is* an ego or that the ego is a necessary element in a self?

I

Consider first the arguments from the awareness of change and from comparison. Campbell states the argument from our awareness of change, made famous by Kant:

> If event B is cognised as sequent upon event A, clearly A must, in
> some form, be present to the same subject as that to which B is
> present. Otherwise A and B would simply fall apart into separate
> worlds of experience, and no discerned relationship—not even
> that of apartness, let alone that of temporal sequence—would be
> possible (*SG,* 75–76).

The argument from comparison is the same in principle. In order
to compare two elements, they must be united in a single consciousness, and this unity is the result of the activity of an indivisible I or self.[1]

It should be noted that both these arguments are effective
against any Humean view of the self. Even Hume admits that we
are aware of a temporal sequence of impressions, but, if there is
nothing more to the self than such impressions, it is impossible to
account for this awareness. As it is often put, a sequence of impressions cannot by itself give the impression of a sequence. The
awareness of change seems to require a changeless "I," just as
change seems to require a "thing" that remains the same through
change. Thus, even a view such as Alexander's, which stresses the
continuity of a complex subject, seems to be open to the same argument.

But it is not clear exactly what and how much this argument
proves. Bradley develops two arguments: In one, he shows that it
does not prove what its advocates think; in the other, he demon-
strates that, even if it did, it would not solve philosophical difficulties with the self (*AR,* 41–43, 98–99). Of course, Bradley admits that for the awareness of change "some kind of unity is
wanted." But what kind? It need not be a timeless unity, for if
our subject is changeless in relation to that sequence of which it is
aware, it can serve as the "I" that contemplates change. And it
cannot be a timeless unity, for the awareness seems to have a
place in the temporal series and to contain succession. But how
can the "I" be qualified temporally if it is not temporal, has no
duration, and does not "occur" in time? The "I" that is aware
must in some sense be temporal because it is qualified by its succession of awarenesses, each of which is temporal. Yet, if the sub-

1. Hermann Lotze states this view in his *Metaphysic,* ed. Bernard Bosanquet (2
vols. Oxford, The Clarendon Press, 1887), 2, 170–71.

ject is in time, it cannot serve as the changeless "I" that was to solve our problems about self-identity; we will want to know how it can be the same and still change.[2] Finally, Bradley points out that, if the argument established a timeless ego, it would not help, for we would still have to explain how this ego relates to the self I experience—a self very much in time. And this seems an unsolvable problem.

II

The second point we shall consider is the claim that the ego is presupposed by experience in general. Against the claims of Bradley and others that no ego is to be found in self-experience, two counterclaims are made. It is said that the absence of an awareness of my self at an early stage of consciousness is irrelevant to the assertion that an "I" exists at such a stage;[3] after all, it is said, the awareness of myself as a subject is the result of sophisticated discrimination; hence, it is not surprising that babies and others lack it. And, about sophisticated adult awareness, it is said that we never should expect to find the ego as an "object." Experience and language both presuppose an "I" that "is the thinker of our inmost thoughts, the doer of all our very deeds—no longer any presentation of self, but the self that has these and all other presentations."[4] This "pure ego" is said to be "the indispensable condition of all actual experience" and, as "first therefore in the order of existence" (PP, 371). Ward characterizes the 'pure ego' as the "limit to which the empirical Ego points" and says that it is known in this way rather than as an object.[5]

Bradley's argument against this way of establishing the existence of the ego is twofold. He tries to show that there is no need for a

2. Thus, Campbell's claim that he is not defending Kant's nontemporal ego is confusing rather than helpful (SG, 81). If his ego is temporal, how can it be the "same" through time as he says it is?

3. For this claim, see James Ward, "The Nature of Mental Activity," *Aristotelian Society Proceedings*, n.s., 8 (1907–08), 232.

4. James Ward, *Psychological Principles*, p. 371.

5. McTaggart claims that it is an ultimate, synthetic truth about experience that it be the experience of a self, that is, be the experience of the substance I perceive to be myself. J. M. E. McTaggart, *The Nature of Existence*, ed. C. D. Broad (2 vols. Cambridge, Cambridge University Press, 1927), 2, 82.

subject presupposed in all experience and that, in those experiences that do involve a subject, the subject exhibits none of the permanence and behind-the-scene quality supposed of an ego. If we go to experience, instead of relying on arguments purporting to prove what must be the case, we find that experience begins with an immediately given and to some extent always contains the given as an element. That is, we are aware of experiences—emotions for example—in which there is no distinction of subject and object. Because immediate experience seems to be describable as "one whole of content," why must there be a subject and, presumably, an object in such experience? Are we systematically deluded about the real nature of immediate experience, or is it just what it proclaims itself to be? McTaggart's "ultimate certainty" seemed far from certain to G. Dawes Hicks who says:

> So far from viewing the texture of experience as being inexplicable except by reference to a "self," . . . we are constrained on psychological grounds to reverse the procedure and to acknowledge that only gradually does thought, so conceived, and along with it recognition of the subject-object relation, come to be—in brief, that instead of experience being the product of the "self," the "self" is rather the product of experience.[6]

This view tends to be reinforced if we examine the subject as we are aware of it. As Bradley says, "When I see, or perceive, or understand, I (*my* term of the relation) am palpably, and perhaps even painfully, concrete." In such cases, the subject "contains a mass of feeling, if not also of other psychical existence" (*AR*, 77). In fact, it is a "concrete form of unity of pyschical existence." And if one claims that the ego is something "before or beyond its concrete psychical filling," he is conceiving of a pure form that cannot exist, can do no work, and is a "metaphysical chimera." Thus, we are restricted to the subject we experience. The difficulty is that this subject has no content that is essentially its own, which it must have to be a subject, and in terms of which the subject might be thought of as a self-dependent and perhaps permanent "I." By having no content that cannot qualify an object, it betrays the fact that, along with the "me" that is its object,

6. G. Dawes Hicks, "The Nature of the Self and Self-Consciousness," *Aristotelian Society Proceedings, 8,* supp. (1928), 192.

it is merely an aspect of the whole "feltness" that, at times, I think of as myself.

Take any content of the subject; may we not, at least in theory, contemplate it introspectively or regard it as an element we deplore and deny is really a part of ourself? A desire, integral to that which "I" am, may, with time, first be noticed by me, then analyzed, and finally rejected as unworthy of what "I" am. Bradley concludes that almost every element of my subject may come to fall "outside" it, and, even if some elements are not objectifiable, they constitute "a residue so narrow as assuredly to be insufficient for making an individual" (*AR*, 81). Similarly, Bradley continues, every element I now experience as other than myself (the subject) may later become identified with myself. Nothing is prevented from becoming "one among the many elements of my feeling" (*AR*, 79). As Bradley says, there is no "absolute confinement or exclusive location of the self. For the self is at one moment the whole individual, inside which the opposites and then tension is contained; and, again, it is one opposite, limited by and struggling against an opponent" (*AR*, 81).

Of course, this would not convince Ward or McTaggart. For them, the fact that I lack awareness of the ego and that some of my experiences are explicitly before me whereas others form an undistinguished background is irrelevant to whether all experience requires an absolute subject. Must we then end with Ward's claim that an ego is required for experience and with Bradley's equally firm denial? This does seem to be so unless we are willing to see the issue in a broader context. According to Ward, the ego is an entity of some sort that is related by its activity to the things it experiences. But four questions immediately arise.[7] How can the ego not be affected by the character of that to which it is related? How can a relation hold between one item beyond experience and another in experience? How can Ward justify the concept of two elements joined by a relation as an ultimate fact? How can the ego be beyond what changes and still be said to be "active"? These questions reveal the theoretical weaknesses in

7. This material is covered expertly in Richard Wollheim, *F. H. Bradley*, pp. 129–38.

Ward's concept of an ego more than does Bradley's own analysis of the subject.

As we have said, some kind of unity is presupposed by the plurality given in experience, but one does not find this unity by abstracting it from the plurality, making it into a distinct entity, and calling it an ego. This natural enough tendency does not bring us a theoretically satisfactory concept of the self. The ego is an abstraction of one element in the self, and the claim is that, so taken, it will give us both unity and the self we seek. In fact, it gives us only a reified abstraction posing as a real thing and the accompanying problem of bringing our ego back into the world of experience.

These last remarks provide the key to Bradley's attitude toward the ego. The ego does not seem to be given either in introspection proper or in immediate experience. Thus, one believes that it cannot be observed, partly because of the apparent testimony of experience and partly because of the very concept of the ego as a *focus imaginarius,* the center of our being, which "has" its presentations but never is a presentation.[8] But neither, Bradley insists, can sense be made of the notion of a transexperiential ego. Why, then, should we continue to believe in the existence of an ego?

All the above shows, it might be said, is that the subject is never an object, and that is trivially true. But we have not shown that the subject does not have an immediate experience of itself. May not the subject be experienced as a subject and not as an object? Evidence for this possibility might be gathered by examining conceptions of self-awareness based on the model of one's awareness of an object. Consider, for example, Ryle's discussion of what he calls the "systematic illusiveness" of the ego. He asserts that the notion of an "I" can be explicated in terms of what he calls "higher order acts." My present activity cannot comment on itself; it can only be commented on my another, later, "higher order" commentary. This gives us the feeling, Ryle says, that my present self or "I" always slips beyond my grasp. But once one realizes that this self and its acts may become the object of my next state of mind, it becomes clear that the "I" is not "systematically

8. See Ward, *Psychological Principles,* pp. 371 and 377.

illusive" in any harmful or mysterious sense. As he says, "Given complete editorial patience, any review of any order could be published, though at no stage would all the reviews have received critical notices." [9]

This argument does not at all show that there is no "I" that *is* systematically illusive in a bothersome sense; all it shows is that my present *thoughts* are, for the moment, illusive to me. But if there be an "I" that is the thinker or commentator and that is active, then this self does not appear as an object either in my present commentary or in my subsequent reflection on this commentary. One might argue that, in reflection, I am aware that I, the same "I" that a moment ago was commenting, am now evaluating my own commentary. Does this not indicate that there is something more to me than my comments and something that I never "stumble on"? One suspects that Ryle has assumed, rather uncritically, that I am nothing but a bundle of comments; certainly Ryle says nothing that shows that my comments do not miss out on the very "I" in question.

The weakness of such views makes it hard to resist the claim of A. A. Bowman that "it is impossible to be conscious at all and not at the same time to experience the self as subject." And, in "primary" self-consciousness, "the conscious subject is aware of a sustained—or, under certain conditions a *recurrent*—identity of being, which underlies the successive phases of his experience." [10] For Bowman, we have a "primary" or immediate sense of the subject, which supports our "secondary" or introspective consciousness of ourselves. The latter is the development and articulation of what is given in the former. As such, it cannot, as Hume claimed, call into question our fundamental consciousness of ourselves as identical subjects of awareness and action.

This is a striking refutation of any view that thinks of the self as merely discrete and one that comes very close to articulating what we feel instinctively about the self. The question that arises is our old one: Precisely what does this description establish? Does it show that we are primarily aware of an ego? Bradley offers two

9. Gilbert Ryle, *The Concept of Mind* (New York, Barnes & Noble, 1959), p. 196.
10. A. A. Bowman, *A Sacramental Universe,* ed. J. W. Scott (Princeton, Princeton University Press, 1939), pp. 260 and 259, respectively.

reasons why not, and they seem to me conclusive. First, in immediate or primary experience, one finds a sense of the continuity and unity of things, but neither subject nor object (*AR*, 219–20); there is merely the given whole of experience. As Bowman says, this is enough to refute a discrete pluralism, but it equally weighs against finding the ego or subject as a fundamental element in the self. Second, in those self-experiences that can be said to be of a related subject and object, both are experienced with a specific character. To be experienced, the ego must have a content—it must be an item within the temporal series of my experiences. But, as such, it is temporal and not a thing that stands beyond events and change. Thus, even if we do have some experience of a subject, it cannot be what is meant by the term 'ego'.

If the ego is not simply an element in my experience, how is it related to those experiences? Various expressions are used in this regard, but none is satisfactory. Campbell says a subject is "something that *has*, rather than *is*, its experiences, since its experiences are all different, while *it* somehow remains the same" (*SG*, 77). Describing pure ego theories, Broad says, "We must further assume a peculiar asymmetric relation of 'ownership' between a Pure Ego and certain mental events" (*MIPN*, 562). "To deny that the self is *reducible* to its experiences is by no means to deny that the self manifests its real character (in whole or in part) *in and through* these experiences" (*SG*, 82). And, "we perceive directly only the mind's manifestations" (*SG*, 126).

One virtue of the critical side of Bradley's philosophy is that he alerts us to the difficulties latent in such expressions. He shows such terms to be meaningless metaphors when applied in their present context. They are metaphors—ordinarily taken as literal and factual—used to rejoin the unity and diversity of experience we have separated by taking experience as we do. What does it mean to say that a thing "has" its qualities or that an ego "has" its experiences? The ego is to be different from its activities, and, yet, they are to be predicated of it. We have, then, the famous 'is' of predication and not of identity. But a man can have or own a car, for instance, because the owner is an identifiable entity and 'having' or 'owning' has a limited, defined sense. But what is the thing that "has" the qualities and how does it "have" them? Take away the qualities of a thing, and what is left to have them? The ego is no more immune from these insolvable puzzles than is Locke's underlying substratum, for both result from the same error. We cannot find the unity requisite for a thing among the qualities, and so we separate it from the qualities and proceed as if it were the "real" thing after all. This gives us neither the thing nor the unity we seek.

The concept of "manifestation" is hardly any better. Are the manifestations of the subject the same thing as the subject or not? If not, then how are the two related? Does the subject "have" its manifestations? Presumably not. If so, then why do we distinguish between the subject and its manifestations in saying that we perceive only the latter? Is not the term 'manifestation' (somewhat like 'potential') designed to say that the thing both is and is not the same as what manifests it? Without elucidation, this is a contradiction, and, yet, is there any possible account that will make this union of differents rational? Certainly, none is forthcoming from Campbell. Further, if I can experience my "states" as manifestations of my ego, then I must in the very act experience the ego as well. For the experience of my states as manifestations is the experience of them as terms related to my ego, and how is this possible unless I also experience the other term of the relation? One cannot experience only the manifestations and experience them as manifestations. If the ego is experienced, one must then explain how it can still be considered the kind of thing (nontemporal, always the same) that seems not to be experienceable.

Such reasons explain Bradley's refusal to make the inference to an ego. At first, this refusal might seem to be mere perversity, for he had made a similar inference to reality. But the two differ in one crucial respect. In conceiving reality, in contrast to its appearances, Bradley was not inferring from one known entity to another partially unknown entity. For him, reality is the world of appearance, but it is that world made consistent. On the other hand, the inference to the ego involves deducing on the basis of my experience of myself an entity that in some way transcends experience. Like Aquinas's proofs for God's existence, it suffers from the fault of attempting to learn about a thing beyond experience on the basis of principles and concepts derived from experience.

To Bradley, the ego represents a misguided attempt to provide the self with unity and identity. In order to have the required "distance" from my changing experience, the ego has to be a contentless abstraction and be beyond my knowledge and experience. Most important, even if this is denied, Bradley insists that the ego once discovered cannot perform the functions for which it was conceived. In the last analysis, the concept of an ego is useless (*AR*, 279; *CE*, 2, 377). (See my discussion below of the argument from 'activity'.)

III

We must next consider the argument that the unity of the self at one moment and its identity through time imply an ego and, therefore, can be accounted for without an ego only on pain of circularity. Obviously, these two points are intimately related; the first makes a claim about the ego, whereas the second states the result of ignoring the ego.

Consider Thomas Reid's statement: "A person is something indivisible, and is what Leibniz calls a *monad*. My personal identity, therefore, implies the continued existence of that indivisible thing which I call myself." The self is permanent and "has the same relation to all the succeeding thoughts, actions, and feelings, which I call mine." How do we know that?

> To this I answer that the proper evidence I have of all this is remembrance. I remember that, twenty years ago, I conversed with such a person . . . my memory testifies not only that this was done, but that it was done by me who remember it.

In short, "The identity of a person is a perfect identity; wherever it is real, it admits of no degrees; and it is impossible that a person should be in part the same and in part different, because a person is a *monad* and is not divisible into parts." [11] I shall put off discussion of these claims until the chapter on personal identity. Suffice it to say here that Reid is faced with explaining how I, in all my complexity, can be a simple entity, and with jus-

11. Thomas Reid, *Essays on the Intellectual Powers of Man*, A. D. Woozley (London, Macmillan, 1941), pp. 203–04.

tifying his claim that memory does or could testify to the existence of such an entity. I am one in some sense, but am I merely one?

Although I know of no philosopher who has stated this second point as such (perhaps Strawson's claim that the concept of a person is an ultimate notion comes closest), it might well seem to be the logical outcome of our analysis. As we have seen, any view that attempts to identify the self with its elements seems to omit the self whose elements they are and, therefore, to become obviously circular when one asks which experiences are to be the same as myself. Perhaps what is omitted is an ego that can act as a center for the experiences that are its own. This comment applies equally to the "continuous" view of Ducasse and to the "discrete" view of Hume. The criticism is effective against any view that tries to reduce the self to a system or collection of related parts. It shows that such views fail to account for the unity and identity of the self, even when they use metaphors (Ducasse's "symphony") that seem to stress those qualities. Something is omitted, but is it an ego? Not at all. The ego only seems to provide that unity and identity, for it must be related to its states, and that relation of elements will not give us the unity we seek either. This is simply a vindication of Bradley's general metaphysical principle that terms and relations never give reality. For him the self, and everything else for that matter, does have a unity that transcends that of a collection or grouping, but we only create problems if we place this unity in an entity called the ego.

It is in this light that we may best understand Bradley's doctrine of "finite centers"

> The self in the first place is not the same as the finite centre. We may even have a finite centre without any self, where that centre contains no opposition of self to not-self. On the other hand we have a self wherever within a finite centre there is an object (*ETR*, 416).

A finite center is "an immediate experience of itself and of the Universe in one" (*ETR*, 410); it is "an experience which is in one with its own reality" (*ETR*, 415). Thus, a finite center is not something other than what I experience and that has these experiences as its states. This is the soul. Nor is a finite center merely a self, for a self is a "limited construction, more or less ill-defined and precarious, built one-sidedly out of materials which fall within my centre" (*ETR,* 436). It is a content with which we are momentarily identified in opposition to an object and which can never be fully brought before us as an object. To some extent, Bradley insists, a self is always felt rather than contemplated.

Bradley accepts the egoist's claim that no conception of the self will satisfy us that pictures it as less than a perfectly unified and identical whole. This instinctive commitment makes us feel that something is wrong with all bundle theories of the self. But, at the same time, he agrees with the bundle theorists that this unity cannot be found within the "self," and he insists that the egoist has failed to explain it. To find the unity we feel is ours, we must go below the level of relations at which both the self and the ego exist. Only in an undivided whole of experience, in a finite center, can I find the one being for which theorists of the self have been searching. In that experience, I find the "whole Universe entire and undivided," as it appears from a single, particular point of view. This immediate experience "is the beginning, and it is the source of all material, and it forms the enfolding element and abiding ground of our world" (*ETR,* 420).

The self and the soul are constructions, secondary products, which are based on the material of immediate experience and arise with the conceptual or relational level of experience. One might say that they represent theories about our experience, ways in which we take or divide our experience to account for differences and emphases that already are beginning to appear there. As constructions, they are inadequate to the unity of feeling, and, if pushed to their limits, both 'self' and 'soul' reveal the inadequacies of any relational scheme. Our concepts of the self and of its identity only dimly reflect the unity of a finite center, and we cannot in our theories make good our claim that the self is a perfect unity. Said otherwise, self and soul exist only in the world of objects, and a finite center is not an object. In this sense, 'self' and 'soul' are not ultimate for Bradley.

Yet, he insists, in a way typical of him, that self and soul are ultimate categories nonetheless. "Selves" are not "real" because they are inconsistent interpretations of experience; their finitude alone condemns them to the level of appearance, and the attempt to think of them as things independent and yet related to other things yields logical difficulties. Nevertheless, 'self' seems to be a concept that, as thinking beings, we cannot do without. As Bradley says, "Our ultimate conceptions, that is, are necessary, and in a sense they are really ultimate. But there are features in them which without any satisfactory insight we have to accept, since we are able to do no better" (*ETR,* 410). As applied to 'self', this means that we find no other way to think of the world than as composed of a plurality of finite centers of experience that exist through an indeterminate period of time and the immediate experiences of which are private to each one. This separation of one center from another, and its being a thing *in* time, which, nevertheless, is said to be the same through time, are notions presupposed in both thought and volition. At the same time, they are not elements present in immediate experience, and they are not logically consistent. They must then be appearances that "are all made good absolutely in the Whole . . . But how in detail this is accomplished, and exactly what the diversity or finite centres means in the end, is beyond our knowledge" (*ETR,* 412).

IV

I shall next consider the arguments from attention, judgment, and volition, which all take the same form. Each is held to be an activity of a certain kind and, as Campbell says, "Activity implies a *subject* that is active" (*SG,* 70). The question is whether activity in general or the character of volition, judgment, and attention require a distinct being, over and above the contents of my mind, who is the author of these actions.

According to Ward, there is a fundamental, simple, indescribable, and indefinable "mental activity" implied "in the very conception of psychical existence." [12] This activity is the ultimate cause of those changes in ourselves and in the world that we ascribe to ourselves when we say that we did something. The case is

12. James Ward, "Mr. F. H. Bradley's Analysis of Mind," *Mind,* n.s. *12* (October 1887), 564. See also Ward, "The Nature of Mental Activity," p. 227.

precisely parallel to Ward's claims for the ultimate subject of experience. The fundamental mental activity does not depend for its existence on our awareness of it, and when we are conscious of the subject's activity, there is always a distinction between the "presentation" of that activity to ourselves (Ward calls it an "internal perception" of ourselves acting) and the activity the subject performs when perceiving itself. Ward adds, "in immediate experience the subject, it seems to me, can only be said to feel and act." [13] And he goes so far as to say that

> The subject is not regarded as merely *capable* of attention [Ward's name for *the* fundamental psychical activity] and as attending, when it chances to attend, by means of an appropriate faculty; but it only is an actual subject as it actually attends.[14]

Bradley is condemned as a "presentationalist" by Ward, meaning that he tries to reduce activity to those elements, ideas, feelings, and the like that we can introspectively observe and to the empirical laws that characterize such elements. Ward charges that such a position simply mistakes genuine activity for something else and that this omission reveals itself in the circularity implicit in Bradley's theory. For example, Bradley speaks of "apprehending" a certain development of psychical elements, which development is supposed to be activity. But he omits to explain what this "apprehending" can be if not our fundamental activity.[15] In addition, if we concede to him that ideas can "realize themselves," "expand," and so forth, we still have not avoided the problem of activity; for we are then faced with explaining how such things can be true of ideas if they are not said to be active in the fundamental sense.[16] Bradley is compared to someone who "because he can't see his own eyes, seems to think he hasn't any" (ibid., p. 234).

Activity, Bradley says, is "self-caused change." "If a thing carries out its own nature we call the thing active" (*AR*, 55). But, he adds, only willing beings are truly active, and entities incapable of will can be said to "act" only in a metaphorical sense. This is because to act seems to be goal-oriented, and in action we feel

13. Ward, "The Nature of Mental Activity," p. 234.
14. Ward, "Bradley's Analysis of Mind," p. 571.
15. Ibid., p. 570.
16. See Ward, "The Nature of Mental Activity," p. 232.

that the nature of the actor is realized. Yet, it is hard to understand how this can happen if the "thing" in question is without ideas, particularly when we also believe that the goal or idea involved cannot merely be an idea *we* have about the "thing" when it really is active. Bradley suggests that no sharp line can be drawn between our awareness of activity, in the broadest sense of awareness, and activity itself. If one does not at all feel himself to be active—if activity be abstracted from the awareness of it—in what sense can he be said to be active? A robot can move or emit a sound, and a person may at times merely react to a stimulus, or act on pure instinct, but are any of these acts in the fullest sense of that term?

What, then, of our perception of activity? For Bradley, we perceive ourselves to be active when we have an idea that is identified with what, in volition, we feel to be ourselves *and* when that idea is realized in fact. In activity, our self is felt to be expanded, and this brings a feeling of pleasure. Finally, there must be the sense that this expansion comes from the self and involves the overcoming of an opposing not-self (*AR*, 82–86; *CE*, *1*, 198–99). Bradley hastens to add that the expansion, as in self-sacrifice, need not involve the entire self, that the not-self may be my present condition, as in cases of self-improvement, and that the idea need not be explicit, as in cases where I merely feel active. If one omits the idea from activity altogether, however, one might be aware that he has changed but not that he has done something.

Now, in attention, some elements gain a "predominance in consciousness" and "in active attention we produce this condition (there is no doubt of that)" (*CE*, *1*, 182). An idea catches our attention. Are we active here? Certainly, we are aware of no "act" of attending; rather, the subjects seem to emerge naturally from our present state of mind. What of the case in which I concentrate on some matter for a time? This, Bradley claims, is a good case of active attention, but it still does not involve any original, simple act of attending. As Bradley says,

> Why am I active? Because the function of itself is interesting or because the idea of the result is dominant. The main idea of the subject favours those activities which further its existence, and it lends them its strength (*CE*, *1*, 187).

Attention, then, is the result of interest, even if it may be said to cause the subject to predominate in our minds; attention is a "derivative product," not simple and fundamental.

If one resolves to attend to something, does he have any "direct revelation of energy"? Not at all. Here also we are drawn on by "the normal working of interest" [17] Several suggestions threaten to take my attention elsewhere, and, finally, I resolve to follow my present course. What has happened? The idea of myself attending to my work, or to something that necessarily involves this work as a condition, causes me to attend to my work through the interest it has for me. The "act" of resolving may be at a "higher" level than my "act" of attending, but it is just as much a product of interest:

> The result of attention will follow the resolve without any mysterious 'act' which intervenes . . . There is no primary act of attention, there is no specific act of attention, there is no one kind of act of attention at all (CE, 1, 193–94).

He concludes that the doctrine of a primordial attention is a mere "revival of the doctrine of faculties," and as such, it is open to two objections. (1) "In its worst form the faculty is a something outside that interferes by a miracle with the course of phenomena." (2) "In its more harmless form the faculty acts by a law, but the objection to it is that in this case it is idle . . . a bad way of stating a law" (CE, 1, 219).

Three things can be said in opposition to Ward's concept of activity, even if we reject some details of Bradley's analysis. There is little evidence in favor of attention as conceived of by Ward; there are strong reasons against it; and it could not do the work it is designed to do even if it were a fact. One might add that the charge of "presentationalism" against Bradley is misleading. If it implies that for Bradley the "self" is only what it is known as in implicit introspection, then the charge is false. Bradley's theory is not identical with Hume's theory. If the charge means that for Bradley the "self," as well as everything else, must be understood on the basis of what is given in immediate experience, then it cor-

17. Bradley says that 'interest' seems to "consist to a large extent in pleasure and pain" (CE, 1, 186).

rectly represents Bradley but without harming him. How can one make sense of experience by resorting to unexperienceable entities, which, of course, can only be understood by referring back to experience? [18]

I think the main evidence in favor of Ward's belief in attention is that derived from ordinary language and opinion. It does seem that we are leaving something out when we explain our activity as the effect that things have on us. Surely we do something when we have an idea or concentrate on a state of affairs. Bradley's theory makes the agent into a passive recipient; a thing comes into the center of my awareness because I attend or act, and I do not attend because the idea does something to me, namely, interests me.

I think Bradley could make two replies to this charge. He asserts that 'attention' refers to a specifiable activity that occurs at some times and not at others. The same is true of 'activity'. If one means something else by 'attention' and 'activity' than these terms normally mean, something simple and primitive, why does he call this thing 'activity' or 'attention'? In short, what is it that is simple and unanalyzable for Ward? Second, Bradley is not confusing or trying to abolish the distinction between activity and passivity, freedom and constraint. In fact, he tries to give a meaning to 'activity' that will make some sense. A pure, simple activity must be inexplicable, a "bolt out of the blue" that lands on some unsuspecting state of affairs or produces some idea for no reason at all. And why I am said to be active when such a "pure energy" invades my self is not clear. But if a concrete "I" is realized in ac-

18. Wollheim suggests (*FHB*, 137–38) that Bradley's conception of activity arises out of an ambiguity in his claim that all knowledge is based on experience. Bradley seems to think that this commits him to saying that everything about the mind must be an experience in the sense of an object of awareness. Thus, he "reduces" the elements of the self to the single level of presentations. However, Bradley explicitly rejects Ward's view that he is reducing the self to what are only objects of awareness (*CE, 1*, 377, n. 1) and so cannot be said to have missed the distinction between feeling and what is felt. And he does not deny the existence of attending or of consciousness; he merely rejects the characterization given them by Ward. Last, he does think of anything real as being an immediate whole of feeling in which there is no distinction of feeling and what is felt, but this is because he finds relational wholes to be unsatisfactory and does not represent an attempt to reduce things to what we are aware of.

tion, then the situation is not correctly described by saying that something is being done to a passive me. When I am "drawn on" by a conception or ideal with which I am identified, then it is understandable why I "act" as I do; and the resultant activity is "mine" because it is expressive of me. The sense of "pure" activity is simply that one is going with his nature and not against it.

Ward's attention is no more observable than is his ego, and it is saddled with the same sort of problems. "Attention—cannot be known *per se;* for it is neither a presentation, nor a relation *among* presentations." [19] It is a relation, existing between a subject and an object, which we know by inference from the fact of presentation itself. But, Bradley insists, we are aware of ourselves as active or as passive, and to have such an awareness, apparently, we must experience ourselves, something "other," and a relation holding between these two entities. If so, how can attention (or the subject) be a merely inferred act? If, on the other hand, as Ward suggests in "The Nature of Mental Activity," we are aware of attention but not as a presentation, then we must experience it immediately. But as Bradley has shown, this immediate sense of my activity is not of a different kind from a more explicit sense of activity and, as such, it involves an experienced relation between an experienced subject and an object. In neither case do we need a transexperiential "act."

Second, how will Ward explain feeling or emotion? Because Ward claims that "All psychical activity is fundamentally one—attention to presentations," [20] he must explain anger, fear, and immediate experience generally as being the awareness of some presentation. Yet, it seems obvious that such states are precisely those in which there is something more than the awareness of a object. Ward's conception of mind is far too suited to explicit cognition to do justice to man's emotional life.

Assuming that there is something in the mind that is totally simple and unanalyzable, how could it be activity? As Bradley says, "Activity implies a happening and a sequence in time." There is always a "before" and an "after" when I am active. Surely, this means that activity is complex, that it has elements

19. Ward, "Bradley's Analysis of Mind," p. 570.
20. Ward, "Bradley's Analysis of Mind," p. 571.

and relations that can be discovered and analyzed. Ward's simple attention, whose very simplicity seems to make it incapable of being any kind of activity at all, is mysterious indeed. Yet, Ward insists that, by whatever name we call it, it is the activity of the self. I can make no sense of this claim.

The concept that judgment is an activity is supposed to supply another argument in favor of the ego. According to the judgment theory of cognition stated by Campbell, knowing involves judging and not merely the passive reception of sensations. If so, we must assume a subject that knows, a fact obscured by the impression theory of knowing characteristic of empiricism (*SG*, 65, 70). It is strange to note, however, that though Bradley is one of the prime advocates of the judgment theory, he denies the conclusion reached by Campbell. But Bradley has not misunderstood the implications of his own theory. For him, reasoning is a process that is in part determined by the nature of the object reasoned about, and the more logical it is, the more it is determined by this object. Reasoning can be objective precisely because it is controlled by the object thought about. In reason, there is the flowering of ideas into a system along the lines of implication suggested by one's previous states of mind, and one feels this process as, in Bosanquet's words, "a necessity gradually revealing itself" more than as the result of some mysterious, undetermined act. In addition, unless we assume that thoughts develop as they do under the constraint of things as they are, we will have lost our one touchstone for theoretical truth—the satisfaction of the ideal sought by thought. The result would be a self-refuting skepticism. Of course, we feel active in judging and we are, but only because we are being determined by an end that is identical with our own and not because we are doing something in a way that requires us to believe in a subject.

Advocates of the ego have also tried to prove their case by a direct appeal to our experience of activity, and particularly that activity present in moral decisions requiring an effort of will. There is no better spokesman than Campbell for this view (*SG*, lect. 8).

His analysis of activity is anchored on one fundamental premise, namely, that "activity, if it is anything, is a function of the subject *qua* subject. It cannot be 'objectified' "(*SG*, 132). To understand activity, we must take the "inner" point of view of the actor and not the "external" point of view of the spectator. Having done this—by reliving the experience of activity—one can characterize activity and see what is wrong in most attempts to understand it. We tend, for example, to explain activity in terms of elements that one might observe about oneself when active (ideas, images, feelings, and the like) and that someone else also might observe (bodily movements). And this is just what activity is not, as someone will be able to verify by comparing his own elements with his direct experience of activity. In addition, he will see how various errors regarding the notion of activity have arisen. For example, philosophers have claimed that the libertarian must be an indeterminist because he claims that certain moral decisions go against the character of the person in question and, consequently, cannot be said to come from that character, the influences to which he is subject, and so forth. This, Campbell claims, is a mistaken interpretation of libertarianism derived from the viewpoint of the external observer. If one relives moral decision-making, he will experience creative activity that is the activity of the self and that, nevertheless, is in opposition to the self's character. One will grasp through this experience what self-determinism means.

Activity, as we subjectively experience it, is a "unique phenomenon" that because of its uniqueness cannot be defined or analyzed in terms of anything else. We can, however, say something about it in general and in particular about its form as an effort of will. The subject knows and only the subject knows whether or not he is making a real effort; self-activity is always directed to some object and differs, thereby, from impulsive action; activity is something I do, not merely something I have, therefore I am the author and not the owner of my activity; in some kinds of self-activity we become aware that this activity is free, that is, that we have made a "creative decision between genuinely open possibilities." We realize that "We could have decided not to make the effort (or in the appropriate circumstances, to make it in less or in greater degree)." [21] When rising to our duty against our inclina-

21. Campbell, "The Psychology of the Effort of Will," *Aristotelian Society Proceedings, 40* (1939-40), 67.

tions (the experience of "moral effort activity"), we experience our choice as transcending and opposing our formed character while still "issuing from the self." This is the highest and most significant form of self-activity and the one that reveals the need for a concept of the self-as-subject that goes beyond thinking of the self as a collection of desires, ideas, and so forth.

There is some truth in Campbell's claim that no theory of freedom that omits something like his "self-determined choice" can possibly account for our sense of responsibility. Yet, it does not follow that Campbell has been able to account for it, for responsibility may be an incoherent notion of which no account is possible. If so, we must reject it as an ultimate fact because of our theoretical commitment to the logical coherence of things, despite Campbell's claim to the contrary. We must give some account of 'free', for man is convinced that he is free in some sense, but our account will necessarily fall short of the full meaning of 'free' that is found in common sense.

Determinism denies real choice. Analyses of 'could' that refer to possible alternative actions rather than possible alternative decisions are a mere refinement of determinism. They simply do not touch on whether I could have chosen to do otherwise than I, in fact, did choose. Idealist theories of freedom are also deficient in this respect. For though they account for one sense of 'free', they have nothing to say about choice. According to idealism, to be free is to be determined in a special way. If one wills something because of causes that are external and opposed to his "higher," rational nature, then his will is not free; and in the obvious case of desire overcoming reason or of external compulsion, this is precisely how I experience my action. But if the will is determined by an ideal adequate to its nature, man is said to be free and so experiences his act. It is the kind of determination that distinguishes compulsion and freedom rather than its presence or absence. Freedom is self-realization or determination by an ideal.

Yet, this does not help us with 'can' or 'responsibility'. For men who give in to their desires will be caused to do so, and men who rise above their desires to their duty will be those lucky ones who, because of their character, are guided by a rational and moral ideal. Why should we either blame the former or praise the latter?

The difficulty with Campbell's analysis of freedom is that he tries to solve this dilemma by introducing the notion of self-determined choice, and, despite his claims to the contrary, this turns out to be undetermined choice. This additional element, rather than solving the problem of choice and responsibility, merely creates more problems and ends by making nonsense of the very concepts it was introduced to save. The situation seems exactly parallel to his ego view of the self, which does not solve the problem of the self's unity and identity but surely brings a host of new problems. The unity of the self is destroyed as surely by the ego as it is by Hume's atomism. Yet, there seems no way to combine Campbell's insight about choice with determinist theories to produce the compromise we seek.

Responsibility demands that an act or a choice be mine, and by 'mine' we mean that it comes from the self I know in feeling and in explicit self-awareness, that is, from the "empirical" self. If a choice merely "happened" in me, I would renounce it as something foreign. This suggests that choices must find their source in the person. On the other hand, responsibility implies that before choosing I really can go in either direction and not merely think that I can. This suggests that my choices cannot find their source in me and must be without a sufficient cause. But these two requirements are self-contradictory and, therefore, cannot be combined satisfactorily into a single theory.

Just as 'self' gives us no coherent account of the unity and plurality of experience, so 'responsibility' is an incoherent account of the determined, yet undetermined, character of freedom. And as the ego represented a one-sided emphasis on one of the conflicting elements in 'self', so Campbell's account of freedom represents a one-sided emphasis on one of the elements in our concept of freedom. The ego and the self it stands for must be replaced by a more adequate concept of the unity of our experience, and Campbell's "undetermined choice," and the notion of responsibility it expresses, must be replaced by a more adequate sense of the self's freedom. Bradley's concept of finite centers in the former case and of determination by an ideal in the latter are steps toward an adequate synthesis, but, as he points out, neither can succeed as a final metaphysical notion.

In his account of self-activity as experienced in moral efforts, Campbell wishes to defend activity as a "unique originative force" and offers the following criticism of Bradley's account of activity. Bradley grants that to have a sense of activity we must feel the expansion of ourself as coming from the self and not from some other source. But, Campbell argues, if we claim that our self is merely the proximate cause of our act, as opposed to a genuinely first cause, we will not have a sense of self-activity; for we will be apprehending the self as merely "one 'link' in the causal chain" and "there is nothing here to generate the consciousness of self-*activity*" (SC, 154). On the other hand, we can only think of our self as a first cause of our self-expansion if we experience ourselves as actively originating it. But then our feeling of self-activity cannot, as Bradley claims, be the result of a certain kind of self-expansion. Rather, self-activity is felt as the original cause of the expansion, and we interpret the expansion as the effect of our activity.

I believe this criticism of Bradley is mistaken in saying that the first kind of experience could not give us a sense of self-activity and is wrong in assuming that we could have or know that we have the experience of ourselves as an absolutely first cause. Why cannot an experience of ourselves as cause, through identification with the idea that leads to action, be one of self-activity, even if in fact there are causes or reasons for the state of myself at the moment in question? The feeling of activity is the sense that I, not someone or something else, initiated this change, with no reference to possible causes for my action. This is quite obvious when one realizes that we are often aware of ourselves as acting without being aware of the causes of our acts. This is precisely why Spinoza, Bradley, and Blanshard would find rather weak Campbell's appeal to our sense that we originate action. We may feel this way, but that in no way proves that such is the case. After all, even if introspection can tell me that I want something and what I want, it cannot tell me the causes, if any, of my wanting. Therefore, the fact that these causes are not found in introspective reports is irrelevant to whether there are such causes. If only we assume that I do not experience some outside force as the total cause of my action, the experience of self-activity is perfectly possible along Bradleyean lines.

It is both possible and necessary to explain the experience of acting against one's character (as so far formed) without referring to Campbell's self-determined act, if we distinguish self from character, seperate the "motive power" of an idea from its power of "psychical perturbation," and if we note the sense in which a self may be said to "rise above suggestions." The first point concedes to Campbell that the self is always more than its character. One's character is that part of himself that has been molded into a more or less systematic whole out of an original disposition and external circumstances. But the self is more than this. There are always dispositional elements that are not systematized into a character, and, given the proper conditions, this "underground self" may intrude into our normal self in the form of a want or desire. Because will is "the reaction of the whole self against the presented object," one cannot be certain of human actions before the fact. In Bradley's words, "Thus the self we have habituated ourselves into is the only self to be counted on, and so none of us is quite safe" (*ES*, 54).

But this latent self gives no warrant for Sartre's claim that we all face a realm of infinite possibilities none of which we must take—although it explains the feeling that Sartre characterizes in this way. Nor does it give much comfort to Campbell, for there is no suggestion that my acts do not follow from my larger self. The point is just that they do not follow from my character (and circumstances) alone.

Second, a principle or end may have more power over me than the strength with which I feel it. Therefore, Bradley says, we "can choose the alternative which produces, and which we know will produce, most temporary trouble and unrest," and I may experience this as acting in the line of greatest resistance (*CE*, 2, 463–64 n.). But this fact in no way suggests that my act does not come from my self in the widest sense, just as Campbell admits most of my acts come from my character. We explain the feeling of resisting the stronger desire without referring to any original, undetermined act of the self.

Third, Bradley admits—even emphasizes—that the actions of the self are not the mere results of the interaction of desires. As he says, "Indisputably the self is able to rise above suggestions. The self can in a manner alienate these from itself, and then, if it does not reject all, can adopt one of them formally" (*CE*, 2, 525). The self is identified with a principle or idea that is higher or more abstract than the ends competing for my allegiance, and this idea in part involves the negation of the particular desires. This identity of the self with a greater end explains our experience of choosing among or rejecting in toto particular ends that suggest themselves to us. It is quite possible to agree with Campbell that we have the experience of acting against our character and our strongest desire without accepting his "self-determined choice."

In fact, we must so proceed, for Campbell is faced with a dilemma. He says that from the "inner standpoint" we have no trouble understanding the meaning of an "act which is the self's act and which nevertheless does not follow from the self's character" (*SG*, 177). But this act either is or is not the logical result of the character of that self. If it is, we have Bradley's view of volition and what might be called a "higher order" determinism. If it is not, then I am at a loss to give any meaning to the claim that the act is the self's act. I suspect that Campbell has the second alternative in mind, and for this reason, his view, despite his claims to the contrary, does make free acts into chance happenings and does result in indeterminism, not self-determination. And if, in reply, Campbell refers to our experience of "creative activity" in effortful willing, this is no help. I want to understand what this experience is and how it can explain the claim that self-determined acts are free in a way that character-determined acts are not, over and above the way provided by Bradley. The experience is not self-interpreting; at most, it provides some data whose analysis may reveal a clue to my puzzlement. We then must show how the nature of experienced creative activity explains how an act can be self-determined, yet free, and this Campbell does not do.

Here we might consider the relation of Bradley's remarks to

those who claim that the experience of the self provides us with the solution to the problem of the union of unity and diversity, or to those who claim that volition is the key to the self. To the former he said:

> Does it give an experience by the help of which we can *understand* the way in which diversity is harmonized. Or, failing that, does it remove all necessity for such an understanding? I am convinced that both these questions must be answered in the negative (*AR*, 90).

To the latter he said:

> But what you offer me appears much more like an experience, not understood but interpreted into hopeless confusion. It is with you as with the man who, transported by his passion, feels and knows that only love gives the secret of the universe. In each case the result is perfectly in order, but one hardly sees why it should be called metaphysics (*AR*, 100).

Finally, I believe that Campbell's conception of self-activity is actually self-contradictory. Campbell claims that our inner experience gives us a self and its activity of a certain nature and gives a meaning to his assertions about the self, but he denies that this experience makes the character of either intelligible. In fact, he points out that by its very nature "creative activity" cannot be understood, and he wonders if we must not accept

> as ultimate certain brute facts which we do not, and in the nature of things cannot, understand; facts which represent the basic conditions of finite experience, and could become intelligible to a finite being only if, *per impossible,* he could transcend the condition of his own finitude (*SG*, 108).

Bradley himself stresses that there are "facts" that we cannot hope to explain (for example, how appearances are "overcome" in reality), or which we must accept as final for us even though we know that they are not ultimately final (for example, the division of experience into finite centers). These are the results of our finitude. But it is one thing to say that we must accept as final for us facts that seem irrational and unintelligible, especially when we have reason to believe that, in reality, these facts are so transformed that they become fully rational; and it is quite another thing to say that we must accept as ultimately and brutally factual "facts" that by their very nature are incapable from any point of view of finding a place in a logical whole. Campbell speaks as if his "self" and "creative activity" were of the first kind, but I think it is clear that they are of the second kind. We have argued that Campbell's creative acts are, finally, undetermined, uncaused acts. They are chance events. But such an event is precisely that that could not have a sufficient reason, no matter in how wide a context we considered it.

Thus, Campbell asks us to accept the irrational as factual, and this is self-contradictory. A fact is whatever is finally the case. We do not determine what the facts are by an appeal to a brute given, for if on reflection our given, no matter how "brute" it is, is found not to fit coherently with other data, it is rejected as some kind of appearance. Facts are what seem to be the case after our theories have worked up a given into a coherent scheme; and any so-called "fact" is subject to reclassification by a wider and more adequate theory. If this is so, a fact must be rational, for it must result from some more or less coherent scheme. Conversely, anything such as chance that defies inclusion into such schemes must be regarded as our ignorance posing as ultimate truth. It then is absurd to claim that creative activity could be both factual and unintelligible, and if Campbell means only that it is unintelligible to us, that leaves the way open for an explanation of freedom as determination-by-my-complete-self along the lines advocated by Bradley. Yet, Campbell rejects this alternative, as his criticisms of the idealist theory of freedom in *Scepticism and Construction* indicate.

14

Bradley's Conclusions
about the Self

When Bradley surveys the various meanings of the term 'self', he finds that none is adequate to the different elements that comprise a self. Concepts of the self either emphasize its unity and changelessness at the expense of the plurality and mutability, or they do the opposite. No sense of 'self' is the "true" one; rather, there just are many fragmentary and unsatisfactory senses of 'self'. The self is, apparently, whatever in a given context and for given purposes one takes it to be. But any concept that, on reflection, shows itself incapable of having a single, consistent meaning must give us appearance and not reality. As Bradley says, "A man commonly thinks he knows what he means by his self," but

> to speak generally, we never know what we mean when we talk of it. But the meaning and the sense is surely for metaphysics the vital point. For, if none defensible can be found, such a failure, I must insist, ought to end the question. Anything the meaning of which is inconsistent and unintelligible is appearance and not reality (*AR*, 64–65).

It is instructive to compare Bradley's view of the self with Bergson's. According to Bergson, there is

> below the self with well-defined states, a self in which *succeeding each other* means *melting into one another* and forming an organic whole . . . Consciousness goaded by an insatiable desire to separate, substitutes the symbol for the reality, or perceives the reality only through the symbol. As the self thus refracted, and thereby broken to pieces, is much better adapted to the requirements of social life in general and language in particular, con-

sciousness prefers it, and gradually loses sight of the fundamental self.[1]

Bergson stresses that empiricism and rationalism are merely different forms of the same error when it comes to the self. Both theories confuse the view of intuition and that of analysis in that they think of their "psychological states" as "real parts" rather than as "partial notions." [2]

That empiricism tries to find the unity of the self between its states, and rationalism in terms of an ego that holds them together, is a rather minor difference for Bergson. More important is that both views leave the unity of the self unexplained. On the other hand, Bergson says, the view of "true empiricism" or intuition ignores our "ready-made conceptions" and, instead grasps the "simple intuition of the self by the self" (CM, 176). In this direct intuition, "because thesis and antithesis [unity and multiplicity] are seen to emerge from the reality, one grasps at the same time how this thesis and antithesis are opposed and how they are reconciled" (CM, 177).

Of course, Bradley would not accept Bergson's claim that all thinking has a practical motive and that this is why it divides as it does, but he would accept much in Bergson's criticisms of these two philosophical theories of the self. For example, Bradley would certainly agree that we know these theories to be deficient on the basis of an immediate awareness of ourselves in feeling. What he would not accept—correctly, I believe—is either Bergson's claim that in immediate experience we have the self as it really is or his claim that such experience shows us how the self is both one and many.

Neither immediate experience nor explicit self-consciousness gives us an understanding of the unity of one and many that characterizes any real thing. In explicit self-consciousness, "The self has become an object that stands before the mind." [3] There is, therefore, a relation between a subject and an object. But the self

1. Henri Bergson, *Time and Free Will*, trans. F. L. Pogson (London, Sonnenschein, 1910), p. 128.

2. Henri Bergson, *The Creative Mind*, trans. Maybelle L. Andison (New York, Philosophical Library, 1946), pp. 172–73.

3. This issue is discussed by F. H. Bradley in *Appearance and Reality*, pp. 93–96.

as observed is never "wholly identical with the subject," for the latter always contains a "felt background" that is not objectified. Therefore, it is a mistake to say, as have some idealists, that in self-consciousness the self is both subject and object in the same sense. There is no total revelation of the self in self-consciousness; what is reflected on is neither the whole self nor the sameness-amid-difference of the present self. Thus, self-consciousness gives us no intuition about the unity of something both one and many.

And if there were such an intuition, would we then understand how such a combination is possible? No, for to understand the self, we would have to think through an intuition, and, in so doing, divide it into a whole of related parts—parts that would "fall asunder forthwith." The intuition in self-consciousness cannot show us the "how" of self-unity, for it omits (rather than contains as a subordinate element) the level of discursive understanding of the self. As such, it "is a mere experience, and it furnishes no consistent view about itself or about reality in general" (*AR*, 94).

Below explicit self-consciousness, below the use of concepts and of relations (as Bergson urges), there is a one-in-many without contradiction. At such a level, we do "experience a concrete whole as actual fact," but it is quite another thing to maintain that such an experience "must be accepted for what it is, and its reality [must] be admitted by the intelligence as a unique revelation" (*AR*, 90). Such a "revelation" is not of the self only or of a self at all, because, without the distinction of self and not-self, how can it tell us of the self? Nor could it explain the relational level of existence because it occurs "below" this level. Yet, any experience that claims to give reality surely must give all reality. In short, feeling gives the material from which to start our understanding of the self and of the world. But it simply reverses the truth to say that it provides a solution to the difficulties that understanding faces. Understanding comes through concepts and not outside of them in some immediately given datum. Bergson mistakes what is *less* than understanding for what is *more* than understanding.

There are three objections to Bradley's theory of the self that I want to consider now. The first I call the argument from complexity, according to which Bradley is said to jump to a conclusion in claiming that the self is unreal merely because no theory of the self seems to be adequate. The fact that we have no satisfactory theory of the self—so the objection runs—only shows how difficult the question is, not that there is no such thing as the self. The question misrepresents the grounds of Bradley's claim, which is not based merely on the negative evidence that no theory is perfect. Rather, it rests on positive evidence resulting from an analysis of the means and end of thinking, in contrast to the character of selfhood, which shows us why theories have failed and must continue to fail. Bradley claims that concepts that we take for granted, and that philosophers often assume can be defined by a sharp-enough mind, are in fact self-defeating. The best we can do is to point out this character and to make as few added mistakes as possible, but we must abandon the notion that there is a single, satisfactory theory of the self. In this sense, Bradley opposes the assumption of both empiricists and rationalists, namely, that there is nothing fundamentally troublesome about 'self'.

The second objection to Bradley's theory is the argument from the imperfection of fact. To be sure, the self is both finite and imperfect, but why should this allow us to say that it is unreal? To the extent that this objection rests on the belief that for Bradley 'unreal' means 'doesn't exist', I hope my previous remarks have shown this to be a mistaken assumption. For the rest, Bradley objects to the kind of imperfection the self exhibits. Because the self cannot satisfy the special activity we call 'thinking', because it is a logically incoherent notion, we must deny its claim to be a fact. Bradley is committed directly only to the claim that reality is logically perfect, and the present objection often carries moral overtones not directly relevant here. As we have seen, Bradley believes that such considerations are indirectly relevant to our metaphysical views, but his claim against the self is not, I want to stress, based on this further point.

The third objection, the argument from "family resemblance," seems to me to be the strongest contemporary argument against Bradley's position. Recall Penelhum's comment that Hume mistook what was really an enumeration of the ways things can be the "same" for ways of "feigning" identity when there is no true identity at all. The present criticism makes a similar point about

Bradley's anaylsis of the meanings of 'self'. It is said: What if a given term, as it actually functions in our thought and speech, has a multitude of meanings similar enough so that they can be said to form a "family of meaning," without at the same time being deviations from a postulated one, true meaning? Then one's failure to find the true meaning may actually be a success, for we may have succeeded in discovering the various, more or less closely related, senses of the term. We regard ourselves as failures because we are under the spell of a traditional view of what philosophers ought to be doing. It is, therefore, our notion of philosophy and not the results of our analysis that makes it seem as if we have fallen short of some always distant goal.

As applied to Bradley, these general remarks might sound as follows. There are actually two Bradleys. One is of a critical mind, constantly showing that certain definitions will not do as the one, true definition. This Bradley has hit on the happy notion that a self is many things, depending on the context and purposes of those interested in identifying the self and is more like a forerunner of ordinary language analysis than a traditional metaphysician. But, alas, there is a second Bradley, one still consumed with the desire to find single meanings for concepts. When he does not do so, he assumes that there must be some deep, metaphysical reason for his "failure." He draws a conclusion from the multiplicity of meanings, when he should be learning a lesson from them. Thus, he says that time, the self, and so forth are "unreal appearances" and that reality lies "beyond" mere appearance. The traditional bias of the second Bradley prohibits the first Bradley from seeing the true significance of his analytical, critical work. We are in a better position to see this, however, and can dispense with the needless metaphysics of the second Bradley. In so doing, we will preserve what is of value in Bradley's philosophy, a great deal of which turns out to be of a critical, antimetaphysical nature.

This is an important criticism, but there are two points that, I believe, rob it of its force. Of course, I can use 'self' with a wider or narrower range, as 'body', as 'mind', and sometimes as both. Yet, it seems to me that I can distinguish between more and less fundamental senses of 'self'. When 'self' is used to mean 'body', this is a less fundamental meaning of that concept than when it is used to mean 'mind'. Second, Bradley claims that the self is "unreal," not because it has many meanings, but because none of them gives a coherent account of all the elements one feels must combine to make a self. One begins with a sense that a self must be one and permanent, yet must be able to change and must contain a plurality of states or activities. No matter how one may take the self at a given moment for a given purpose—such as that in which one's chief interest lies—one knows that no account of the self will give theoretical satisfaction unless it combines the above elements in a coherent way.

The different senses of 'self' may all be perfectly legitimate ways of considering the self given a certain point of view and a certain purpose, but I cannot give up my belief that the self is something regardless of how I may take it and that it is the philosopher's task to find out what this self is. I have a vague feeling of what I want to say about the self, and I measure the various meanings given to 'self' against this feeling. When I make the requirements of this feeling somewhat explicit, I realize that no account can do justice to them, and at this point, I assert that the self is "unreal," an incoherent notion that could never be an ultimate fact. In philosophy, our purpose is to understand the self, to give a coherent account of what we feel a self to be, and we can be satisfied in philosophy with nothing less.

For this reason, I distinguish what the self is from the many ways in which I may regard it. If no one viewpoint or combination of viewpoints can possibly give me an adequate concept of the self, then I have a good reason for saying that 'self' is a poor way of interpreting my experience. Thus, the critical side of Bradley's philosophy should be understood as a detailed revelation of the incoherence of basic notions, and this analysis, in conjunction with his claim that reality is rational, leads to his condemning these notions to the level of appearance. The critical part of his thinking displays not merely many senses of self but, rather, many incoherent attempts to say what the self is. The fact that these attempts are incoherent again—in conjunction with Bradley's concept of thought and reality—seems to me to have metaphysical implications, even if the mere fact that 'self' has many senses does not.

15

Three Contemporary Views
of the Self or Mind

In our attempts to define the self, we have assumed that it is an entity in some sense different from the body and have treated it much as one would a physical thing. Now, if the mind could be shown to be a physical thing, or if it could be shown that the mind is in no sense a thing at all, these assumptions would be incorrect. It also might be claimed that attempts to conceive of the identity of a mind, or to discover its nature, are at best misleading, or that they focus our attention on something that does not exist and divert our attention from the real things whose nature and identity should interest us. There are three main contemporary theories that in different ways attempt to undercut the implicit dualism of our discussion of the self. In order to defend that discussion from the charge that it has fundamentally misconceived its object, I shall consider each of these theories.

The Identity Theory

According to Smart,[1] sensations—or "conscious experiences" he says at one point (*PSR,* 88)—are "strictly identical" with brain processes. More specifically, the experience of having an afterimage or a pain is identical with the brain process, whereas there are said to be no such entities as afterimages (*PSR,* 97). One assumes that this holds for pains as well. When I report having an afterimage, I am reporting an experience or process that is like

1. See J. J. C. Smart, "Sensations and Brain Processes," in *The Philosophy of Mind,* ed. V. C. Chappell (Englewood Cliffs, Prentice-Hall, 1962), and the chapter on "Consciousness" in his book *Philosophy and Scientific Realism* (New York, Humanities Press, 1963).

the experience I have when my eyes are open and that is, in fact, a brain process.

Smart seems to hold this view for two kinds of reasons. Negatively, he finds that the objections to his view are either based on misunderstandings or can be accommodated by his view. Positively, he invokes Occam's razor and "scientific plausibility." That is, he finds it "frankly unbelievable" that physics should be able to explain everything except the occurrence of sensations, and he goes on to say that the assumption that it can do this has the advantage over any Cartesian-like dualism by using only one "stuff" and one set of laws. If the brain-process theory and dualism both account for the facts, "then the principles of parsimony and simplicity seem to me to decide overwhelmingly in favor of the brain process theory" (PM, 172). The appeal to Occam's razor is important because Smart insists that no experiment can decide between the two theories. For him the issue is not a factual one but, rather, one of which theory is more simple, given the facts.

One might think of Smart's view as a compromise between the Wittgensteinian view (as interpreted by Smart) and the dualistic view. He agrees with the former that, in a sense, there are no such things as sensations, though he disagrees with its claim that first person pain reports are not really reports. On the other hand, though he agrees with the dualists' claim that pain reports are genuine reports, he disagrees that what they report is "an irreducibly psychical something." If one then combines physicalism with reporting, and if one feels that a behavioristic account will not do for all psychological concepts, one may well say that what one reports in sensation-talk are the brain processes that are, in fact, the sensations reported.

It seems to me that this is an unacceptable philosophical theory. As Smart admits, there is not a scrap of evidence in its favor. No observation that is even conceivable could support it to the slightest degree. The most that experience could establish is the correlation of brain states and sensations. Yet, it seems to me absurd to say that "There is no conceivable experiment which could decide between materialism and epiphenomenalism" (PM, 172). There is evidence bearing on this issue; it is just all on the side of some kind of dualism, and it is conclusive. That is why I am perplexed that Smart speaks as if we have two theories equally consistent with the facts, with the result that simplicity is the only criterion for deciding between them.

If one has pain, he will have no trouble noticing that the object of his awareness is totally different from any physical behavior or process. This experience of mental states tells us, far beyond the power of any argument to the contrary, that the mental can never be reduced to the physical.[2] And such "processes" as judging, inferring, wishing, and desiring are even more obviously different from brain processes. For one thing, they all involve consciousness or ideas, and how is one going to make something physical out of them? If the identity theorist refuses to admit that this evidence is conclusive, then I cannot persuade him that it is so, for there is nothing more certain that I can first get him to admit and that entails the irreducible mentality of sensations. But all arguments must begin somewhere, and if they could all begin with evidence as clear and as certain as this, there would be far less disagreement in philosophy.[3]

In the light of introspective evidence, much that Smart says seems very strange indeed. For example, the dualist does not beg the question when he says that his sensations are not spatial in the way his brain processes are (*PSR*, 96). He reports the findings of introspection, and Smart has only his faith in physics to support him. But why should the attitudes and needs of the physicist have any weight at all when it comes to a matter of philosophic truth? The philosopher cannot dictate to the physicist what assumptions he should or should not make, but why should those needs and assumptions dictate to the philosopher what conclusions he should draw about sensations? There is a reason why sensations and brain processes have different logics and meanings; they refer to different entities. Again we know this; it is not a matter for speculation or future confirmation. Thus, no one need argue that they are different because they have different logics, or cannot be the same because 'sensation' does not mean 'brain process'. Rather,

2. See A. C. Ewing, *The Fundamental Questions of Philosophy*, p. 101, for a beautiful statement of introspective awareness.

3. Smart does not expressly extend his analysis beyond sensations, but his "aversion" to "nomological danglers" indicates that he would want, ideally, to identify all mental activities with brain processes.

the argument, if one can call it that, goes in precisely the opposite direction.

I append the following criticisms, less central than the above but worth noting. How does Smart know that kidney processes do not have "the right sort of complexity of structure" to be sensations? One would have thought that this is known by relating sensations and brain processes, and seeing that a change in the latter results in a change in the former, whereas the same is not true of kidney processes. But, then, sensations and brain processes are distinct, though related.

What does Smart mean when he denies the existence of pains but not the experience of having a pain? How can he distinguish so sharply between the "act" and the "content" of sensation when there seems to be no such distinction in experience? Is there no "content" in sensation? I can make nothing out of Smart's claim here. In saying "It is the *experience* which is reported in the introspective report," does he mean that I report only the "experiencing" and omit the "experience?" (*PM*, 168). But in sensation, these are indistinguishable, and one wonders whether they are distinguishable at all.

When we report a sensation, do we merely omit to mention its spatial character, as I omit to identify a person as my wife when I say, "Somebody just came in"? (*PSR*, 97). (This is the basis of Smart's claim that sensation reports are "topic neutral.") Not at all. I do not say this—or say that my sensation is swift or circular —because I see that it is none of these things. There are no conditions under which I would include these characteristics in a complete list of what introspection tells me about sensation.

According to Smart, lightning "really is" a movement of electric charges. Then, I suppose, red "really is" a certain set of light waves. But Smart just assumes an extreme scientific and perceptual realism, two highly questionable positions; and what happens to the red I see on Smart's analysis? That is what I mean by 'red', and that is itself and not another thing, no matter what its cause may be. Is the scientist a type of metaphysician as Smart believes? If so, he is a bad one, for he tells us that the world "really is" what any observation tells you it really is not.

If it is "simply obvious" that sensation reports are genuine reports, why is it any less obvious that what they report are sensations and not brain processes? Some day we might be able to construct beings who behaved in such a way that we felt obliged to say that they felt pain, but why would this in any way encourage or force us to say that sensations were brain processes? How can Smart prove his thesis, which is obviously supposed to be true and not be a mere recommendation? Can he prove it by showing that views to the contrary are not effective, or by showing that science is better off by adopting his thesis? In fact, Smart says nothing that indicates directly that his thesis is true, and there is nothing he could have said. Does this cast no doubt on his claim? For example, how does Smart show that the brain process theory and dualism cover the facts equally well, so that his appeal to Occam's razor is not question-begging? Does Smart admit the privacy of sensations? (*PSR*, 99). If so, how can they be brain states that are, in principle, publicly observable?

In general, what is wrong with Smart's identity thesis is that it pays too high a price for the unified view it brings to our investigation of nature. In his hurry to eliminate "nomological dangers" by means of Occam's razor, Smart ignores the difference between the mental and the physical. His is an easy monism, won not by finding the unity that underlies different elements but, rather, by ignoring the different elements altogether. Thus, though one can sympathize with his desire for intellectual unity, one objects to the means by which it is obtained. If we reject Cartesian dualism as a final account of things, as we must in Bradley's view, because of the external relation of mind and body, then let us do so by demonstrating some logical connection between the two and not by denying the divisions that we find in our experience.

The Behavioral Thesis

In a general way, everyone who has read *The Concept of Mind* knows what view Gilbert Ryle is opposed to: the view held by some philosophers that the mind is a ghostly thing that exists in a machine called the human body. The difficulty comes in being certain of precisely what elements, according to Ryle, either comprise this view or are direct consequences of the view. Put another way, does Ryle intend to show that everything that forms part of the doctrine of the "ghost in the machine" and its immediate surroundings is to be rejected, because it either is a "category mistake" or at least is something one would hold only if he had first made a category mistake? Or, does Ryle intend that only certain more extreme claims that are part of, or are associated with, the "ghost-in-the-machine" theory are to be rejected, allowing that other, less extreme elements that seem to be parts of the theory are to be considered legitimate?

Roughly, one might state this dilemma as follows. Are we to understand as the general thesis of *The Concept of Mind* that there are in existence no ghostly entities that certain philosophers presumably were attempting to characterize in the theory attributed to them by Ryle? Or, are we to understand only that certain claims made by these philosophers about these ghostly entities are without foundation? Commentators such as Ewing and Hampshire have been justifiably puzzled by whether Ryle is pressing the weaker or the stronger thesis. The preponderance of evidence, however, appears to be on the side of the stronger-thesis interpretation. The wholesale, all-or-nothing, categorical tone of *The Concept of Mind,* as well as specific remarks that occur over and over again, lead me to believe that Ryle intends to show that there is no "ghostly" world at all, that the belief in it leads to certain logical absurdities, and that statements we may take to be about it are in fact about certain behavioral dispositions. If Ryle is advocating only the weaker thesis, what he says is immune from my criticisms, but I do not see how most of *The Concept of Mind* could be brought into line with that interpretation.

Let us examine the doctrine of the "ghost in the machine," which, according to Ryle, is without qualification a category mistake, by seeing both what Ryle says about the ghost in the machine and what he claims the mind is not. (When the denials are significant, they can, in the stronger-thesis interpretation, be assumed to oppose theses of the "ghost" theory.) In general, the theory Ryle criticizes is that the mind is a thing related in some "paramechanical" way to the body. We must not, however, in understanding the "ghostly" theory, place too much emphasis on the notion that the mind is a thing, for it is possible to embrace the theory and reject the concept 'thing' when applied to the self. Hegel's claim that the mind is a subject and not a substance, for example, is precisely the claim that we distort the mind if we conceive it in the analogy of a thing, but it is made only to clear the way for a truer conception of the mind as an active entity.

For Ryle, the mind is not an entity or collection of any kind; any such conception is a variant of the "ghost" hypothesis. In thinking of the mind as an invisible entity, one mistakes certain human abilities and capacities—capacities that are knowable as behavioral elements in our interpersonal world—for private, inner happenings in a world far different from the one we learn about through our senses. On my interpretation of Ryle, then, the category mistake committed by the defenders of the "ghostly" hypothesis consists in part in thinking of the mind as a thing within the body, but more generally in thinking of the mind as an existing entity of any kind. In short, the fundamental mistake of Cartesian theorists is that they subscribe to the "inner world" thesis, and Ryle, in fact, directs his attention to the absurdities involved in this thesis. It is the difference of mind and body and their subsequent relation that he attacks.[4]

The more specific elements in the "ghostly" view are: (1) There are such things as "mental happenings"—"occurrences taking place in a second-status world." [5] (2) Only I can be directly aware of these happenings and only I can know if one of them is taking place. (3) I am necessarily aware of any happening of mine when it happens. (4) I can deliberately scrutinize these happenings; this is introspection, a way of knowing my inner world comparable to the perception that tells me about the outer world. (5) Both the awarenesses described in (3) and in (4) are "exempt from error," and they are "prior in genesis" to my awareness of physical things. (6) Some of these happenings, called "volitions," are the causes of bodily movements. (7) Mental happenings are not spatial nor subject to mechanical laws.

Ryle seems to have at least four general objections to the

4. Ryle seems to imply that he is denying "the existence of the second theatre" (*CM*, 158), and he says that the hypothesis of the ghost in the machine is "entirely false, and false not in detail but in principle" (*CM*, 16).
5. This is denied by Ryle (*CM*, 161).

theory, all of which lead to the conclusion that the happenings in question are "mythical." First, the happenings believed in by the Cartesian theorist are not observable (*CM,* 66), nor are they referred to in our talk about our actions (*CM,* 65). Second, the claims made on their behalf are often known to be false. Thus, we often think we know our state of mind when we really do not (*CM,* 162); or we know what goes on in another's mind, though this should be impossible in the "ghostly" theory (*CM,* 54). Third, certain logical objections can be raised about mental happenings, for example, the theory of volitions results in an infinite regress. Fourth, another, more satisfactory, analysis can be given of "mental happenings."

Before evaluating Ryle's arguments in detail, I wish to make an initial observation. Ryle's claim that it is a category mistake to think of the mind as similar to a physical thing is not obviously true, for in order to make the mistake of confusing a college with a university (Ryle's example of a category mistake), one would have not to know how to use 'college' and 'university'. Conversely, as soon as one could use these words—as soon as one knew what they meant—he would admit to his former confusion. But there is no parallel here with 'mind' and 'thing'. I seem to know the meaning of these words well enough to use them correctly, and yet I am not aware of any type confusion in speaking of them in similar ways. Ryle himself says that the mistake of confusing a college with the university "arose from inability to use certain terms in the English vocabulary" (*CM,* 17). But, surely, the same is not true of a theory that treats the mind as a thing. Similarly, Ryle says that

> A man would be thought to be making a poor joke who said that three things are now rising, namely the tide, hopes, and the average age of death. It would be just as good or bad a joke to say that there exist prime numbers and Wednesdays and public opinions and navies; or that there exist both minds and bodies (*CM,* 23).

Yet, we might laugh at the former and have no tendency whatever to laugh at the latter.

I do not think we can conclude from these nonparallelisms between obvious mistakes and jokes on the one hand and certain ways of using 'mind' on the other that Ryle is wrong in thinking such usages to be in error. But, at least, it seems to follow that the mistake is not merely one that philosophers make, as Ryle claims (*CM*, 7). Our ordinary opinion and word usage is itself dualistic and "paramechanical," and Ryle is, therefore, going against the grain of such usage in *The Concept of Mind*. He is not merely doing away with mistaken accounts that say things that common sense finds queer; rather, he is attempting to revise our common-sense view of the mind. He thinks that we ought to think of the mind in ways other than we usually do. Therefore, his program is very like that of those metaphysicians who want to reform the character of our ordinary opinions, which they think systematically deceive us. This is important, for it shows that the burden of proof lies more heavily with Ryle than he seems to think and that from the point of view of common sense, he is "denying well-known facts about the mental life of human beings," whatever he claims to the contrary (*CM*, 16).[6]

About Ryle's program, let us first agree that certain elements of the "official theory" must go. For example, there is no reason to think that introspection is generally infallible; philosophers such as Broad, who have believed in introspection, have insisted that it is not at all infallible. Nor would one want to defend the claim that one is explicitly aware of everything that goes on in his mind when it happens, or knows his mind before he knows physical objects. The question is: Do Ryle's arguments show that the whole "official theory" is wrong?

Consider Ryle's first line of argument. It seems that at times one is aware of having decided on a certain course of action and that what one is aware of is an inner episode. Why does Ryle deny it? Of volitions he says, "If we do not know how to settle simple questions about their frequency, duration or strength, then it is fair to conclude that their existence is not asserted on empirical grounds" (*CM*, 65). But this is a non sequitur. It would follow only if everything observable had to fall under such categories. It seems, on the contrary, that one might better argue that

6. See Stuart Hampshire, "The Concept of Mind," *Mind*, n.s., 59 (April 1950), for a clear statement of the involvement of common language and dualism.

because we know introspectively that volitions are often not discrete entities, we know that such questions about them will have no point.[7] And in the cases of explicit decisions, one can perfectly well give them a time location, say whether he decided quickly or slowly, and so forth. We *do* describe our behavior by saying that we spent the morning making an important choice, or that we made a number of important decisions in one day. Ryle has failed to show that volitions are not mental happenings.

Ryle's second line of argument shows at most that certain claims about introspection were exaggerated, but it does not show that there is no such awareness. Consider four points. (1) Ryle insists that all introspection is retrospection, because "such an act of inner perception would require that the observer could attend to two things at the same time" (*CM*, 164). But if our awareness of ourselves indicates that we can split our attention in this way, is it not "empirical" to say that it is so rather than to deny it on some other grounds? In fact, one might accuse Ryle of thinking of self-awareness too much on the model of normal perception, and this is the very category mistake of which he accuses the defenders of dualism. (2) Even if he is correct, what is retrospection? Ryle says that "there is nothing intrinsically ghostly about the objects of retrospection" (*CM*, 166). Why? If one is aware of wishing for a hamburger a moment ago, is he not aware of a "ghostly" event? Ryle does not show otherwise. (3) Ryle claims that "there must be some mental processes which are unintrospectable," for one can only attend to so many things at once (*CM*, 165). But then, Ryle continues, our knowledge of mental processes must be obtained in some way other than by introspection, and if so, it is questionable if it is ever obtained by introspection.

Now this seems to me to be a maze of confusions. First, why must the Cartesian hold that one knows himself only through introspection, or that no one else can know one better than he knows himself in introspection? It is obvious that a person watching one's behavior, or a psychoanalyst listening to what he says, may know far better than he what he believes or feels. But

7. See A. C. Ewing, "Professor Ryle's Attack on Dualism," *Aristotelian Society Proceedings*, n.s., 53 (1953–54), 64 and 68, for the characterization of will as "continuous striving."

that one does know what he is thinking, for example, and that one knows this introspectively and with far greater certainty than could any observer is also quite possible. All the Cartesian must maintain is that even in the former cases no one but the person has "direct access" to his mental states, although the inferential knowledge of others may be better than his own "direct" information about himself. Second, one may dimly feel what he cannot at any moment explicitly introspect, and this may tell him something of his mental background. (Of course, this awareness when made explicit is not infallible.) Third, the fact that some mental happenings are not known introspectively and explicitly when they happen is no reason to question whether one ever knows such events in this way. One knows that he does. If one had claimed that he knew everything about himself immediately and explicitly, he would have to withdraw the claim. But who is anxious to make such a claim?

(4) Ryle asserts that one finds things out about himself much as I find things out about others, the only difference being in "a residual difference in the supplies of the requisite data," caused by the speaker's constant "presence" to himself (*CM*, 155, 179).[8] Is this sometimes the case? Of course. Is it always the case? Of course not. When one knows that he is imagining a centaur, he knows this as no one else can, because he has not merely more data but a kind of data and a way of getting at it that no one else can have. This seems so clear that one wonders how Ryle could possibly have denied it.

Nor do I see why the Cartesian theory makes knowledge of other minds an impossibility, unless 'knowledge' implies absolute certainty. In any dualistic theory, it is logically possible that my common and natural belief in other minds is mistaken. But why is that conclusion a liability to the theory? It merely states that our belief is an inference and that all inferences may be mistaken, no matter how certain they seem. The belief in other minds does make sense of the behavior of other people in a way that makes

8. It is interesting to note that almost the same point was made by Perry when he said that I know myself better than others do only because I enjoy certain "inductive advantages" over others in this case. R. B. Perry, *Present Philosophical Tendencies* (New York, Braziller, 1955), p. 276.

its truth highly probable, just as my belief that the American
Civil War occurred in 1861 makes sense of many reports, accounts, and so forth. Its power for coherence is why I take it to be
a bit of knowledge.[9] And in any case, because no analysis of pain
in terms of behavior could possibly succeed—as we saw in the case
of the identity theory—we must accept the inference from behavior to a ghostly world qualitatively different from the physical
world whatever difficulties this involved. There may be certain ex-
aggerations in the privileged access view (the errorless claim),
but does Ryle really mean to deny that there is privileged awareness and that, therefore, there is no direct awareness by me of another's mental state? He seems to mean exactly this, for he says,
"When we characterize people by mental predicates, we are not
making untestable inferences to any ghostly processes occurring in
streams of consciousness which we are debarred from visiting"
(CM, 51). He adds that such inferences could never give us the
"slightest understanding" of others' actions because we cannot test
our inferences by direct observation, the laws describing the
"ghostly" causation of actions are quite mysterious, and the argument from analogy would be "pitiably weak," based as it is on a
"single instance" and applying to actions often quite different
from one's own (CM, 52–53).

I do not find this convincing. When one ascribes pain to someone, is he referring to his behavior? The answer seems clear. One is
quite certain on reflection that he, in fact, is referring to an experience that he believes the person is having. One is more certain
of this than of any possible proof to the contrary; therefore, I do
not see that Ryle's analysis of mental states is at all plausible. Nor
are his particular objections convincing. Ryle presupposes a simple correspondence test for truth, but one's inference to other
minds, like his historical claims, may well rest on the coherence
power of his hypothesis. That we cannot see "how" volitions cause
actions is not disturbing, because one does not see fully how anything causes anything else to happen. What is mysterious is not
thereby nonexistent. Last, though one's belief in other minds has

9. See Ewing, "Professor Ryle's Attack on Dualism," pp. 54–55, for the point that
Ryle assumes a naïve realism for physical objects, thus concealing from himself the
fact that our belief in such objects is based on the same test of coherence.

a narrow base, it is amazingly fruitful in explaining and predict-
ing the actions of others, and I do not see why these qualities may
not well overcome the weakness of the sample. What is true in
Ryle's account is that one often is not aware of making an inference to a person's mind on the basis of his behavior; we seem (unreflectively) to apply our mental predicates to the actions themselves. And normally, one certainly is unaware of the possibility
that his belief in other minds may be incorrect. I do not see, however, that any of this shows that we, in fact, do not make such inferences, nor that we would not admit doing so on reflection. For
example, imagine a being who had no feeling of pain, but who
learned his pain-behavior from watching others and learned,
therefore, how to use 'pain' correctly. Would he understand fully
what 'pain' means? It seems obvious to me that he would not, although everyone including himself might be unable to discover
his lack of understanding.

Ryle's third mode of argument is masterfully met by Ewing. He
points out that the "self-intimation" of mental states need not
lead to an infinite regress if we distinguish 'felt' from 'consciously
known'.[10] Perhaps no mental state may occur unfelt, but that
does not mean that every such state is the explicit object of some
other state. As Ewing says, "I can be conscious vaguely of a whole
without being conscious of all of its parts." The concept of a "felt
whole" does not seem to me to involve any infinite regress. For instance, what reason is there for thinking that volitions must be
voluntary, in the same way that actions are, in order to be wicked
or virtuous? [11] One wonders if Ryle is again committing the category mistake of thinking of the mind as too closely analogous to
the body. If Campbell is right, volitions are free only if they do
not follow from a sufficient cause; and even if we reject this view,
why cannot a volition be either wicked or virtuous because of the
actions that it tends to cause without it being either voluntary or
involuntary? Whether or not we want to say that volitions are
free, or whether we want to restrict 'free' to actions, is a real phil-

10. Ewing, "Professor Ryle's Attack on Dualism," p. 58. Ryle makes this point in
The Concept of Mind, pp. 162–63.
11. Ewing makes this criticism in "Professor Ryle's Attack on Dualism," p. 64.
This point is made by Ryle, *The Concept of Mind*, p. 67.

osophic problem with important consequences. But I do not see how either solution involves the belief that volitions explain human behavior in a vicious regress.

Fourth, does Ryle's own view of 'mental' carry conviction? According to Ryle, when we speak of the mental we are speaking of the "powers and propensities" of which actions are the exercise, or of "certain ways in which some of the incidents of his one life are ordered" (CM, 167). 'My mind' stands for "my ability and proneness to do certain sorts of things" (CM, 168). Thus, mental talk is of a "higher order" than talk about my behavior, without at the same time being talk about "a second theatre of special-status incidents." I do not find this characterization of the mental convincing for the simple reason that, though much of our psychological talk *is* dispositional ('belief', for example), it need not be dispositional. When one is mulling something over, or believes a friend to be doing something, doing or believing is an activity occurring now and not a power or propensity. And when one thinks, one is aware that what is going on is private to him as no physical activity can be. Last, even when one speaks dispositionally of the mind, one speaks of powers that manifest themselves in private, mental activities. Therefore, these powers are not behavioral, but can only be classed as mental.

Consider a single example. Ryle constantly refers to doing problems "in one's head," but one looks in vain for what this phrase could mean on his own grounds (CM, 35–40). If what goes on "in my head" is primarily "imaginary," is it or is it not actually occurring? On what basis does he say that "The phrase 'in the mind' can and should always be dispensed with" (CM, 40), especially when he claims that "occult" mental processes do not exist? (CM, 54). Ryle is not an ordinary behaviorist, for he does not equate the mental and actual behavior, nor is he a simple materialist, for he does not say that man is simply the same as matter. Yet, because he agrees with both these theories in denying the existence of anything distinctively mental, his view is fundamentally no more plausible than they.

Why does Ryle hold this view? I will make one tentative suggestion. He begins with the correct observations that we always use behavioral criteria when we ascribe mental states to others and that we sometimes use these criteria when we ascribe such states to ourselves. These observations may easily become the view that we always use such criteria, particularly when Ryle develops his view against the supposed claim that we never use behavioral criteria. Ryle may also have noticed that behavior sometimes even forms part of the meaning of the state ascribed, as in the case of 'volition' (as distinct from 'resolve'). Combined with the above view, this could easily become the claim that behavior (or a tendency to behave) is always all of the meaning of our mental terms. Ryle does say that Descartes should have formed his problem according to the criteria by which "intelligent behavior is actually distinguished from non-intelligent behavior" (CM, 24), and this way of formulating the problem already suggests a solution along the lines provided by Ryle. Yet, it seems perfectly clear that we often do not use behavioral criteria to judge mental states, that at no time is behavior all of the meaning of such states, and that often it is no part of that meaning at all. (Thinking of something is an example of both kinds of exception.) Ironically, Ryle has tried to combine meaning and verification precisely in that area in which one might demonstrate how they fall apart. Our ordinary conviction that they do fall apart in our references to the mental states of others, based on our observation of the relation between our behavior and our own mental states, is simply stronger than any argument Ryle has presented. Like Smart, he wants to believe a unified view of the person at the cost of denying that the bodily and mental aspects of a person really are different in the way they seem to be. Surely, the way to proceed is to find the unity we seek in the different elements themselves, especially when this difference is beyond question.

The Self as Person

There is a position of some influence today that holds that philosophical talk about selves and self-identity is in fact misleading talk about persons and personal identity. The suggestion is not merely that philosophers should change from one term to the other, but rather that, if we take 'person' as our basic notion, we will avoid certain problems associated with 'self'. We shall stop re-

ferring to an imaginary entity called the "self" and shall instead
concentrate on what really exists, namely, persons. The theory of
persons shares with *The Concept of Mind* a dislike for Cartesian
dualism and the resulting reference to unperceivable, private
things called "selves," and to some degree the doctrines overlap.
In fact, in some of its forms the theory of persons seems to be the
doctrine of *The Concept of Mind,* whereas in other forms it seems
to give the mental a status not allowed by that work. However,
even in its more moderate form, the theory of persons agrees with
The Concept of Mind that minds are not distinct things that, in
the case of others, we know of only by analogical inference from
their behavior. In fact, the theory of persons (in its milder form)
can be seen as a compromise between the more extreme claims of
Ryle (that one knows his mental states as one knows those of others, that there is no privileged access, and so forth) and the
equally extreme results of Cartesianism (that one can never know
of the existence of other minds, that the self has its own identity,
and so forth).

It is hard not to have sympathy for the general program. If one
could construe talk about selves as talk about persons, without
slurring over the qualitative difference between mind and body, it
would eliminate some vexing problems. For example, as Strawson
points out, if we cease to consider the self as a "primary particular," then there will be no need for a special and apparently illusive principle to explain its identity. We will merely have to
apply the ordinary criteria for personal identity and "once disen-
tangled from spurious questions, this is one of the easier problems
in philosophy." [12] Nor will it still be a mystery how we can know
of the existence and character of other minds.

Indeed, from Bradley's point of view, there are conclusive reasons for saying that we know that mind and body, and any other
two terms for that matter, cannot be independent, yet related,
things. The soul taken as an independent thing shows itself to be
an inconsistent abstraction.[13] And in his analysis of volition, he

12. P. F. Strawson, "Persons," in Donald F. Gustafson, ed., *Essays in Philosophical Psychology* (Garden City, Doubleday, 1964), p. 402.
13. See F. H. Bradley, *Appearance and Reality*, pp. 261–63, for Bradley's denial that the self is a self-subsistent thing.

argues that it necessarily involves some behavioral element if it is to be distinguished from mere resolve. Nevertheless, mind and body are different, and the question for Bradley—the question one has about the theory of persons—is whether any account can show how they form one thing without ignoring some significant aspect of their difference. It seems to me that the theory of persons fails to make the union of mind and body intelligible or even to show that they are aspects of a single thing. Therefore, we cannot replace questions about the self with questions about persons nor avoid the problems of Cartesian dualism.

The more extreme form of the person theory is held by Ryle. He states that "Assertions about a person's mind are therefore assertions of special sorts about that person" and that " 'I' is not an extra name for an extra being . . . it indicates the person whom 'Gilbert Ryle' names, when Gilbert Ryle uses 'I' " (CM, 167–68). The "extreme" nature of this claim becomes clear only when one remembers that for Ryle a person is a being who behaves or is disposed to behave in various ways and that when I refer to myself I can only be referring to such a being. Yet, because many of my activities are not behavioral, it seems that such a self cannot be identified with "me" considered as a physical entity. Indeed, the public bodily self is often thought of as quite foreign and as a hindrance to the inner, private self. Ryle's talk about persons, thus, is talk about the public self, and he desires so to construe all references to the self. Because, as we argued above, mind and body are qualitatively distinct, this program cannot be carried out. Strawson seems to restate Ryle's point when he says that 'I' does not suffer from "type-ambiguity." [14] We do not refer to a "pure subject," nor merely to a certain body that is related to a certain set of thoughts, feelings, and so forth. We refer to the person, the "I," about which both kinds of description are possible.

We shall see Strawson's reasons for saying this in a moment. Here I will say only that on the surface it looks as if 'I' does suffer from "type-ambiguity." At different times, I seem to talk about myself as if I were my body, or something that could not possibly be my body, or even in ways that require both a mental and a bodily component. Because the first two kinds of referring make

14. Strawson, "Persons," p. 392.

me aware of the radical difference between mind and body, even the third type does not seem to be free from ambiguity. When speaking in this way, I seem to refer to two things at the same time. We then ask: How can 'I' refer to one and the same thing when it can refer to entities so disparate as mind and body? One can say that, in stating "I am thinking of my favorite elephant," one is referring to the same person as when he says "I weigh a hundred pounds," but what does this mean? What or who is the person who is the same and yet so different?

I seem to be faced with Descartes' problem. There seem to be two mutually exclusive categories, minds and bodies; and I do not seem able to conceive (not "not able to imagine," as I cannot imagine my mind, either) of them as aspects of some "third thing," or as unified in any intimate way at all. Therefore, 'person' is from this standpoint in danger of being an empty "promissory note." It is a promise that with greater insight we would see mind and body as parts of one whole, but it has no power or content beyond that. Strawson must make good the claim that we can think of persons in the way described and that, therefore, this concept is not empty. And if one says, "Of course I can think of persons; it is 'self' that *I* find mysterious," then the question is whether on analysis 'person' does not also dissolve into two somehow related entities. (The problem is similar to that in the case of Spinoza's substance.)

Consider one other formulation of the person theory. According to Richard Taylor, 'self', 'man', and 'person' are "absolutely coextensive" notions. Thus, "We can say, not that selves, but that men are the causes of their acts . . . We thus can avoid any reference to selves or egos just by speaking instead of men." [15] In addition, when I say that men do things or act, "There is not the slightest difficulty in understanding what is being said," whereas talk of selves causing actions may suggest that "some 'self' which is not identical with me but is instead something that I 'possess' and which is a veritable agent in its own right is the cause of them. And this, plainly, would be *inconsistent* with saying that I cause them" (*AP*, 135). Taylor claims that when one person refers to

15. Richard Taylor, *Action and Purpose* (Englewood Cliffs, Prentice-Hall, 1966), p. 137.

another, "He is not referring to some *self* which is something other than a man and perhaps inside of him" (*AP,* 136) and that "No one has any doubt as to what a man is" (*AP,* 138). In short, speaking of selves is at best merely a mystifying and misleading manner of speaking of men.

About the mind, Taylor asserts that no one has ever "discovered such a thing within himself." Thus, all we are saying when we say that a desire causes action is that we do not have a simple mechanical explanation of the act. Then, "a 'desire' is postulated just in order to supply the missing element." To say that men have minds is to say that "they are capable of doing all sorts of things which machines, for example, cannot do, just because they are only machines" (*AP,* 246–47). This is the meaning of "men have minds," not mere evidence that they have minds. Thus, minds and selves, Taylor suggests, are not nonobservable, ghostly, mental in nature, distinct from an animal body, or the cause of bodily movements.

I find these comments either very ambiguous or wrong. For example, to say that "men act" is perfectly clear seems obviously wrong to me. Depending on what 'men' and 'act' are taken to mean, it might be either false or true. And, it seems to me, one can avoid reference to the self in referring to actions only if one ignores the basic ingredient in acts. Saying that "men act" is perfectly clear either slurs over this element or denies it. Neither seems to be in the interest of truth and clarity. Thus, I can make no sense at all of Taylor's claims that we "postulate" desires as the causes of actions merely because we lack another explanation or that one does not know by observation that he has a mind. What do I know better than that I am a wishing, thinking being, and what is the source of this certainty if it is not self-observation? And though there are philosophers who believe that volitions are reasons and not causes of actions, it seems hard to deny that some connection between volitions and performances is a matter of observational record. To deny that we are acquainted with an inner self is surely to contradict the most convincing empirical testimony we have.

Taylor's assertion that 'capable of deliberating, choosing, etc.' is what 'having a mind' means is ambiguous. If 'choosing' is defined as a "mental act," then perhaps such acts are what mind is —although what the mind is when it isn't acting would remain a real problem, unless, with Aristotle, one holds that the mind always acts. But if 'choosing' is defined in terms of behavior, speech, and the like, this is mere evidence that men have minds, for it is the expression of real choice. And, of course, the self that "causes" bodily performances is not correctly described as being different from me, possessed by me, or any like expression. Rather, the self *is* me and is so recognized in action. Thus, reference to the self is unavoidable in speaking of actions. In short, it seems that Taylor's identification of 'self' and 'person', or 'man', denies the existence as well as the efficacy of private acts of my mind, but how he plans to substantiate the denial is not clear. And he substitutes 'man' for 'self' as the cause of actions, without realizing that this takes us nowhere until we know what a man is or what it means to say that such a being acts. Such an analysis inevitably leads us back to a concept of the self.

The most persuasive theory of persons has been expressed by P. F. Strawson in his famous essay "Persons." There he asserts that we must take 'person', and not 'self', as "logically primitive," for 'person' is demanded by the conceptual scheme in which we ascribe mental and physical characteristics to ourselves and to others. Conversely, if we take 'self' as primitive we cannot explain how we come to ascribe properties to even this self, let alone to other, possible selves. Because Strawson claims that a person does ascribe mental properties to himself (that he can confirm that he is in pain) and that when he says 'I' he refers to the same person and in the same sense that someone else does using the person's name, he concludes that 'person' is a primitive concept.

I believe that Strawson is right in saying that we do "genuinely ascribe one's states of consciousness to something, viz., oneself . . ." rather than only *think* that we do this.[16] Thus, for me his essential point lies in his reasons for saying that this fact can be understood only if 'person', not 'self', is taken as primitive. Why must the person "own" both physical and psychic properties, rather than my body "own" the former and my self or mind the latter?

16. Strawson, "Persons," p. 384.

Strawson begins with what he calls "a very central thought: that it is a necessary condition of one's ascribing states of consciousness, experiences, to oneself, in the way one does, that one should also ascribe them (or be prepared to ascribe them) to others who are not oneself." [17] As interpreted by Strawson, this principle means both that, whether I ascribe a mental state to myself or another, the sense of the ascription is the same and that I cannot ascribe such states to myself in this sense unless I am prepared to do so in the same sense to another. This does not mean that I use the same criteria in both cases. Strawson rejects Ryle's claim that one knows about himself and others in the same way. Strictly, there is no method of verification in cases of self-ascription; thus, we cannot use the behavior criteria that we use in cases of other-ascription. To say that the sense is, nevertheless, the same, is to say that there is no more or less certainty in other-ascription than in self-ascription, no more or less difficulty in identifying the subject to whom the mental state is ascribed when it is another than when it is oneself. (I am not certain of this interpretation of 'same sense' because Strawson does not say much about it, but it does seem consistent with his over-all aim.)

But, if so, Cartesian dualism is doubly wrong. It is wrong in asserting that we know the states of others only by analogical inference from their behavior. As Strawson says, "the behavior criteria one goes on are not just signs of the presence of what is meant by the P-predicate, but are criteria of a logically adequate kind for the ascription of the P-predicate." [18] It is not the case that one knows that he is in pain but can only infer that you are in pain; your behavior tells me that you are. Cartesian dualism is also wrong in stating that first one knows that he is in pain (when one is a pure subject of experience) and only secondly, and by means of your body, identifies you as the subject who is also in pain. This is wrong because the identification of me rests logically in the ability to identify you, and one could not identify you if all one had to go on was private experience. Such experience yields nei-

17. Ibid., pp. 385–86.
18. Ibid., p. 393. Strawson characterizes P-predicates as all those predicates that we apply to persons other than those which apply equally to material things. For example, "is smiling," "is thinking hard," "believes in God," and so forth (p. 391).

ther the idea of you nor of me. Therefore, one must be able to identify you as a person with certain physical and mental traits, and this is what makes it possible for one to know that he, a certain person, is in pain. The mistake of the "no-ownership" view lies in thinking that one could assert that an experience is his without using the concept of a person who "has" the experience. But, then, one must already be able to identify other persons who have experiences, and this commits him to the view that behavior is a "logically adequate" criterion for the ascription of P-predicates.

My fundamental problem with Strawson's account is twofold. I fail to see how anything he says justifies his thesis that self-ascription depends on other-ascription and his examples of how behavior can be a "logically adequate criterion" for P-predicates seem to me unconvincing. This failure reinforces my belief that his thesis that self-ascription depends on other-ascription remains unproved. Apparently, Strawson's case amounts to saying that if we are to overcome Cartesian dualism, then behavior must be something stronger than a sign of mental states, and my knowledge that certain states are mine must rest logically on my knowledge (or ability to know) that certain states are yours. If the reverse of these statements holds, then the argument from analogy, the division of self and body, with all of its inherent problems, seems the necessary consequence. Yet, one is tempted to turn the argument around and say that, because the evidence is in favor of dualism, therefore we must reject Strawson's claim that 'person' is more basic than 'self'.

Consider an example of Strawson's. He says that "X's depression is something, one and the same thing, which is felt but not observed by X and observed but not felt by others than X." [19] If 'depressed' means (partly) certain kinds of behavior, then of course that behavior is a "logically adequate criterion" for being depressed in the sense that one would not be depressed if he did not behave in certain ways. Yet, even in this case, observing the behavior in question would not tell us that a person was depressed, for he might not also feel a certain way. Because the presence of the behavior does not guarantee the presence of the feeling, it is

19. Ibid., p. 395.

not a "logically adequate criterion" for it, only a sine qua non for
'depression'. In addition, I don't see that 'depression' does mean
(in part) certain kinds of behavior. Depression seems to me to be
a state of mind or experience, which is expressed by certain kinds
of behavior. If so, it seems quite possible that I could be depressed
and not behave as depressed people usually do, or might so behave and not be depressed. That one does not logically entail the
other is admitted by Strawson when he admits that behavior can
be faked or disguised.[20] But, then, how can behavior be a "logically adequate criterion" of P-predicates?

Ayer is right, I believe, when he says that 'logically adequate'
lies in a nonexistent no-man's-land between 'logically entails' and
'is a sign of' (*CP*, 95). For example, crying is a form of pain-behavior that we do not learn, as we do learn self-control. It is a
natural expression of pain. Yet, it seems possible—though on
grounds of coherence extremely unlikely—that others may cry
without feeling pain. I believe that the behavior is a trustworthy
sign of the feeling—and thus of 'pain'—but, on reflection, I see
that this need not be the case. We may prefer to say that crying
expresses pain rather than is caused by it, as the former suggests
more intimacy between the two than does the latter; but they are
still different and logically separable. In any case, crying or anything like it is in no way part of the meaning of 'pain'. There are
other cases of P-predicates in which the P-predicate obviously involves no behavior and the behavior is a mere sign of the mental
state.[21] For instance, thinking of a mathematical proposition
seems to be an activity "in" or "of" my mind and to have no behavioral component either as part of its meaning or as a certain
indicator of it. How would Strawson handle such cases?

Nor am I convinced by Strawson's second example. He asserts
that we know our own actions without observation or inference.
Thus, something beside private experiences can be known,

20. See ibid., p. 396.
21. Strawson does speak of a "crucial class of P-predicates" and "at least some
P-predicates," "Persons," pp. 394 and 396, respectively, thus suggesting that his remarks have only a limited scope. I think, however, he intends us to understand
that if we concentrate on predicates which involve doing something, we will grasp
the nature of all P-predicates more accurately. Otherwise, what is left of the primi-
tiveness of persons?

namely, the present and future movements of our body. Once we accept this, he seems to suggest, it will be easier to see how we can take the observed bodily movements of others as actions, without using these movements as signs of some private intention. But I fail to see that either claim is correct. As Ayer points out, it is in doubt whether we know our own bodily movements on the basis of certain kinesthetic sensations. If we do, we know them by inference, just as one is perceptually but inferentially aware of any object. Nor are our intentions infallible guides to what we are doing or will do. Second, it is not clear to me why, even if we accept some kind of immediate knowledge of our own bodies, this helps us see that we have immediate knowledge of the actions of others. One sees a movement as an action, but that does not preclude his having inferred from the movement that it expresses an intention. Because one easily and unreflectively takes certain movements as actions does not prove that one knows for certain that the P-predicate in its entirety applies as he believes it does.

Thus, it seems, Strawson's case rests on his basic principle. And what does it amount to? As far as I can see he claims that one must already know when to say that a certain P-predicate applies to another before he can apply it to himself, thus reversing the order suggested by the Cartesian model. Now Strawson says that he is not doing *"a priori* genetic psychology," but what is this principle if not an account of how we come to apply P-predicates to ourselves? No doubt we learn to apply 'pain' to certain behavior of others and to not think of the behavior as a sign of pain. Perhaps one learns to refer to certain feelings as 'pains' because they are those (or like those) associated with physical events, such as skinning his knee. Thus, when one says that he is in pain, he may already know when to say that you are in pain. But does this prove that your pain and my way of telling that you are in pain are not logically distinct? Does it prove that one takes 'pain' to refer to the same thing as 'five feet tall'? Does it prove that one does not infer your pain from your behavior once he comes to realize that pain is in no way behavior? Strawson must show that one cannot even refer to his experience as "his" unless he knows that you are a person and that, therefore, P-predicates in all their fullness apply to you.[22] One suspects that this claim rests on a prior rejection of the argument from analogy and therefore does not really show why this argument is deficient.

Assume that one must know how to ascribe P-predicates to others on the basis of behavioral criteria. How does this prove that one does not use behavior as a sign, or lead to the conclusion that I ascribe both M-predicates and P-predicates to the same thing? Strawson's examples do not lead to these conclusions, and his other arguments seem to me to assume that the argument from analogy will not work. Most important of all, it must be shown that 'person' is not an empty concept. What is it to be both mental and bodily? When asked to conceive of such a thing, I seem to think of two things intimately related, but their union as one thing seems inconceivable. The relation of mind and body, although intimate, does not seem to be intimate enough to form a single thing, and the qualitative difference between the two seems to make such a union unintelligible. Of course, Strawson's theory represents a vast improvement on the views of Smart and Ryle, for he tries to account for the unity of mind and body without denying their difference. Yet, I suggest, he has failed to find a ground for their connection that both preserves their difference and binds them together into a single whole; and I further suggest that the reason for this failure lies in the impotence of our intellect to see the "why" that explains the connection of any two elements within our experience.

22. On this point, see Ayer, *Concept of a Person*, pp. 105–06.

16

Personal Identity and
Its Criteria

I begin this chapter by making some assertions about personal identity, which I try to defend later.

Personal identity cannot be the same as, or defined in terms of, bodily identity. The self or person is not the same as the body, and, thus, even if the identity of the self rests on the identity of the body (as Ayer thinks is the case), when one claims identity with his past and wonders about his identity in the future one would not necessarily be thinking of the continuous existence of his body. Nor would he necessarily *mean* by his claims for self-identity that his body is now the same as it was in the past. I say "not necessarily," because just as one can use 'I' or 'person' to refer to his body, so one can be wondering about bodily identity when worrying about personal identity. But one can also wonder about the identity of his mind, to which only he has direct access and which manifests itself in bodily change and behavior. My claim is that he can attend to his self or mind in this way and that, when he does, he is not attending to his body. Therefore, no answer in terms of bodily identity will be relevant to the attempt to define self-identity, even if the identity of the mind is causally dependent on the identity of the body.

Nevertheless, just as we judge the state of mind of others by their bodily states and actions, so, in fact, we determine the identity of other persons by some bodily state or action. We may use bodily criteria by themselves in different ways. A detective may know that I am the same person who committed a crime because he followed me home from the crime, never taking his eyes off me. Or, lacking this conclusive evidence, we may rely on similarity of appearance. My wife looks much the same as yesterday and so I take her to be the same person. Or we may rely on certain characteristic gestures, facial expressions, and mannerisms, which tell us instantly who the person before us is. We may rely on all or a combination of these criteria, but, interestingly, only the first two could be used to identify the sameness of the body.

If we exhume a corpse to see if it is the same body that we buried, we cannot use the first criterion, but would rely on some form of the second, including the use of fingerprints if necessary. That the third criterion would be out of the question reveals that the criteria of personal identity may be the same as the criteria of bodily identity, but they may also—even when they refer to the body—not be criteria of bodily identity at all.

On the other hand, we may take what people say and do as evidence of certain expected personality traits. Here, we seem to make that troublesome inference to other minds; we seem to take the bodily action as a sign of a personality trait, thus repeating an inference that we have made in regard to this person in the past. Or, if we are convinced that his reports about his past are genuine, we will believe that he must be the person who witnessed, endured, or felt so-and-so yesterday. A different person, we say, could only imagine, not remember, such things.

I have two general comments about the above criteria of personal identity. First, insofar as we decide questions of personal identity by appealing to observable bodily facts, we make them easier and less mysterious than if we regard such facts as irrelevant to personal identity. (I note in passing that such a view assumes a certain theory of perception—a fact often overlooked in discussions of the mind-body problem.) But it is important to remember that even if we confine our attention to bodily criteria, and even if, disregarding difficult cases, we know how to determine bodily identity and are satisfied that our tests do tell us when someone is the same, this is a matter of practical convenience rather than of theoretical satisfaction. A body is a thing, and unless we can say what 'thing' means, I do not see how we can be certain of the conditions under which a "thing" remains the same. If we cannot answer such questions as "How much can a thing change and yet still be the same?" "What sense does it make to speak of things changing?", then questions about whether an object is or is not the same remain fundamentally unanswerable. We do answer them, of course, but only because we ignore the theoretical difficulties in some of our basic concepts. When we ask for the criteria of bodily identity, we find certain vague guidelines, and without a satisfactory meaning for 'thing', we settle questions of sameness in more or less arbitrary ways. The point is that our difficulties about 'same' when applied to the self are not erased when we speak of the body instead, for we still cannot say what 'same' means when applied to the body. Hence, we cannot answer in any theoretically satisfactory way the question, "Is this the same body as the one that . . . ?"

Second, in settling questions about the personal identity of others, we never do precisely what we do when we settle questions about bodily identity, even when we use the same criteria. The difference lies in the fact that with personal identity we take bodily sameness as a reliable sign of self-sameness. We assume that if it is the same body, then it is the same self, for we do not believe that selves "float" around from body to body in a haphazard way. Thus, we find, bodily identity can settle questions about personal identity, but not, I suggest, because a person *is* his body plus his behavioral dispositions and tendencies. Contrary to what physicalists would have us believe, meaning and mode of verification are not the same in establishing the identity of other persons. It is true that we do not explicitly think of the self as qualitatively distinct from the body when we identify or re-identify someone. Yet, on reflection, we would admit that our concern was not primarily with the body at all.

But I must admit that the issue is difficult to argue. Because I believe that our criteria for self-identity are bodily and behavioral, I do not think that we can demonstrate our interest in the "inner" self by showing that in some cases we, in fact, suspend and contradict our normal bodily criteria. Thus, all I can do is appeal to my own sense of what we mean by self-identity. And it seems to me that when making an arrest, for example, we want to catch the being who intentionally stole the money and not merely the "vehicle" by which he did so. In taking heed of bodily or speech acts, which we quite consciously take as signs of the character and identity of the "ghost in the machine," we reveal that we are not primarily interested in the body at all. The body is our means of identification, but it is not that that is identified in cases of personal identity. Such remarks are most unconvincing, I fear, but it is hard to see how one might formulate convincing arguments in this area.

Problems about personal identity involve the notion of criteria. But what is a criterion? If an art critic decides that a painting is beautiful, one can justifiably ask him what was his criterion. We want to know what standard he applied to the fact or facts before him in order to classify the painting as he did. We have a standard or principle and a candidate that, in some degree, either is in accord with the principle or is excluded by it. The standard may contain the meaning of the concept it involves. That is, it may be a definition—a thing is beautiful if so-and-so, and the criterion-as-meaning may or may not be the working standard we use in characterizing the thing in question. For example, if 'true' *means* 'coheres with', then the meaning of 'true' may indeed serve as the way we decide whether to call a given proposition true. But if 'true' means 'corresponds with fact', as philosophers have often thought, then obviously we do not classify many or all propositions by the criterion of correspondence. In fact, we may test by logical coherence, on the assumption that reality is logically coherent and that a truly coherent (and comprehensive) theory must correspond with fact. The criterion-as-meaning may or may not be the actual standard by which we judge such an issue as the reality of other minds.

Alternatively, the criterion may only give us characteristics by which we can recognize the presence of the thing in question—a proposition is thought true if it coheres with other propositions, but truth is not coherence. What I am saying denies Pierce's dictum that a thing is its visible effects, but then that seems to be nothing but the old confusion between meaning and verification.

In judging the identity of physical objects, what we mean when we say that something is the same is the standard by which we judge things to be the same. When one says that this pen is the same pen he had yesterday, he does so on the basis of its likeness to yesterday's pen (and on the unspoken belief that it has been continuously existing since then). That evidence is not an external sign of identity; it is the very meaning of that concept. Thus, identity judgments are made on the basis of some aspect or quality or character that is the same. In addition, such judgments obviously involve memory; one must be able to refer to yesterday's pen and to compare that memory with today's pen before he can decide the question of sameness. The judgment of sameness is reached on the basis of evidence and in terms of a criterion.

It has been suggested that memory is a criterion of self-identity, indeed that it is *the* criterion of self-identity in first-person identity claims. Clearly, one knows that he is the same person who witnessed, endured, felt so-and-so without having to know anything about his body or having to check with those who do, and it is natural to think that, when one does not apply the bodily criterion of self-identity, he must apply some other criterion, which could only be memory.

The problem of considering memory as a criterion of self-identity can be stated in several ways. For memory to be such a criterion, it must be an element in a principle, such as "If X remembers doing, feeling, enduring P, then X must be the same person as the one who did, felt, endured P." But does this principle give us the meaning of self-identity or only some evidence by which we can test the presence of self-identity?

The first view has been thought to have been advocated by Locke when he said, "For as far as any intelligent being *can* repeat the idea of any past action with the same consciousness it had of it at first, and with the same consciousness it has of any present action, so far it is the same personal self." [1]

G. Dawes Hicks seems to express the same idea when he says that one's ability to remember "constitutes the continuity which he ascribes to his own inner life" and "lies at its very basis." [2] The idea seems to be that, at any one moment, what makes a pain and a wish elements of a single self is that they are felt together as part of a common "field of consciousness." A self is unified or one just because of this common feeling and not, for in-

1. John Locke, *An Essay Concerning Human Understanding* (2 vols. New York, Dover, 1959), *1*, 451.

2. G. Dawes Hicks, "The Nature of Introspection," *Aristotelian Society Proceedings, 8,* supp. 1927), 74.

stance, because there is a particular existent that "has" these elements. The identity of the self must then reside in my ability to
unite the past and the present self into a common whole. But
memory enables one to reunite the self in this way, and so it is
natural to understand Locke to be placing the identity of the self
in its hands. (He does not use the word 'memory' in this connection.)

Perhaps Locke means something like this: The self is one to the
extent that it can "re-create" the mental elements that, in fact, ac-
companied a certain act or perception and insofar as the (present) self can feel that these elements "belong" with those elements whose unity in "one consciousness" *is* the unity of the (present) self. One reason in favor of this view might be that the alternative is to base the oneness of the self on an underlying substratum or ego whose presence or absence makes no difference to
the sense of oneness within my awareness.

If Locke simply means that a self is identical with the self who
did X if the present self can in fact have an idea of that act, then,
as Berkeley knew, he is simply abandoning the distinctness of
selves and any distinction between memory and imagination.
Many memory claims can be parts of my present consciousness,
but that gives me no warrant for saying that, therefore, my present self is the same as the self referred to in the memory claim.

Even if the substratum view is absurd, that is no ground for believing that a view of identity-through-consciousness is any less absurd. If the first point is a valid criticism, then Locke, in fact, has
given up the view that memory or consciousness "constitutes"
self-identity, that is, that self-identity means "can remember."
Locke must mean that self-identity is co-extensive with, and determined by, true memory. But, as Bradley, following Butler and
Reid, said, "this admits that identity must depend in the end
upon past existence, and not solely upon mere present thinking"
(*AR*, 73). Memory is knowledge about what I have done, felt,
perceived in the past, and so forth. If so, it presupposes the self-
identity that it is supposed to "constitute."

Thus, even if I can remember all of my past (in some "logical"
sense of 'can'), 'self-identical' does not mean 'can remember',
and, as there are things about myself that I cannot remember (in

some "empirical" sense of 'cannot'), memory and self-identity are not even co-extensive. In short, once one uses 'memory' seriously, he must distinguish between memory and the self remembered, and that forces him to recognize that our memories form a fragmentary and hardly unified "bundle," which lacks unity as much as the self our memories are supposed to unify.[3]

H. P. Grice has attempted to reformulate Locke's theory of personal identity in order to avoid certain criticisms and yet retain its main feature, namely, that the self is "a logical construction and is to be defined in terms of memory." [4] Grice conceives of the self as a series of "total temporary states" that form one self when each such state could, under certain, unspecified conditions, have as an element a memory of some experience of the "temporally preceding member of the series." A "total temporary state" is defined as follows: " 'A t.t.s. occurs at t.' means 'experiences occur at t. which belong to the same t.t.s.'; and 'experience E and E′ belong to the same t.t.s.' means E and E′ would, given certain conditions, be known by memory or introspection, to be simultaneous." [5] Specifically, Grice hopes that his view will overcome Reid's objection that, according to Locke's theory, two selves could be the same as a third self and not be the same as each other and the objection that, because very few of our distantly past experiences are remembered, very few of them could be experiences of myself.

Granted that Grice does overcome these specific objections to Locke, his theory does not come to grips with the underlying point of objections to the logical construction view. For example, I do not see why, as in James's view, we should not speak of the self as a series of selves united by a certain relation, rather than as a single entity whose past is revealed by remembering. I say this because at any given moment a TTS may not contain a memory of an immediately previous TTS, as Grice admits. But what is the relation between the present TTS and the TTS it remembers at the time T_2 when it does not remember it at time T_1? At T_1,

3. On the analogy between the weakness of the inference to other minds and the weakness of the inference, through memory, to my own past, see F. H. Bradley, *Appearance and Reality*, pp. 226–27.

4. H. P. Grice, "Personal Identity," *Mind*, n.s., 50 (October 1941), 340.

5. Ibid., pp. 343–44.

how can we even speak of a single series of TTS's at all? Before an actual memory occurs, there are merely a plurality of present and past TTS's none of which forms even a series, let alone one self. In short, Grice defines the unity of many TTS's in terms of the possibility of memory and the unity of a single TTS in terms of the possibility of knowing two experiences to be simultaneous by memory or introspection. But I am now one self, even if I am not remembering or introspecting; and Grice cannot account for this "need" any more than phenomenalism can explain what I mean by saying that an object now exists unperceived.

Indeed, looking closely at Grice's view, we see that the real unity presupposed in our concept of the self emerges despite the intention of the theory. For example, what are the "certain conditions" for remembering a past experience or introspecting a present one? Presumably, one of these conditions is that the experience was or is mine and not someone else's. Yet, Grice could not admit this without admitting that the self is one in a sense other than that which memory or introspection could make possible, and this would make his view circular. (Butler's criticisms of Locke bring out this point.) Grice claims that his view avoids this kind of circularity, but I do not see how it possibly could when it employs a concept such as memory, which presupposes the unity that Grice wants to explain away.

My objections to Grice's theory are as follows. Although he is correct in noting fatal objections to the pure ego theory, his own view suffers from equally serious objections. In particular, there is one fact that any theory of personal identity must account for, but for which Grice's theory cannot. Why am I convinced, in a way that no theory can question, that I can remember only certain TTS's? (The same question could be asked for introspection.) Any view that holds that personal identity consists in memory or possible memory cannot answer this question. Yet, we cannot accept a theory that, by its very nature, remains silent on this point. We are convinced that the answer lies in the fact that there is a bond between my present self and my past self that is totally unlike that between my present self and the past of some other self. Grice's theory tries to replace this bond with the possibility of memory, but it cannot be done.

If memory does not supply us with the meaning of self-identity, is it then a standard or way by which we can test claims about self-identity? Regarding bodily identity two things are obvious. (1) Memory is *not* a criterion. The criterion is, let us say, qualitative similarity between the body I now see and the body I remember; memory merely supplies one half of the material in terms of which an identity judgment can be made. (2) The material provided by memory may or may not allow me to say—when I apply my criterion—that the man before me is the same as the man I remember. The mere fact that I remember the man in the past correctly is neither here nor there when it comes to the judgment of sameness.

If memory is to be a criterion for self-identity, it must apply either to others or to myself, or to both. Consider others: We do conclude that someone is the same when we are convinced that his memory claim is a genuine memory report. The police think they have their man if a suspect tells them something they think only the criminal could have known. Their reasoning goes: If he isn't imagining it (which is logically possible but can be checked against other facts that have not been released), or if he isn't piecing it together from news reports (it wasn't in the reports), then he must be remembering it. (This "must" isn't very strong; we would want to check on his whereabouts at the time of the crime.) If he is remembering it, he's the man. This last point is hardly a separate step and is certainly not taken as such; it is assumed as obvious. More extremely, if I seem to "remember" details about the life of Louis XIV, which only later are discovered, then one might say: How could he have known such things unless he was Louis XIV? As Shoemaker says, "The fact that such cases so much as incline us to admit the possibility of bodily transfer, or leave us in doubt as to what to say, seems to me to be *prima facie* evidence that memory is a criterion of personal identity." [6]

But, as applied to myself, memory does not seem to be a criterion at all. Either we do not need a criterion, or if we do, no criterion based on memory will help. In the first case, remembering is

6. Sydney Shoemaker, "Personal Identity and Memory," *Journal of Philosophy* (October 22, 1959), p. 879.

the same as remembering that I X-ed, I did X, or something of the sort. If so, in determining whether my memory claim is genuine or not (by comparing it with those of others and with my other claims), we have already settled the issue of self-identity. There is no need to take my verified memory claim and apply some criteria to it to see whether the present self is the same as the remembered self. So to speak, memory in this case supplies the fact of self-identity along with the X I did. As Shoemaker says, what I report looks like a memory statement and not a conclusion based on what I remember and guided by the criterion that I remember it. I am "too close" to what I remember for the situation to be described in those terms. If it be said that I remember a headache (owner unspecified) and conclude that I had the headache from my remembering it, then how does remembering the past differ from merely knowing about it? If all I can claim is that I know there was a headache, then Shoemaker's point seems unanswerable. He says, "If . . . what I remember is that someone had a headache, or that a headache occurred, it is clear that the remembered facts provide no grounds for the conclusion that I had a headache." [7]

Nor is memory in this case merely a way of gathering facts about the past. If it were, then I could take the remembered fact and judge by some criterion (let us say psychical similarity) that I am the same as the person who did X. But memory already tells me that, and so no criterion is needed to confirm self-identity. One might say that, because we are not employing criteria, there can be no knowledge, for where one cannot err (and I cannot be wrong that memory-knowledge is self-knowledge), there can be no truth either. But, as Shoemaker concludes, we do want to say that we know ourselves by means of our memory, as no one else can know anything about us. It is our private access to our past life, as introspection is our private access to our present experiences. Thus, we conclude that we can know about our own past without applying any separate test that tells us that it is our past that we know.

What can one conclude concerning the self and its identity

7. Ibid., p. 875.

from what we have said about memory? For example, are we to
agree with the editor of *An Analysis of the Phenomena of the
Human Mind* when he says:

> My personal identity consists in my being the same Ego who did,
> or who felt, some specific fact recalled to me by memory. So be it;
> but what is Memory? It is not merely having the idea of that fact
> recalled; that is but thought, or conception, or imagination. It is,
> having the idea recalled along with the Belief that the fact which
> it is the idea of, really happened, and moreover happened to my-
> self. Memory, therefore, by the very fact of its being different
> from Imagination, implies an Ego who formerly experienced the
> facts remembered, and who was the same Ego then as now.[8]

Memory does presuppose, in some fundamental sense, the indivisible unity and identity of the self. Any other account ignores
our instinctive claim that I can remember only what I did or felt
and is, therefore, ultimately circular. Bradley's distinction of self
and finite center is an attempt to distinguish the appearance of
that unity in time from the timeless unity that the self implies.
For Bradley, the self is a constructed thing in which we cannot
find the identity or unity we seek.

It does not follow, however, that self-identity can be conceived
of in terms of an ego. Even if memory presupposes identity, does
it presuppose that *kind* of identity? If our above comments on the
ego are accepted, it does not. As Hicks states, the unity of the self
is "of a type totally different from that which we encounter in the
physical world," but that does not mean that "The term 'I' is the
proper name of a certain existent. . . ." Rather the "I" is its mental states at any given time and not their "owner," while the mental states are "The transient modes or phases of an indivisible
individuality." [9]

As Bradley points out, if one avoids metaphysical talk about
finite centers and remains within the confines of the self, one does
not find the always-the-same element that memory presupposes or
requires. Rather, all one can say is that "Memory depends on re-
production from a basis that is present—a basis that may be said

8. James Mill, *An Analysis of the Phenomena of the Human Mind* (2 vols. London, Longmans, Green, Reader, & Dyer, 1869), 2, 173–74.
9. Hicks, "The Nature of Introspection," pp. 75–76.

to consist in self-feeling" and that "As long as there remains in the self a certain basis of content, ideally the same, so long may the self recall anything once associated with that basis" (*AR*, 71–72, 97). Self-feeling may presuppose much more, of course, but self-feeling and a content ideally the same permit changes in degree. Thus, the self may remember and be somewhat different while not being so different that we refuse to label it the "same." On this level, memory presupposes only sameness-within-limits, whereas on a deeper, metaphysical level, it presupposes a self-identity not resolvable into an always-the-same ego and its states.

17

Bradley's Theory of Personal Identity

In an article on spiritualism, Bradley argues that bodily identity is a necessary (though not perhaps sufficient) criterion for self-identity (*CE*, *2*, 595–617). He argues that we identify a man—in a law court, for example—by showing that the body before us is the same as the body we are after; to accomplish this we must show that the body is descriptively similar to that sought after and that it has existed continuously since we last identified it. The latter qualification is necessary if we are to distinguish between one identically the same body and two qualitatively identical bodies. A break in existence (if that be possible), or the substitution of one object for another, destroys identity. We cannot prove continuity of existence, Bradley claims, but we can establish it with a "certain probability." "We try to prove that the facts are in favour of continuity, and that nothing suggests an opposite hypothesis" (*CE*, *2*, 608). We argue indirectly that the man before us may be the one we seek because he seems like the man, his story makes sense, and so forth. Last, we argue that he must be the man, for no one else could be so like him. Of course, this last step is open to possible error, but Bradley insists that without it we cannot move from qualitative sameness to identity.

Now, he asks, when we cannot identify in the above manner (as when a medium identifies a certain spirit), do we have some other means of identification? The answer is no. We cannot argue that because a certain spirit has the same disposition, knowledge of facts, and so forth as our friend that, therefore, he is our friend. This is because we have no way of rendering improbable such hypotheses as that the spirit we speak to is an impersonator ("my kinsman or the devil"), or is our friend's duplicate, or has ceased to exist at some point and now exists again. Thus, we cannot with any degree of confidence claim that this is the same spirit and so forth. And, Bradley adds, when it comes to identifying selves in supposed cases of souls interchanging between bodies:

> In this (impossible) case could we get to know the identity of their souls? I do not think that we could. A man might say, 'This woman C is no longer my wife; she is at present not the same with the woman I married.' But nothing could entitle him to find the soul C in the body D (*CE*, 2, 609).

The necessity of identifying selves by their bodies has been urged recently by B. A. O. Williams in "Personal Identity and Individuation." [1] Williams argues, somewhat like Bradley, that "bodily identity is always a necessary condition of personal identity" (*EPP*, 325). This is because, without the body to identify and individuate persons, we cannot distinguish between identity and exact similarity. Thus, if someone claims to remember what some historical or contemporary personage did or felt, we have no way of deciding whether he really remembers this—and, hence, was in that body but is now in this body—or whether he simply has the mysterious power to know what some other person has done or felt. (I assume a case in which we can rule out the possibility of fakery or hallucination.)

Even in the case of oneself, it is hard to see how we could render probable the fact of bodily interchange, for one's memory claim is not self-validating. Yet, can we test it except by seeing if it fits with the memory claims others make about what they saw us doing, that it, saw our bodies doing? If I can report nothing that others can check and that only the person I claim to have been could have known, how can I decide between the possibilities of hallucination and bodily transfer? And even if I do know such things and they are found to be true, how can I decide between occult powers plus hallucination, on the one hand, and bodily transfer, on the other? As Bradley said, we can know when something very strange happens to others or to ourselves, but how can we know that that person or ourself has come to inhabit an-

1. B. A. O. Williams, "Personal Identity and Individuation," in *Essays in Philosophical Psychology*, p. 325.

other body? If my own memory claims were certain, or if I could distinguish the genuine memory reports of others from other kinds of knowledge by some intrinsic mark, then, assuming that I can remember only what happened to me, perhaps we could decide about bodily transfer. But because neither alternative is genuine, I do not see how we can decide. Of course, as Bradley admits, "We, I presume, are not sure that one soul might not have a succession of bodies. And, in any case, we certainly do not know that one organism can be organic to no more than one soul" (*AR*, 272). How could we, unless we know what a self is and how it is related to the body? Nevertheless, the possibility remains an empty one, because no one, including the person in question, could ever verify a case of bodily transfer or of mutliple personality. There can never be any reason for doubting that bodily identity is a necessary criterion of personal identity.

In holding that bodily identity is a necessary means of determining self-identity, while denying that it is all or part of the meaning of self-identity, I hope to overcome an objection raised by Ayer (*PK*, 192). He points out that, if self-identity depends on bodily identity, as Williams claims, then survival after death must be a logically absurd notion and not merely an unlikely possibility. But, Ayer continues, in regarding it as unlikely we concede that it is possible. It seems hard to see how we can know that there cannot be such survival, for although 'man' logically implies 'body', 'self'—whatever its causal relation to the body—does not. In my view, an afterlife is possible, but only under strange conditions, for one would have no way of determining whether his experience as disembodied was genuine, and no one on earth could identify any disembodied spirit, even if contact were made with the spirit world. Chisholm takes the opposite view when he says, "If I woke up tomorrow and found that I had a body vastly different from this one, I would probably conclude, not that I was some one else (whatever that might mean), but rather that my body had changed." [2] But how would one know that he "really" woke up and "really" found himself in this situation? If later one found himself back in his own body, how would he decide whether he had imagined the entire episode? It might have been

2. Roderick M. Chisholm, "The Concept of a Person," *The Monist*, *49* (1965), 33.

as Chisholm described, but might it not equally be the case that I know things about another person that are most strange? And how can one eliminate the possibility that there is another spirit, exactly like myself, who occupied the body of someone else for a time? Seemingly, there is no way of testing identity claims once we imagine a situation in which we cannot apply the criterion of bodily identity.

Our use of bodily criteria for self-identity implies, it seems to me, that in worrying about self-identity we must assume that selves or minds "stay put" in one body. But bodily identity and self-identity are not the same. Thus, in wondering about self-identity, we wonder whether the self that is "in" the same body is such that it can be said to be the same. That is, if we eliminate the possibility of the substitution of one self for another, we still have the problem of whether what we normally think of as the same self, but changed, can be shown to be the same by any principle, or whether, on the contrary, we might just as well think of it as many selves that more or less resemble one another. In asking this question, we are asking for a justification of the ordinary notion that a thing may have changed and yet still be the same. Bradley's answer, like Hume's, is that there is no such justification and that, therefore, one is free to say about the self's identity whatever suits his given specific purposes.

The problems are these. (1) If self-identity is known through bodily identity, then the immediate difficulty is in justifying our claims for the sameness of the body. Because, Bradley argues, we cannot say what is "this general character which is taken to make the thing's essence," we have no way of answering in a final way whether or not the thing is the same after some change (AR, 63). If you ask me whether it is the same in some particular respect, I at least understand you, though even here we are hard pressed to say whether a particular respect is the same if it is also slightly different. (2) To the extent that we can be concerned directly with the self's identity, we find ourselves in no better position. Like the body, the self is the same if it has some degree of qualitative sameness and continuity of existence. But we cannot say which qualities must be the same, whether they are the same even if they are also different, whether any break in continuity destroys sameness (if in sleep consciousness lapses, am I on awakening the same or not? "If the same soul lived twice, at the interval of a century, would it really be the same?" (*CE, 2*, 610), or how much weight should be given to each criterion in judgments of sameness. What justification is there for saying that a person radically changed is the same merely on grounds of continuous existence? In fact, if there be no qualitative sameness, what is thought to have existed continuously?

According to DeWitt Parker, the self preserves its identity in two ways. Experiences, purposes, thoughts, and so forth, which exist at one time as elements in a self, may themselves exist at a later time, thereby giving a sameness to the self. Thus, Parker says, "The very same experience that was can exist anew at separate moments of time; and these reappearances are not duplicates of the old; they are just the old recreated." [3] Parker distinguishes between the "focal" and the "matrix" self. He says that the former "consists of that activity, or complex of compresent activities, now in operation" and that it "overlies a relatively deeper and larger background of expression, conception, and volition of a relatively systematic character, out of which it springs and to which it contributes." [4] The "larger background" is the matrix self that provides a core or essential self, remaining the same for long periods and providing the whole self with stability and identity. Parker then finds *within* the matrix self an "essence," which is "that part without which the person ceases to be himself" (*ES,* 63). Though the matrix self alters slowly, presumably the "essence" remains unchanged for the life of the self.[5] Thus, personal identity is a matter of "more or less," depending on how much of the present activities are the same as those of the past (*SN,* 38, 49–50).

Parker's theory is full of solid commonsense, but it does not withstand Bradley's critique of our commonsense notions. For instance, how could Parker possibly know that some experiences recur that are numerically the same as certain past experiences?

3. DeWitt H. Parker, *The Self and Nature* (Cambridge, Mass., Harvard University Press, 1917), p. 40.

4. DeWitt H. Parker, *Experience and Substance* (Ann Arbor, University of Michigan Press, 1941), pp. 43 and 44, respectively.

5. On this point, see Parker, *The Self and Nature*, p. 32.

Because our standard of identity insists on continuity of existence, how would we know what to say when asked if such an experience were the same? What principle would we invoke to make our decision other than arbitrary? By what possible observation could we distinguish an item that was numerically distinct but qualitatively indistinguishable from a previous experience from the numerically identical experience reappearing in my mind? Because there is no such test, Parker's hypothesis is beyond proof and can be dismissed with safety. Second, how does one decide what the essential self consists of? If this essence is complex, are all of its elements essential to it, or does it have an essence? From some points of view, certain of my "elements" are more essential to me than others, but what elements are absolutely essential from any point of view? I know of no way to draw such a line that has the support of an absolute principle.

Last, if real self-identity depends on an unchanging core, where is one to look for such a core? The fact that the matrix self changes more slowly than the focal self will not help, for self-identity should span this slower change as well. But are we to believe that from birth to death the real self does not change? Then Bradley's dilemma must be faced. Either there is no such essential self, or what does not change is a "bare remnant" too simple to be the self. In short, Parker's theory leads me to the conclusion that self-identity is a matter of convenience and point of view rather than a matter of principle.

This is precisely Bradley's conclusion. For him, "Personal identity is mainly a matter of degree" (AR, 73). If one wonders whether a self is the same from a certain point of view, or in a certain respect, then headway can be made on an answer, although, Bradley cautions, we must recognize that the points of view we occupy are arbitrary and the answers given assuming these points of view involve "more or less of convention and arrangements." For the features we select will be themselves somewhat different than before and we will have to say, "So much change and they can be considered the same; any more and they are to be considered different."

To ask about the general sameness of the self, without specifying a respect or point of view, is to ask a meaningless question.

The self seems to be a thing that I "construct" on no sound basis; it is something about whose identity I can say what I like.[6] Of course, we do not ordinarily think this way, but that is because we (unjustifiably) trust such notions as 'self' and 'change', believing them to be coherent notions that refer to real entities or facts in the world. Bradley attempts to call to our attention the confusions and makeshift character of such notions so that we will realize that there are no right or wrong answers to general questions about sameness or identity. As Bradley says, our failure to answer questions about self-identity stems from the fact that "We will persist in asking questions when we do not know what they mean" (*AR*, 60). For instance, what would count as evidence for an answer to the general question whether a certain person is the same as before? The word 'general' excludes questions about the sameness of one's 'personality', and what other sense can the question have?

It is important to remember, however, that the self for Bradley is only an aspect of the "felt totality" that is a finite center. Whenever within a finite center there develops the opposition of subject and object (either theoretical or practical), we have a self. It is a fluctuating part of a greater whole and, as such, is not simply one or simply many, but rather is more or less of a collection that reveals no principle of unity or identity. Yet, the finite center of experience retains its characteristic unity or "point of view." It is not a construction in time, does not change, and is not an object for our awareness. It is the felt whole, the unity of content and existence, out of which we construct or separate a self and a not-self. The self is a fragment; as such it is mere appearance. Thus, when Reid says, "The identity of a person is a perfect identity; wherever it is real, it admits of no degrees" (*EIPM*, 204), he seems to be stating a theory of the self diametrically opposed to that of Bradley. Nevertheless, if one substitutes 'finite center' for 'person' in the above quotation, the result is a view entirely compatible with Bradley's.

Finally, let us return to the notion of responsibility. In the *Ethical Studies*, Bradley says, "Without personal identity responsibility is sheer nonsense" (*ES*, 36), and he used this claim as an argu-

6. See Bradley's remarks on the soul (*AR*, 268–69).

ment against the Humean theory of the self. Now we may agree that in failing to give us a theory of the self that makes sense of responsibility, Hume is faced with explaining our instinctive belief that we are responsible for our past acts. But does not Bradley's treatment of personal identity, so similar to Hume's, run afoul of responsibility in the same way?

To some degree, we must, I think, concede this point. For Bradley, responsibility must be only a matter of degree, and we do not usually think of it in this way. If personal identity is not absolute, then responsibility cannot be either. Yet, I think Bradley might be defended. Because he does not think of the self as merely discrete he is not forced simply to deny responsibility. There will be responsibility to the extent that the self is the same.

Connected as it is with the concept of freedom, responsibility is a "queer," if not illogical, notion and is, therefore, in need of some kind of alteration. Even though at times we think of responsibility as absolute, we also admit circumstances that in some undefined way limit responsibility. Thus, if a man commits a crime under the influence of a passion, or if he is apprehended many years later, at which time he seems completely changed from the person who committed the crime, we are likely to feel that the present person is not fully responsible for the act he committed.

In fact, Bradley does argue that responsibility is a matter of degree. In his view, will is "the self-realization of an idea with which the self is identified" (*CE*, 2, 474). But he points out that there are cases in which I am in some sense identified with an idea and yet also disown that idea as antithetical to my "genuine" or "natural" self. For example, this may happen when I act under the influence of an abnormal idea. Then the question is whether I acted willfully and, therefore, whether I am responsible for my action; and no simple answer is possible. On the one hand, the result seems to be formally a volition; on the other hand, I do not feel that *I* have acted and may claim to have been compelled in some strange way. Bradley concludes: "Human responsibility is not a thing which is simple and absolute. It is not a question which you can bring bodily under one head, and decide unconditionally by some plain issue between Yes and No" (*CE*, 2, 472). It follows that "It is indefensible to insist that I am absolutely accountable for all that has issued from my will." If we have good reasons for saying that responsibility is a matter of more or less, then a theory that makes personal identity a matter of degree cannot be inadequate to the extent that it entails the same result for responsibility.

Index